Love, Death, and Revolution in
Central Europe

Previous Publications

Popular Sovereignty and the Crisis of German Constitutional Law: The Theory and Practice of Weimar Constitutionalism (1997)

Dictatorship, State Planning, and Social Theory in the German Democratic Republic (2003)

Love, Death, and Revolution in Central Europe

Ludwig Feuerbach, Moses Hess, Louise Dittmar,
Richard Wagner

Peter C. Caldwell

First published in 2009 by PALGRAVE MACMILLAN® in the United
States - a division of St. Martin's Press LLC, 175 Fifth Avenue, New York,
NY 10010.

Where this book is distributed in the UK, Europe and the rest of the world,
this is by Palgrave Macmillan, a division of Macmillan Publishers Limited,
registered in England, company number 785998, of Houndmills, Basingstoke,
Hampshire RG21 6XS.

Palgrave Macmillan is the global academic imprint of the above companies
and has companies and representatives throughout the world.

Palgrave® and Macmillan® are registered trademarks in the United States,
the United Kingdom, Europe and other countries.

ISBN-13: 978-0-230-61496-3
ISBN-10: 0-230-61496-5

Library of Congress Cataloging-in-Publication Data

Caldwell, Peter C.
    Love, death, and revolution in Central Europe : Ludwig Feuerbach,
Moses Hess, Louise Dittmar, Richard Wagner / Peter C. Caldwell.
        p. cm.
    Includes bibliographical references and index.
    ISBN 0-230-61496-5
    1. Feuerbach, Ludwig, 1804–1872—Influence. 2. Hess, Moses,
    1812–1875. 3. Dittmar, Louise, 1807–1884. 4. Wagner, Richard,
    1813–1883. 5. Radicalism—Germany—History—19th century.
    6. Radicalism—Religious aspects—History—19th century. I. Title.
    B2973.C27 2009
    193—dc22   2008051798

A catalogue record of the book is available from the British Library.

Design by Macmillan Publishing Solutions

First edition: July 2009

10 9 8 7 6 5 4 3 2 1

Printed in the United States of America.

There is no other road for you to truth and freedom except that leading through the stream of fire [*Feuerbach*]. Feuerbach is the purgatory of the present times.

Ludwig Feuerbach,
"Luther as Arbiter between Strauss and Feuerbach," 1842

The new worlds [that form "out of the nebulous gases of decadent, old orders"] are the arsonists who come into contact with the old, extinct, and petrified during their development, and who present to us the sublime drama of a heavenly revolution. Death and resurrection, solidification and dissolution, are the means of eternal reproduction.

Moses Hess, "Physische Beschaffenheit und
Geschichte der Weltkörper," 1857

There are times when a new perception, a new light seeks to animate the world. This is the time of rebirth. The old gods are diminished in the eyes of their former adherents [*Bekenner*]. Nordic mythology shows a transition and names it the twilight of the gods [*Götterdämmerung*], which is followed by the night of the gods. . . . So then the two parties, the Æsir and the Jötnar, the irresolvable opposites, fight a battle of annihilation. The world is corrupted and must perish. Forward to battle against the corrupt world of fog!

Louise Dittmar, *Zur Charakterisirung der nordischen
Mythologie im Verhältniss zu andern Naturreligionen. Eine Skizze*, 1848

Whenever murderers and thieves now set fire to a house, the deed rightly strikes us as base and repugnant:—but how shall it seem to us if the monster that is Paris is burned to the ground, if the conflagration spreads from town to town, and if we ourselves, in our wild enthusiasm, finally set fire to these uncleansable Augean stables for the sake of a breath of fresh air?

Richard Wagner, letter to Theodor Uhlig, Oct. 22, 1850

Contents

Acknowledgments

I would like to thank Christian Emden, Jeff Kripal, Michael Maas, Jan Palmowski, Mark Swofford, and Joel Wolfe for discussing the project with me. Comments from Michael P. Steinberg, Alex Byrd, and an anonymous reviewer were of exceptional value as I completed the manuscript. A number of students have slogged through the raw material for the project with me, providing essential help on the way, including Ryan Foster, David Getman, Liz Machol, and Marty Wauck. Joseph Abel provided an expert and committed reading at just the right moment. Christopher Chappell of Palgrave Macmillan proved to be an exceptionally helpful editor. Not one word appears in print without Lora Wildenthal's having read it. I also realized that several voices from my past were part of this book, most important Randy Kim, John Ringman, and Mark Rubin. They will be surprised to be mentioned here; neither they nor anyone else mentioned here bears responsibility for my errors. Last but not least, Vera Caldwell refocused my attention on the practical-sensual elements of Feuerbach's thought at just the right moment.

Abbreviations

Dittmar, *WdE*   *Das Wesen der Ehe von Louise Dittmar nebst einigen Aufsätzen über die soziale Reform der Frauen* (Leipzig: Wigand, 1849)

Feuerbach, *GW*   *Gesammelte Werke,* ed. Schuffenhauer (Berlin: Akademie Verlag, 1969ff)

Feuerbach, *EC*   *The Essence of Christianity,* trans. George Eliot (1854) (Amherst, NY: Prometheus, 1989)

Hess, *Briefwechsel*   Moses Hess, *Briefwechsel,* ed. Edmund Silberner (The Hague: Mouton, 1959)

Hess, *NQHF*   Moses Hess, *Neue Quellen zur Hess-Forschung,* ed. Wolfgang Mönke (Berlin: Akademie, 1964)

Hess, *PSS*   Moses Hess, *Philosophische und sozialistische Schriften 1837–1850. Eine Auswahl,* 2nd ed., ed. by Wolfgang Mönke (Berlin: Akademie, 1981)

Marx and Engels, *MECW*   Karl Marx and Friedrich Engels, *Collected Works* (New York: International Publishers, 1975–2004)

Wagner, *PW*   Richard Wagner, *Richard Wagner's Prose Works,* trans. William Ashton Ellis (London: Routledge Kegan and Paul, 1892–1899)

Wagner, *SL*   Richard Wagner, *Selected Letters of Richard Wagner,* trans. and ed. Stewart Spencer and Barry Millington (New York: W. W. Norton, 1987)

INTRODUCTION

Love, Death, and Ludwig Feuerbach's Philosophy of Revolution

Ludwig Feuerbach's psychological theory of religion pervaded radical political thought in Germany in the 1840s. Radicals found in it a way of thinking that questioned the legitimacy of established institutions and authorities. The critique was radical: not just of the established church, but of religion in general; not just of the existing, undemocratic state, but of the state and its institutional forms (especially army and bureaucracy) in general; and not just of the existing patriarchal family, but of legalized forms of interpersonal relationships in general. In the hothouse political atmosphere of Vormärz Germany, the young men and women informed by Feuerbach found that even he was an institution to be attacked. The strongest criticisms of his thought appeared before the revolution from those heavily under his influence, such as the socialists Karl Marx and Friedrich Engels and the anarchist individualist Max Stirner.

These battles over the meaning of religion and the function of philosophical critique were not idle play. The new Prussian monarch Frederick William IV, a Pietist, drew a direct connection between Protestant orthodoxy and the exercise of monarchical power. The radicals experienced repression in the 1840s. Some, like Arnold Ruge, landed in prison; others, like the poet Georg Herwegh, were forced into exile. All had to struggle with the reality of censorship. Herwegh's *21 Sheets from Switzerland* of 1843—so named since all publications of fewer than 20 sheets, or about 400 pages, were subject to censorship in Germany—was a tour de force, consisting as it did of pieces by Marx, Ruge, Bruno Bauer, and Moses Hess.[1] It was at the same time a document of impotence, as it revealed that many of the best German thinkers were writing anonymously or from exile. The existing political order excluded the radical thinkers; even a reclusive philosopher of Feuerbach's stature had almost no chance of gaining a secure position in the state-run universities of the day. Advocates of moderate, gradual change, like Moses Hess and Karl Grün, became radicalized under the combined influence of political reality, Feuerbach, and other radicals including the French anarchist Pierre-Joseph Proudhon.

By the mid-1840s, what had begun as countercultural rhetoric was transformed into open revolutionary discourse. This was not a discourse about the proper form of institutions, or a debate over the specific meaning of rights and their institutional protection, or a discussion of the specifics of governmental policy. Instead, the radicals called for the dramatic destruction of what existed in the name of a not-yet-specified future. At stake were not specific reforms demanded of the existing state. At stake for the radicals were the experiential extremes of everyday life, the authentic moments of meaning beyond the artificiality of institutions. Discussions of revolution turned on problems of love, death, and the meaning of the universe. They turned on the question of what life meant after traditional religion.

This book examines the radicalism in Feuerbach's work. It then traces Feuerbachian critique in Moses Hess's cosmology of revolution, the radical democrat and feminist Louise Dittmar's turn from established religion to self-imposed ideals, and Richard Wagner's revolutionary opera, which posed the problem of death for narratives of human progress. Other followers of Feuerbach could have been chosen for this study. But these three are important insofar as their differences both with Feuerbach and with each other indicate how divergent the paths were that Feuerbachian critique opened up. Underlying the book is the recognition that the issues that arose—from the meaning of religious illusion in Feuerbach to Richard Wagner's quest for a new kind of political religion, from Hess's search for cosmic meaning to Dittmar's demolition of institutional marriage—persist in countercultural thinking today, a full century and a half later. The specific criticisms have shifted, of course, but two elements have remained intact. First, death is a reality for all humans, whose souls are not eternal, neither saved nor damned, but part of the earth. Death raises the constant possibility of the meaninglessness of life, which can both undermine the sense of existing institutions and raise the question of whether any institution, as well as any revolutionary aim, makes sense. Nihilism is a constant possibility in the counterculture of modernity; Wagnerian ruminations on destruction are everywhere, both in contemporary pop culture and in contemporary politics. Second, love presents a hoped-for alternative to the false objectivity of institutions and systems, an immediacy that implies something beyond the present order. Love in turn means sex, both in the work of Feuerbach and his readers, and in our own contemporary popular culture, which positively drips with the praise of sex and the night against the inauthentic world of the day invoked in *Tristan and Isolde*. The culture industry has been highly successful in harnessing revolutionary forces of death, nihilism, love, and sex. Meanwhile, the removal of intimacy and meaning to the private household, concealed through solid walls and legal curtains, rights of property and rights of privacy, corresponds to the mass production of standardized housing. In fact, revolutions in everyday life are perfectly compatible with the maintenance of existing institutions. The process of revolutionizing everyday life began more than a century before the 1960s, as politicized intellectuals on the margins of society before 1848 transformed Romantic concepts into political ideals. The countercultural world of mid-nineteenth-century Europe (while my focus is on Germany, there were similar developments in England, France, and Russia) is not alien to contemporary America.

The Feuerbachian critique was specifically German in one respect: its adoption of a radical, antistatist, even antilegal language of communitarian nationalism. Feuerbach's remarks on patriotism were not incidental to his communitarian ethics: an "I" and a "Thou" were part of the same natural community, the nation, as he and the national democrats from Friedrich Hecker to Georg Herwegh proclaimed. Whatever anti-German position Hess took at the end of his life, his radical Jewish nationalism made use of cultural elements common to German nationalism, from a biological conception of race to a sentimental glorification of the mother of the nation. Dittmar's search for a separate Germanic worldview in ancient Nordic and Germanic sagas was not alien to the worldview of a radical democratic politician like Robert Blum or a radical feminist like Louise Otto. Indeed, Wagner's work on the *Ring of the Nibelung* came out of a discussion in the mid-1840s on the need for a new national and nationalist German opera making use of the sagas; Louise Otto had contributed essays and an original opera on the Nibelung saga to that discussion.

These motifs point to important precedents for the 1840s radicals, to be found in German Romanticism, the Young Germany movement in literature, and radical nationalism since 1813. In the 1840s, Feuerbach stood at the center of a specifically philosophical radicalism, which had developed out of the contradictions of Hegelianism as progressive hopes for the Prussian state slowly died.[2] Others, such as David Friedrich Strauss, with his realistic approach to Jesus, undermined the transcendent claims of religion by splitting Jesus Christ into a historical figure, the empirical data of whose life scholars could research, and a mythic figure. Strauss, Feuerbach wrote, was a man who "finally spoke freely and openly, who spoke directly to his age."[3] It was Feuerbach who spelled out the significance of these challenges, and who lived these challenges, as a thinker too radical for existing institutions, maligned by the contemporary press, as a convinced revolutionary disappointed with the Revolution of 1848 almost as soon as it began, and as a critical observer of the dismal political scene in Germany between 1849 and his death in 1872. Central to Feuerbach's thinking—and indicative of the rarified nature of German radical politics—was his radicalization of Hegel's critique of Descartes.[4] Descartes had posited a dual nature of the human, on the one side concrete, material, and determined, on the other side abstract, spiritual, and free; Hegel had sought to put these two sides into motion: bodily substance and consciousness were two sides of the Spirit that governed the whole process of the world, and the historical end of the process was self-knowledge, the coming together of body and spirit. Feuerbach's initial rejection of personal immortality was still within a Hegelian spirit, where the "immortal" could exist beyond the individual; by the early 1840s, he had discarded Hegel's world-spirit entirely.

In 1830, Feuerbach published anonymously his *Thoughts on Death and Immortality*.[5] The work was an affront to the official Protestant church in Prussia, and indeed to the state-endorsed churches across the German lands, insofar as it rejected personal immortality—the basis of much religious authoritarianism, which used the threat of damnation to promote ethical behavior. But this was also a work solidly in the Hegelian tradition. Spirit did not disappear; it consisted of the knowledge acquired by humans over the course of their lifetimes, and this body of knowledge bore the higher unity of all mankind, the product of human consciousness, spirit. By producing knowledge, the individual became immortal.[6] Feuerbach became increasingly dissatisfied with this formula over the 1830s, as he turned back to his earliest interest, religion and theology. There he found something else at work: the individual yearning to be something more than a mortal being. His radical critique took on a paradoxical form in his 1841 *Essence of Christianity*:[7] on the one hand, the human is completely within an immanent, restrained universe, rendering claims to transcendent foundations, whether of God or of the state, an absurdity; on the other hand, the human is aware of this finitude, and that awareness points to a sense of belonging to a species that has infinite potential. The consciousness of death points to a surplus capacity of humanity—but the latter is always susceptible to the critique of meaning in light of inevitable death, as the chapters in this book will show.

The critique of abstraction from the point of view of the finite human led Feuerbach to a second set of questions, closely related to those facing the French sensualists of the eighteenth century. If there is no abstract God or Idea setting down rules of human conduct, then where do these rules come from? Feuerbach's father, the renowned Bavarian legal reformer Anselm Feuerbach, would have said, following Kant: from an inborn, abstract, logical sense of the ethical, of what "ought" to be.[8] His son's anti-idealist thought had to deny the Kantian categorical imperative; he sought the solution on a different level, that of "love"—by which he meant the concrete relationship between I and Thou. Concrete relationships were not the same as abstract institutions; they were not ideals but concrete realities. They were physical, not spiritual. In his final years, Feuerbach would come to appreciate the aspects of Kant that criticized idealism and pointed toward empiricism, but he could never accept Kant's abstract ethics. Physical love between man and woman was concrete, not an abstract institution like marriage. Love, in short, was the key to ethics, to politics, to social organization. Feuerbach never wrote on the French or German utopian socialists who sought to make "love" the center of their systems, but it is no surprise that the German utopian socialists—Moses Hess, Karl Grün, Hermann Kriege—turned to Feuerbach for their philosophical foundations.[9]

The third element of this study is revolution. The concept itself underwent a shift already during the French Revolution, where the call for the emancipation of the people as a whole in the form of representative institutions became the demand for a complete transformation of the world in all its aspects, from eating to temporality to fashion. Revolution haunted the political culture of the nineteenth century. In Germany, even before 1848, political discussion was dominated by conservatives seeking to preserve absolute power against the onslaught of French radicalism, moderates seeking a nontraumatic way to usher in an era of limited political participation through constitutional monarchism, and democrats seeking the direct role of the people. These debates helped paralyze the Frankfurt National Assembly in 1848–49. Social history over the last few decades has ripped apart mythic accounts of the events and gradually dissolved the notion of a real, unified "revolution" in 1848 into a multitude of localizable conflicts, misunderstandings, and resentments. It has provided a far more accurate view of what happened.[10] Nevertheless, many of the leading participants, especially among the radicals, sought to comprehend the events as a unified process, and used the idea of "the revolution" to organize their thoughts and actions. The year 1848 revealed the conflict between the practices of revolution—themselves multiple and contradictory—and the ideal of revolution itself. The main characters in this book were witnesses to one or another moment of the revolution. Feuerbach was an observer at the Frankfurt National Assembly and held lectures on religion in Heidelberg organized by the democratic students of that university, an early example of a radical teach-in. In the Rhine-Main region, Louise Dittmar gave public lectures as a single, radical woman—in itself a revolutionary deed—and published books of bloody, radical democratic poetry. Richard Wagner was, despite his later protestations, active on the barricades in the Dresden Uprising of May 1849, the Russian anarchist Mikhail Bakunin by his side. Moses Hess was part of the radical "workerist" fringe in the 1848 uprising in Cologne, before being marginalized by Marx and Engels, and witnessed the June Days in Paris in 1848, correctly seeing in them the coming crisis of socialist endeavors.

While Feuerbach, Dittmar, and Hess demanded some kind of rights as part of their notion of revolution, rights in themselves were not their main objective but rather a means to other ends. Dittmar's 1849 essay on Charlotte Corday, who assassinated the radical "friend of the people" Jean Paul Marat in 1793, affirmed the terrorist revolutionary act over abstract and universal human rights, for example; Hess's revolutionary catechism stressed love, i.e., solidarity, not rights. Love and revolution were to trump mere rights; the new world was not one of individualized rights-holders. The political radicals developed their attack on rights-oriented liberalism even before a system of civil rights and democratic voting rights existed. The critique of liberalism began before liberalism triumphed. The radicals of mid-nineteenth-century Germany were suspended between two worlds; on the one hand, they confronted a set of institutions and a way of thinking that had become implausible; on the other hand, the institutions of liberal capitalism, whether democratic or not, did not yet exist, which helped bar the way to rights-oriented social theory of neo-Kantian thought in Germany, pragmatic philosophy, and later theories of rational choice in the Anglo-American world. The radicals dismantled before the new construction had begun in earnest. Perhaps for this reason they have been held responsible for the crises of the century that would follow.

From very different political perspectives, Karl Löwith and Georg Lukács developed this Feuerbachian critique.[11] Löwith saw in Feuerbach's philosophy the dissolution of a stabilizing worldview developed by Goethe and Hegel, the one with a notion of balance and harmony in nature, the other with a notion of the coherence of the historical process, including the French Revolution. Goethe and Hegel's backward-looking approach to the world was replaced, on Löwith's argument, with the attempt to smash the old and usher in the not-yet-known new. The disruption of an existing worldview led to new conceptions of the future exemplified by Wagner, for whom the world was a stage subject to the commands of its conductor. It is unclear whether Löwith was aware of Lenin's use of a similar metaphor to describe socialism.[12] Lukács certainly was, and came to see Leninism as the solution to the crisis of the nineteenth century, namely, the destruction of a realistic view of the world and the rise of a conception of the future dominated by myth and nihilism. Both Löwith and Lukács saw Nazism as one logical result of the intellectual crisis of the twentieth century. For Lukács and for official

Marxism-Leninism, the atheism of Feuerbach and the political economy of Marx offered a way out of this nihilistic end of the world. For Löwith, by contrast, Marxism-Leninism embodied the logic of modernity, infused with both nihilism and hubris.

Löwith and Lukács still today make compelling reading of the crisis of modernity, and their ideas inform much of this book. But at the same time, they are philosophers and political thinkers seeking to make a single, strong argument; the historical legacies of Feuerbach and his followers are more complex. Feuerbach's reduction of myth to man could mean the destruction of myth in a positivist spirit, but it could also lead to a reevaluation of myth itself, now viewed as a way for humans to conceptualize value and meaning in an austere, cold world. And such recognition of the value of myth could it-self lead in several different directions: toward Feuerbach's republican natural-ism, toward Wagner's authoritarian cult, or toward a Nietzschean anarchism. Indeed, the turn from myth to nature itself could lead to a "remythification" of nature in the form of a science-based cosmology. In fact, Hess's work on gravity was part of a larger movement in the 1850s and 1860s associated with the natural scientists Ludwig Büchner, Jakob Moleschott, and Karl Vogt, to find a new Weltanschauung based on the natural sciences, a kind of ersatz religion in the finite, material world. Myth, especially mythic thinking about the origin and order of the cosmos, did not disappear even as the world of Hegelian abstractions and speculation gave way to a very different intellectual culture of positivism and materialism. These were examples of a posttraditional cosmology that in some cases foreshadowed New Age notions of later decades. And, like later experiments in esoteric thought, the movements included not only serious elaboration of philoso-phy but also cosmology, not only a turn to physiology but also odd diets. As Moses Hess explored the parallels of cosmic, biological, and social orga-nization, he also turned to acupuncture and homeopathic medicine;[13] as Richard Wagner considered the grand scheme of mythic world history, he also experimented with radical hydrotherapy;[14] as Dittmar developed her critique of formal marriage, she delved into the myths of the pagan North to find a new vision of the world.[15] And Feuerbach himself went beyond a physiological account of consciousness ("You are what you eat") to the concrete proposal that a revolutionary people should eat lentils rather than potatoes.[16] (Of the four, probably only Feuerbach retained a sense of humor about his arguments.) Out of the counterculture can come many different kinds of politics and many different diets. In the end, the story of the Feuerbachian radicals is one of the birth of politics neither from pure reason nor from theology, but from the contradictory, scattered pieces of an anti-liberal, antiformal counterculture.

The subject of Chapter 1 is Feuerbach's influential 1841 work, *The Essence of Christianity*. There Feuerbach makes two arguments that reappear throughout this book. On the one hand, Feuerbach asserts that humans are part of the world, finite and mortal, limited in knowledge and ability by the matter that makes them up: in short, that humans are *not* divided into a transcendent or spiritual, "higher" soul and material substrate. As already noted, the critique of transcendence has immediate bearing on aspects of the world that claim to have a higher standing than the individual, such as God and state (to use Bakunin's chief examples).[17] On the other hand, Feuerbach wants to retain some notion of the infinite potential of humanity—otherwise why the critique? That potential he finds in the very notion of God. Since God is a creation of humans, then His characteristics are also potentially the characteristics of humans. The species-being has possibilities that the individual does not. The contradiction between finite ability and infinite potential, the limited human and the unlimited humanity, comprises the key radical move of Feuerbach's text: in essence, an attempt to pull the Christian dichotomy between man and God down to earth.

The Essence of Christianity criticized religion but did not abandon what Feuerbach viewed as its core significance for humanity. Indeed, after 1841, Feuerbach would plunge ever deeper into religion and mythology, not at the level of abstract theology, but at the level of concrete stories. Positivistic, natural science, in his estimation, would not answer the human questions raised by myth and religion. As Feuerbach put it in a letter to an admirer, "Anatomy, physiology, medicine, chemistry know nothing about the soul, God, etc. We only know about them from history." While he agreed with the materialists that the human is a natural being, his main focus was "the fantastic beings and the thoughts that arise from humans."[18] Myth and religion revealed something about humanity. The question was how to read these obscure stories, how to translate the sacred language of the high priests and formal institutions into the reality of a concrete humanity. The chapters that follow, on Hess, Dittmar, and Wagner, explore three different approaches to the hidden human meanings of myth.

Moses Hess is the subject of Chapter 2. Hess is notoriously hard to place in the intellectual world of midcentury Europe. A Rhenish Jew, he abandoned Judaism for an ill-defined worship of Spinoza at an early age; was one of the first German speakers to discover the French utopian socialists; fell in with Marx and Ruge at the time of Feuerbach's greatest influence, and with Marx developed a critique of Feuerbach's contemplative side; moved with Marx toward communism, then broke with Marx over the latter's authoritarian political style; found his way to discussions of natural science and worldview; developed an early socialist Zionism at the same time as he worked with Lassalle on a new workers' movement in Germany; and ended up close to the newly formed Social Democrats at the same time that his final sympathies lay with France, reflecting his dismay with German radicals' anti-Semitism. The chapter reads Hess as a radical in search of a revolutionary lever able to change the course of world history, and seeking signs in nature and society indicating the coming harmony of the world. The revolution for Hess—and for Feuerbach—was to realize the human, to open up new horizons for humanity. What is most embarrassing about Hess to his defenders, namely, his amateurish forays into natural science, becomes understandable as a way to conceptualize what the revolution should mean, indeed why the finite human should be capable of a revolutionary world in the first place.

Over the past two decades, Louise Dittmar's unapologetic, democratic feminism has finally received some attention. Few women were as direct in their philosophical and political critique of marriage. Chapter 3 provides a systematic interpretation of her work, arguing that Feuerbachian motives and ways of thinking structured it throughout. Dittmar was a political radical, but more specifically she was a Feuerbachian, seeking the deeper meaning of humanity in the "hieroglyphics" of myth.[19] If one takes her work on Nordic religion and Feuerbach seriously, one finds a disturbing endorsement of violent, bloody revolution, of a *Götterdämmerung* in fire and destruction as the prerequisite for a new, authentically human world. Beneath the images of violence is a serious philosophical point: in the modern world of mature citizens, religion is no longer something one is born into, but rather a consciously chosen, self-imposed God or ideal or worldview. The individual must set his or her own values.

Chapter 4 continues to explore the post-Feuerbachian appropriation of myth and religion in the works of the composer and writer Richard Wagner. Both Feuerbach and Wagner attacked political and religious institutions of the day. Yet both also saw in myth-making an essential human activity, and furthermore an activity that was important for communities rather than merely for individuals. The results of their work differed greatly, however, as Feuerbach sought to see myth as a momentary creation of ideals that should be immediately subject to destruction by new ideals, while Wagner's work culminated in a brute juxtaposition of utter nihilism and the creation of a new institution around himself, Bayreuth. Wagner asked what came after religion, and had no clear answer—itself an important response to the problem.

The people in this study were all outsiders. Feuerbach was an outsider at least in part by choice: initially intending to study Lutheran theology at Heidelberg, he shifted to idealist philosophy at Berlin in the mid-1820s,

quickly falling under Hegel's influence. His intellectual trajectory was thus
within the two dominant traditions of Protestant, academic Germany in
the nineteenth century. Feuerbach knew that his writing would probably
lead to his being barred from the profession, since professors as civil servants
were expected to conform to the official ideology of the state. Feuerbach
proclaimed in 1842 that an authentic philosopher could not be a professor
of philosophy, backed by the authority of an institutionalized discipline, but
should, like Spinoza, Descartes, Bruno, and Campanella, descend from the
lectern to engage the matters of a whole, free human.[20] Wagner was not a
serious student and came at the scholarship of German mythology and at
politics as an outsider. He was a dilettante in high culture, and some have
made the argument that his musical innovations also reflected—and perhaps
even derived from—a dilettantism. His most transformative work appeared
after his programmatic criticism of opera in *Opera and Drama* of 1851.
Hess and Dittmar were both autodidacts. Their appropriation of philosophical and political materials reflects their marginal position. Neither was
at home in the world of the German *Bildungsbürger*. Though from a leading
family in Darmstadt, as a woman Dittmar was an outsider to higher education and public debate; it was a political event when she first took the stage
to hold a lecture in Mannheim in 1847 and began to publish under her
own name. Hess came from an unassimilated Jewish family. The Judaism
he grew up with was not intellectual, nor was it mediated through nineteenth century Christianity; unlike assimilated or converted Jews, like Karl
Marx, Hess was a true outsider, even learning German in private lessons in
his teenage years.[21] Hess, more than Marx, was aware of the prevalence of
anti-Jewish sentiments among the radicals (Jewish or otherwise), and developed his late, harsh criticism of the limits of German "universalist" radicalism on this basis. In short, the countercultural thinkers described here
indeed formed a culture outside of the institutionalized culture of the
German academy, whose representatives had secure jobs, secure pensions,
and a secure sense of their own importance.

Feuerbach is the only true insider in the story—and he made a series of
conscious choices that ensured his exclusion from the academy and, by the
1860s, put him outside the mainstream of German intellectual life. The
final chapter of this book explores the late Feuerbach, and in particular his
view of ethics. Feuerbach was less obsessed with a gigantic view of world
history, of the world on fire, than were Dittmar, Wagner, or Hess. His late
readings of myth and religion focused instead on the intensely personal and
individual world of concrete relationships, practical ethics, and morality
embedded in everyday life. Feuerbach's image of a truly human life took

place apart from the worlds of finance and capital, legislation and rights, infrastructure and grand systems of planning, the worlds that he, like Kierkegaard, would have considered in some sense inauthentic. His image of the truly human world imagined revolution in the form of the victory of love and the coming to terms with death. Nothing less.

CHAPTER 1

Feuerbachian Radicalism: The Finitude of the World and Infinite Human Potential

In 1841, Feuerbach took the German intellectual world by storm. *The Essence of Christianity* proclaimed loudly and clearly what David Friedrich Strauss's *Life of Jesus* had insinuated: religion, including Christianity, was the product of human thought and emotion, and one could only understand religion by understanding humanity. The book stated openly what conservatives had suspected over the 1830s, that Hegelianism, whatever its claims to reconcile politics, religion, and society, was at its heart actually atheistic and radical. Feuerbach's work, along with that of Strauss and Bruno Bauer, marked the turn to open radicalism of the Left Hegelians. But his work was also the document of a fallen Hegelian. It not only took on the establishment connected with Pietism, it also marked part of Feuerbach's own break with his philosophical roots. The tensions between the new approach and the residues of Hegel in the book, this chapter argues, were precisely what made it so important as a radical text in the German *Vormärz*, the years before the March Revolution of 1848.

At the heart of *The Essence of Christianity* was a tension between the finite world in which humans lived and died and the infinite potential of the mind. The contrast between finitude and infinity was hardly a new one. Indeed, the notion of the human as part animal and part angel was central to Christianity. Feuerbach seemed to replicate the Christian notion of the human in his book. If the qualities imputed to God were really those of humanity, then was not humanity itself divine in its potential? The notion of the divinity of humanity would attract radicals seeking both a break from established religion and some new notion of what was sacred in the secular world. But along with the first argument went a second that seemed to contradict it: that any notion of the divinity of humanity, of its infinite potential, was necessarily limited and finite, since human experience itself was limited and finite. On this reading, Feuerbach's critique of religion became a critique of ersatz religious tendencies as well, including the deification of humanity. The divine could always be reduced to the finite; any hermeneutics of religious styles of thought had to be suspicious, had to be at the same time a critique of ideology.

These arguments existed side by side in *The Essence of Christianity*. At times, Feuerbach seemed to use the tension between them to make his points; at others, he seemed less in command of the relationship between ideology and utopia. That tension nonetheless was productive. It allowed his contemporaries to engage in multiple interpretations of what Feuerbach's radicalism was about. The first part of this chapter examines the arguments in more detail, in the context of Feuerbach's life. Feuerbach himself quickly became aware of the contradictions in his work, and his work of 1842–44 sought a new approach, which the chapter next examines. All the while, he himself was part of a discussion about revolutionary political and cultural change. The chapter finishes with an account of Feuerbach's activities, or rather his own passivity, during the revolution itself. The problems he posed in *The Essence of Christianity* said very little about actual revolutionary politics. They were rather problems that confronted humans in their everyday lives, problems more of culture than of politics.

Feuerbach's Context

Feuerbach's background itself exemplified the political, religious, and philosophical traditions that would be central to German radicalism in general. His father, Anselm von Feuerbach, was a leading legal reformer in the famous Montgelas government, and too liberal and too Protestant for the restoration in Bavaria. Ludwig's three older brothers were all investigated by the Prussian police in 1824. One of them, Karl, was kept in solitary confinement for a year, where he tried twice to commit suicide; no charges were brought against this suspected terrorist, and he was eventually released, a broken man. Ludwig's interests seemed less overtly political. An interest in popular Protestant theology in his youth led him to study theology at Heidelberg, following the advice of his father. There his family's name prompted observation by the police, who were, however, unable to uncover any direct connection to political activities.[1] His interests were meanwhile shifting away from theology. Against his father's wishes, Feuerbach went to Berlin in 1825 to study philosophy, and soon came under the sway of Hegel. By the late 1820s, he was a devoted follower—but also penniless. Defending his dissertation in 1828, at the age of 24, he moved to the intellectual backwater of Erlangen, where he became a *privatdozent* at a university devoted primarily to training Protestant ministers.

Feuerbach's time in Erlangen was limited. Not only were his philosophy lectures of little interest to the provincial, conservative students—and a *privat-dozent* lived on the fees of students—but his work soon ran afoul of the state. In 1830, he published anonymously his *Thoughts on Death and Immortality*, a thoroughly Hegelian attack on the concept of personal immortality. The content was offensive enough to a conservative government, but the sarcastic poems at the end sealed its fate. Referring to Pietists as "loathsome worms" and Pietism as the "eliminated waste of the food that humanity long ago digested" could endear him to few religious conservatives, Pietists or not. The work was instantly attributed to him, and he lost any chance at a career in the state-run universities of his time. He must have been aware of what a book like this, published in the same year as the July Revolution in France, would cost him. After all, the work revealed the radical streak in Hegel and questioned the individualism and orientation toward personal immortality that had become so central to conservative religious and political thought of the time. By the mid-1830s, Feuerbach was one of the leading figures of the critical Left Hegelians. The theological faculty at Erlangen banned their students from attending his lectures, leaving him without a clear future in the university.[2]

The 1830s saw a radical transformation of philosophy. At the beginning of the decade, Hegel still represented something of the conservative establishment, despite growing tensions. But by the end of the decade, the Left Hegelians had begun to make their radical positions in philosophy, politics, and religion public. Part of the transformation was rooted in an internal transformation of Hegelian thought itself; as John Toews showed in his important work on Hegelianism, the delicate Hegelian syntheses of religion with philosophy and of the existing Prussian state with a notion of historical flux began to fall apart, especially as anti-Hegelian conservatives occupied the leading positions in the state bureaucracy.[3] Eduard Gans, because of his Jewish descent never fully at home in the restored Prussian state, gave Hegel's political thought a critical, dynamic thrust, oriented toward freedom and the fulfillment of the principles of the French Revolution.[4] David Friedrich Strauss's 1835 account of *The Life of Jesus Christ* pulled the empirical, finite Jesus of history away from the mythical, "infinite" Jesus of religion, opening the way to a critique of established religion.[5] Bruno Bauer pushed Strauss's critical distinction between the finite and the infinite even further, eventually calling for the demolition of theological consciousness in general, in the hopes of finding a new, higher synthesis in fully human self-consciousness.[6] Gans, Strauss, and Bauer all remained within the framework of Hegelian thinking but raised problems not easily resolved by it.

The late 1830s for Feuerbach, by contrast, were occupied with a volume on the late eighteenth-century religious skeptic Pierre Bayle.[7] Even while he followed the disputes of the Young Hegelians with care and penned defenses of the Hegelian tradition in a series of essays from the 1830s, even as he participated in Arnold Ruge's venture in radical philosophical publishing, the *Hallische Jahrbücher für deutsche Wissenschaft und Kunst*, his mind was in a different, more skeptical world. Feuerbach announced his break with Hegelian philosophy in a controversial article in 1839. As Marx Wartofsky has showed, that was just one of the steps toward his new, critical, sensualist philosophy of the 1840s.[8] The threads of thought that would preoccupy Feuerbach for the rest of his life were already present: the inadequacy of thought alone as a means of grasping the world; the necessity of sensual, empirical knowledge; and the critique of the divine. With his criticism of the primacy of self-consciousness, Feuerbach went beyond Strauss and Bauer, too—and pointed toward a new kind of philosophy.[9]

The Essence of Christianity went beyond denying personal immortality to declare all of religion, including God himself, the product of humanity, stating systematically what Strauss had implied in his *Life of Jesus*. The grand gesture overturned the field of theology, replacing the study of God with the study of man. The work was bound to be viewed as a radical statement by the leading critics of German politics and society of the time: Karl Marx, Friedrich Engels, and Moses Hess on the far left; Arnold Ruge, Karl Grün, and Bruno Bauer among the republicans; Julius Fröbel and Karl Ronge among the democrats. Strauss and Feuerbach would become the "prophets" of the Free Religious movement—and the symbols of anarchy for the establishment.[10] Once Feuerbach's latest book had taken the radical world by storm, his fate in the academic world was sealed: barring radical change, there was no way he would ever find a path into the university.

The finite and the infinite were in tension in Feuerbach's prose, and exactly this tension was what transformed his hundreds of pages about God into a statement about the existing polity. The critique of transcendent notions in favor of the immanent world implied the destruction of ideals—king, church, property. "Humanity" would remain, as the foundation of a new religion of infinite potential in the finite world. The tension between finite and infinite, critique and glorification of the sacred, runs throughout Feuerbach's work before 1848. His work raised questions on two separate levels. On one, it implied a limited, finite human being deprived of the foundations of God, Truth, and Right; on the other, it implied an immense, even divine potential for human self-improvement, since humans bore the nature of God. He proclaimed, for example, that the essence of God is man: did that mean that God is the figment of a weak animal's mind, a kind of psychological wish-fulfillment, or that the human is God, capable of controlling the universe? He proclaimed that human knowledge is determined by the finite world: does that mean that humans can never raise themselves above the world, that this knowledge is always determined and constructed by external forces, or that they have the potential to know the entire universe? Feuerbach found in love the expression of intersubjectivity, and saw in intersubjectivity the source of knowledge: does this insight into the social nature of knowledge point to the social construction of perception, or to a socialist utopia, the brotherhood of man? At heart, Feuerbach saw the truth of religion in its expression of human desire rooted in scarcity and dependence and its lie in theological abstraction: is religion part of the human's limited and dependent place in the world, or can it be superseded? Both Van A. Harvey's interpretation of Feuerbach as protoexistentialist and Karl Löwith's discovery of an unmoored humanistic hubris find expression in Feuerbach's own writing.[11] Indeed, this combination of the finite and the infinite, ideology-critique and utopia, gave his work its political force in the 1840s and after.[12] For in a German political world marked by monarchical rule and religious Pietism, ubiquitous censorship and growing critique, police controls and radical movements, the critique of religion and focus on the world of concrete things accessible to all men was a political event.[13]

The Essence of Christianity and the Essence of Humanity

Feuerbach wrote *The Essence of Christianity* as a prophet of change. His aim was not merely to develop a theory of Christianity but to uproot it and the entire social order on which it was based, to prove that theology was a "psychic pathology,"[14] and that the essence of religion was not God but man. Even the style of his work exhorts the reader to revolt.[15] Like a German Jean-Jacques Rousseau, Feuerbach called on the reader in second person, as intimate interlocutor, to recognize the obvious, the natural, the radical truth of Feuerbach's rejection of Christianity, the sacrament of real life: "Let friendship be sacred to thee, property sacred, marriage sacred— sacred the well-being of every man; but let them be sacred in and by themselves," i.e., without reference to an imagined God.[16] In rejecting Christianity, Feuerbach did not want to give up religion; he sought to provide a new religion of what was truly divine and in the world, a religion of love, marriage, property—of, that is, the concrete world of real humans.

Feuerbach's book provided a two-pronged revolutionary message: it sought to smash false idols of the establishment, reducing the sacraments of institutional religion to finite, concrete, material things, and it yearned for a new beginning, a new world of infinite human potential.[17] Even as Feuerbach moved away from his anthropocentrism in the years that followed, as he began to bring nature into his work as a frightening, inhuman entity, he continued to present his philosophy as radical, even "communistic" politics. Feuerbach viewed himself as a reformer, a new Martin Luther, as the embodiment of radicalism in Germany before the Revolution of 1848.

In the first, dense chapter of *The Essence of Christianity*, Feuerbach located the "essential nature of man" in consciousness: it was humans' consciousness of themselves as a species, as a set of subjects who possess a collective knowledge, he asserted, that distinguished humans from other animals. This distinction between human and animal on the basis of consciousness could lead to two quite different conclusions: either that humans had a quantitatively better knowledge of the world than animals, or that they had a qualitatively different one. Humans were either a higher order of finite being able to exercise "divine" powers or a limited, finite being unable to escape their physical definition. Already, then, he elucidated the tension between the finite and infinite potential.

Human knowledge was, in Feuerbach's definition, knowledge of the human being, i.e., of self; human contemplation of an object was therefore always also contemplation of human self-consciousness:

> We know the man by the object, by his conception of what is external to himself; in it his nature becomes evident; this object is his manifested nature, his true objective *ego*.[18]

These obscure words expressed a basic principle of epistemology for a philosopher in the tradition of Kant and Hegel: that the matter of the world revealed to the sensory organs depended on what the sensory organs themselves are capable of comprehending. And human nature provided knowledge not just of immediate surroundings but of "the remotest star": "Man alone has purely intellectual, disinterested joys and passions; the eye of man alone keeps theoretical festivals. . . . The eye is heavenly in its nature."[19] Humanity, then, by virtue of its ability to observe the stars, was heavenly, cosmic, and able to rise above the world. The origin of philosophy, the origin of theory, lay in the ability of the human eye.

An individual example of cognition illuminated the nature of the species. Humanity as a species distinguished itself from animals insofar as humans were "absolute," able to elevate themselves "above the earth" in theory;[20] they were conscious of their abilities as (theoretically) infinite[21]—humans felt the divinity of their own being in the potential that was limited by their own finitude; they reached beyond the self to the divine, which was the absolute potential of the species itself.[22] In his 1843 *Principles of the Philosophy of the Future*, Feuerbach made evident the connection to humanist conceptions of a thinker like the Renaissance philosopher Pico della Mirandola: the human, as over against the animal, was universal and able to appropriate and manipulate all potentialities of nature.[23] By "the human" Feuerbach meant something other than the individual. The individual human was a finite being—as shown above, Feuerbach rejected as illogical the notion of personal immortality long before he overturned idealism per se.[24] By contrast, the human species was capable in toto of knowing all and doing all: "The knowledge of a single man is limited, but reason, science, is unlimited, for it is a common act of mankind."[25] The abilities that Feuerbach ascribed to humanity were none other than those of God, omniscience and omnipotence. God's qualities, Feuerbach argued, were the qualities of humanity, qualities that revealed themselves in the advancement of human knowledge and human community. The "new religion" that Feuerbach called for resembled nothing less than Comtean positivism, with its worship of science and vague promise of social reorganization.[26]

But the image of the cosmic human eye allows for another possible interpretation: why go beyond the limits of the human?[27] "Every being is in and by itself infinite—has its God, its highest conceivable being, in itself. . . . The leaf on which the caterpillar lives is for it a world, an infinite space."[28] Thus, "to a limited being its limited understanding is not felt to be a limitation."[29] By implication, humans were also irrevocably mired in the finitude, the immanence, of the human world:

> Man cannot get beyond his true nature. He may indeed by means of the imagination conceive of individuals of another so-called higher kind, but he can never get loose from his species, his nature.[30]

The clear implication of this statement was that humans, like all creatures, were indeed in a physiological circle: they, like caterpillars, could not be aware of their own limitations, even as a species. Humans were existentially tossed into a world not under their control. Indeed, "every limit of a being is cognizable only by another being out of and above him"[31]—like, perhaps, a superintelligent space alien. Feuerbach completed his thought with a note on the essentially human conceptualization of alien intelligence:

> There may certainly be thinking beings besides men on the other planets of our solar system. But by the supposition of such beings we do not change our standing point—we extend our conception *quantitatively* not *qualitatively*. For as surely as on the other planets there are the same laws of motion,

so surely are there the same laws of perception and thought as here. In fact, we people the other planets, not that we may place there different beings from ourselves, but *more* beings of our own or of a similar nature.[32]

For Feuerbach, human attempts to conceptualize higher beings, be they God or creatures on other planets, necessarily assumed that human intelligence was capable of accurately comprehending the universe, and was not limited by its finite place in the world. Alien intelligence, by implication, had to be the same as human—although perhaps more. Far more radically than the positivists of the second half of the nineteenth century, who would claim to follow in Feuerbach's footsteps, he raised the problem of finitude, of the limits to human cognition, of its self-referentiality (a sensory organ may only receive what it is physically capable of receiving, i.e., what it already potentially "knows").[33]

Feuerbach's discussion of intelligent alien life related directly to his discussion of religion. Indeed, the idea of beings with a higher intelligence paralleled Feuerbach's exposition of the Christian God. In this sense, his brief aside on the essential similarity of alien and human intelligence shed light on his continued belief in the centrality, even godlike place of humans in the universe. Feuerbach's humanism likewise reduced God to the human—and, like his discussion of alien intelligence, excluded the possibility of a radically different God incomprehensible to humans. A God that was fully abstracted from human experience would not be comprehensible to humanity, or indeed of any use to it. This God was the one Feuerbach considered that of the theologians. This God was the target of his criticism.

The theologian's understanding of Christianity, Feuerbach maintained, abstracted from the human self and in the end alienated humans from their essence; it consisted of abstract concepts and faith, which were, Feuerbach maintained, at the root of most violence in human history. The theological understanding of Christianity contradicted popular religion, which embraced the concrete, suffering self of Jesus; popular religion, unlike the religion of the theologians, recognized warm, human qualities in God as well as human love and desire. Feuerbach attacked the theologians for their cold abstractions; indeed, he rebelled against all abstraction, a way of pointing to the radical, existential materiality of the human experience. This search for the radically material, immanent truth of worldly life was not only a standard aspect of the Young Hegelian revolt of the time but was also to characterize much radicalism for the next century. At the same time that Feuerbach condemned abstraction as human alienation, however, he also reintroduced another kind of abstraction, this one associated with the telos of the radical gesture: humanity. Feuerbach hoped that his criticism would reveal not a dependent, finite, often helpless individual but a finite, collective being, the human race, with an infinite nature. In other words, he sought to discover the divinity of humanity.

As noted above, Feuerbach argued that the theologian's God was an abstraction from human activity. Instead of seeing a specific object, God was the power *to see*. While the individual human was able to do things, God was able *to do*: He was omnipotent. He did not know something, He was able *to know*, He was omniscient. God was, in a way, the grammar of infinitive constructions—not concrete reality, where verbs were delimited. But according to Feuerbach the human was in fact concrete: he or she was not abstractly human in life; rather, "personality is essentially distinguished into masculine and feminine,"[34] and this distinction, which broke apart the abstract human, "penetrates not only bones and marrow, but also his inmost self, the essential mode of his thought, will, and sensations."[35] And a human was also concrete in his or her work, devoted to the "essential mode of his activity," which determined judgment, mode of thinking, and sentiments.[36] The human was a limited individual, the human had a definite, concrete existence, as man or as woman, as hunter or planter, writer or day laborer; the human was his or her ability to comprehend the world, in his or her experience of the world. Awareness of this limitation was for Feuerbach the source of religiosity—an issue that would take on ever more importance in Feuerbach's work over the next decade.

Feuerbach showed sympathy for precisely the concrete aspect of popular religion in *The Essence of Christianity*: Mary, the mother of Jesus, whose divine status the Protestants sought to eliminate;[37] the human Jesus, who brought Mary's love back into Protestantism;[38] the suffering of the Son on the cross;[39] God as a person, as a father;[40] immortality, not as participation in the abstract perfection of the theologian's God, but as the resurrection of the individual—as the affirmation of the good aspects of the existing world, the wish that it continue after death.[41] Popular religion expressed the essence of man as determined by external forces, as suffering, as finite rather than infinite, and as multiple and divided rather than as a whole.

Even though Feuerbach rejected theological abstractions, not all abstractions disappeared from his thought. As noted already, the individual human was part of a larger unity he called humanity:

> [H]uman nature presents an infinite abundance of difference predicates, and for that very reason it presents an infinite abundance of different individuals. Each new man is a new predicate, a new phase of humanity. As many as are the men, so many are the powers, the properties of humanity.[42]

Indeed, the totality of humans—an inexhaustible totality—replaced God for Feuerbach. Hegel continued to resonate in Feuerbach's work as he recounted the development of a unified, expanding consciousness of mankind:

> In isolation, human power is limited, in combination it is infinite. The knowledge of a single man is limited, but reason, science, is unlimited, for it is a common act of mankind; and it is so, not only because innumerable men co-operate in the construction of science, but also in the more profound sense, that the scientific genius of a particular age comprehends in itself the thinking powers of the preceding age, though it modifies them in accordance with its own special character.[43]

Feuerbach's humanity had a scientific flavor reminiscent of French positivism. And, as he himself admitted, "humanity" was an abstraction that provided little in the way of feeling.[44]

Feuerbach, then, discovered two different essential truths about humanity that are concealed under the figure of an alien, nonhuman God—two truths that had quite different political implications.[45] On the first, existential reading, God embodied the wishes of a finite, dependent being for love, sympathy, succor, and power. God was essentially wish fulfillment.[46] If a practical-political project were to arise from this existential understanding, then it would involve coming to terms with one's own limits, taking responsibility for one's own life, perhaps also an unheroic and stoical liberalism. On the second, positivist reading, humans projected their own collective being, their humanity, onto a being they worshipped as objective.[47] A political project that focused on this alienation would have a strong, revolutionary thrust: to grab that essence back from the fetish, to transform the alienated self into an independent subject. Progress would involve reclaiming humanity from the alienated God—but not losing the redemptive category of "humanity" itself. The radical Young Hegelian Max Stirner, part of the circle around Bruno Bauer in Berlin, quickly saw that when Feuerbach replaced "God" with "man," he replicated what he attacked. "Haven't we seen the priest again then? Who is his god? Man with a capital M! What's the divine? The human!"[48] And the resulting political order, Stirner argued, would be more oppressive than that of the old regime, as certain individuals came to be declared not human: "[T]he Christian *essence*," namely, the focus on abstract God rather than the concrete man, "would only be fixed yet more oppressively."[49] The redemption that Feuerbach sought in this critique of God seemed to reverse theological priorities, but it did not dismantle theological structures. The same was true of the many movements and individuals that tapped into Feuerbach's ideas. By the mid-1840s, the German Catholic and Free Religious movements, for example, called for a turn away from formal structures of religion and instead to a movement for human dignity, for the realization of humanity's potential. They still had ideals—in Stirner's view idols—that drove their movements, but now these were worldly and consciously chosen; no wonder that a Feuerbachian feminist like Louise Dittmar, in search of a real movement for radical change, would gravitate toward these groups, as Chapter 3 discusses.[50]

Feuerbach was certainly sympathetic to these groups and others, arguing for a progressive repossessing of human nature from formal institutions like the church. But at the same time, even though he apparently replaced "God" with "humanity," his grand historical narrative contains aspects that resist a narrative of redemption. At these moments in *The Essence of Christianity*, the full complexity of his vision becomes evident. For he both engaged in a radical critique of the ideology of grand historical schema and sought to recreate one; he both dismantled an ideology and sought to create a new world of meaning, a new utopia. It was this tension that Stirner grabbed onto, but only partially comprehended. At several points in *The Essence of Christianity*, Feuerbach described the history of religion as the history of human consciousness itself in its childhood, youth, and adulthood. So long as humans are in a state of nature, their gods are personifications of natural forces—and necessarily plural. "Zeus is the strongest of the gods" because "physical strength, in and by itself, was regarded as something glorious, divine."[51] The abstractions from human characteristics, in other words, remained fragmented and relatively concrete in the polytheistic world. And so did the conception of the human: the individual was both distinguished from the species and subordinate to it, or rather to one species of man among many, or one commonwealth among many.[52] Judaism represented, according to Feuerbach, a break with paganism in light of monotheism, but not a step forward. Judaism set "egoism," not "subjectivity," at its foundation: nature was created ex nihilo by God for the Jewish race, it was "the abject vassal of [man's] selfish interest, of his practical egoism."[53] Judaism was "absolute intolerance, the secret essence of monotheism" in general,[54] and its doctrine of creation ex nihilo by the God of the Jews precluded Jewish contribution to the scientific progress of mankind:[55] careful study of nature could only constitute idolatry for monotheism, whereas "the polytheistic sentiment" was "the foundation of science and art."[56] The logical next step for Feuerbach might be to view Christianity as a mere extension of Judaism, as Marx would do in 1843.[57] That Feuerbach did not make this step reveals to what extent he remained embedded in 1841 in the usual anti-Jewish affect of the secularized Protestant tradition in Germany.[58] As he turned away from grand philosophizing about history a few years later, Feuerbach dropped such statements about Judaism, as discussed in Chapter 5.

Instead, Feuerbach seemed to view Christianity, not least in certain respects, as the true step forward to real universal subjectivity (i.e., the self-consciousness of the species) rather than the egoism of one small part of humanity. Christianity, according to Feuerbach, overcame the "self-humiliation of man" implied in Jewish subordination to God's law through the mediation of Jesus, God-become-man: "The Christian religion . . . distinguished the impulses and passions of man according to their quality, their character; it represented only good emotions, good dispositions, good thoughts, as revelations, operations . . . of God."[59] In short, Christianity "distinguishes inward moral purity from external physical purity" imposed by alien law;[60] Feuerbach evoked Jewish dietary rules as an example of such alien law-giving, arguing that "the Israelites did not rise above the alimentary view of theology."[61] By contrast, Christianity abstracted from individual abstractions to create one, unified center of positive qualities, God, and in so doing was able to represent the unity of humanity in its godlike character:

> "God is love": this, the supreme dictum of Christianity, only expresses the certainty which human feeling has of itself as the alone essential, i.e., absolute divine power, the certainty that the inmost wishes of the heart have objective validity and reality, that there are no limits, no positive obstacles to human feeling, that the whole world, with all its pomp and glory, is nothing weighed against human feeling.[62]

By expressing love as a generalized feeling of solidarity, Feuerbach spoke the language of the utopian socialists, employing a vague notion of socialism as a kind of sentiment of unity.[63] Love offered to Feuerbach a way out of an existential reduction to the individual egoist.

Faith, Feuerbach noted, contradicted love: the demand that humans serve one God broke the unity of humanity. "To be a Christian was to be beloved by God; not to be a Christian was to be hated by God, an object of the divine anger"—and thus "the maxim 'Love your enemies' had reference only to personal enemies, not to public enemies, the enemies of God, the enemies of faith, unbelievers."[64] Like so many other radical thinkers of the time, Feuerbach viewed the errors of Christianity as those aspects that it inherited from Judaism. Christianity may have "overcome" Judaism (in Feuerbach's conception) with its doctrine of the God-become-man in Jesus, but it remained within the "fanatical" and "egoistic" doctrine of Judaism, in its theological demand of faith.[65] God is both that which renders the world an object of aesthetic contemplation, which renders theoretical and scientific work on the world a positive matter and not mere idolatry—and remains "tainted with egoism."[66] Feuerbach called for casting off the bad aspects of Christianity; in its place appears a religion that would believe that "the Divine Being is the subjective human being in his absolute freedom and unlimitedness." "The beginning, middle, and end of religion is MAN."[67] And in conclusion, Feuerbach stated: "If human nature is the highest nature to man, then practically also the highest and first law must be the love of man to man. *Homo homini deus est* [Man is God to man]: this is the great practical principle: this is the axis on which revolves the history of the world."[68] Once again, Stirner's critique of Feuerbach is on the mark: "Our atheists are pious people," Stirner proclaimed, and Feuerbach's notion of redemptive history, however much it claimed to cast aside theology, fit well within the Protestant story of liberation from false idols and return to the concrete suffering of the man Jesus. The concept of humanity seemed to retain the idealist notion of a universal history of redemption.[69]

Without a doubt, Stirner hit his target with his criticism of Feuerbach's notion of humanity. But to conclude this section on *The Essence of Christianity*, it is important to keep in mind the tensions in the book itself. For Feuerbach himself was not finished thinking the topic through, and considering what the break with Hegel actually meant. There are hints of an overarching narrative of human consciousness, in which pre-Christian naturalist polytheism is overcome by Christianity, and Christianity finally resolved into a form of fully reclaimed human consciousness. But there are also hints of a sympathy for the ancients that went against the narrative. Indeed, already in the mid-1840s, he began to take polytheism more seriously as a religion of science. Even more than his covert admiration of the pagans, however, his doctrine of the relationship between I and Thou pointed toward a concrete and individual rather than universalizing and abstract notion of human community and communication.

Love for Feuerbach was the sensual encounter of an I and a Thou, of two conscious subjects, who in exploring each other become aware of the limits to their own consciousness and thereby able to grasp an outside world: love explained consciousness in a concrete and finite world, without recourse to God or idealism.[70] "Consciousness of the world," he writes, "is the consciousness of my limitation: if I know nothing of a world, I should know nothing of limits."[71] But his notion of consciousness, as noted above, pointed toward a closed circle, in which humans, just as much as caterpillars, could not be aware of their own limits. Humans escaped this cognitive circle by way of communication, speech, social action, and most important through "love," which meant feeling of an other, communication—both sensual and linguistic—of an I with a Thou:[72] "Without other men, the world would be for one not only dead and empty, but meaningless. . . . A man existing absolutely alone would lose himself without any sense of his individuality in the ocean of Nature; he would neither comprehend himself as man nor Nature as Nature."[73] The key here lay in recognizing the other as an other with similar human qualities, that is, offering and demanding respect and understanding. Mutuality meant recognition of mutual dependence as well. Love was not only active, it was also passive, insofar as it meant that the human being had to receive and accept the actions of another person:

> The heart, however, does not invent in the same way as the free imagination or intelligence; it has a passive, receptive relation to what it produces; all that proceeds from it seems to it given from without, takes it by violence, works with the force of irresistible necessity. The heart overcomes, masters man.[74]

And a new world would take shape.

"The Necessity for a Change": Revolution and Philosophy in the Vormärz

I have argued that *The Essence of Christianity* had at its core the tension between finite determinism and infinite potential, a paradox that far from being a logical error in fact made for the text's radical thrust. The three years after the book's publication saw a remarkable and intense debate over the meaning of philosophy, God, religion, state, citizenship, and revolution, all concepts central to the radicalism of the Vormärz.[75] Feuerbach's work stood, with all its tensions, at the center of the controversy. He was already aware that his work still contained residues of Hegelianism, although Stirner's work would not appear until 1844; in 1842, he felt compelled to publish an article clearly distinguishing his work from that of Bruno Bauer, whose work continued to be based on Hegelian concepts, and to write an unpublished essay as well, indicating the "necessity for a change" in his thought.[76] In a remarkable series of writings from 1842–43, he began to trace out a new position, turning against abstractions and toward an immediate, sensual notion of the world, what he called a "practical atheism."[77]

"Atheism" for Feuerbach did not mean that the essence of religion, what it said about humans' place in the world, would come to an end; Feuerbach never viewed religion as merely a lie. The categories that humans had set up between themselves and their own senses or between each other, rather, would disappear. Atheism meant the end of false idols and false mediations. Feuerbach called for replacing the mediation of institutional forms, including the church, holy writ, and the monarchy, with the immediate unity that he described as "love." "The Necessity for a Change" made clear that Feuerbach had a political intention in mind. Religion, Feuerbach wrote there, was the "heart of humanity"; but Christianity, he argued, had gradually lost its heart to theology and in practical terms had died.[78] Hegelianism had sought to retain Christianity, not in its original form, but as a set of abstractions—without the "fire, energy, truth" of a religion at its origins. Feuerbach proclaimed that little more than convention remained, the mere ghost of the departed spirit of theology.[79] The only way forward was a new, atheistic philosophy that was itself "religion"—in the sense that it explained the original needs that led to religion. Politics itself, he stated, "must become our religion," in the sense of immediate and common bonds among people, which was the anthropological content of religion.[80] Christianity had broken these bonds by promoting individuality. It would have to be replaced by direct faith in the human being itself. But Feuerbach was no anarchist; this new religion of atheism was to be embodied in the state, which for Feuerbach seemed to be the kind of harmonious unity represented by the ancient Greek polis: "The state is the unlimited and infinitely true, perfected, divine human. The state is precisely human—the state is the absolute human, who determines himself, who relates to himself; in the state, my being depends on the human. That is why," Feuerbach continued, "the state has the right of capital punishment."[81] In these unpublished remarks, Feuerbach seemed to proclaim a coming religio-social order, not founded on an external God but on man, a polis to which people belonged immediately; the comment on capital punishment may be an implicit reference to the Jacobin phase of the French Revolution.

It is worth noting that Hegel's intervention into the creation of the new constitution in Württemberg in 1818 had precisely the opposite aim: not to discover the immediate unity of demos and polis, but to create systems of representation, rights, and executive power that mediated civil society and the state.[82] Feuerbach's demand for an immediate unity of the people implied a break with the constitutional, liberal aspects of Hegel that went along with his abandonment of Hegel's speculative philosophy. In this break with liberalism, as Chapter 2 will discuss further, he was not alone in the early 1840s, as radicalism differentiated itself from liberalism prior to the revolution.

This radical republicanism, even Jacobinism, corresponded to a radical sensualism in Feuerbach's thought now. The senses, Feuerbach asserted in his works of 1842–43, preceded and determined thought; being determined consciousness: "Thinking comes from being, but being does not come from thinking."[83] Feuerbach's "Provisional Theses for the Reformation of Philosophy" appeared in Arnold Ruge's *Anekdota zur neuesten deutschen Philosophie und Publicistik,* which was published in Switzerland in 1843 to avoid the increasing repression in Prussia and Saxony. The aphorisms sharpened Feuerbach's new arguments. He made his method clear: to reverse subject and predicate in order to reach the truth, such that God no longer created Man, but the reverse. "We only need always make the *predicate* into the *subject,* and thus, as the subject, into the *object* and *principle.* Hence we need only *invert* speculative philosophy and then have the unmasked, pure, bare truth."[84] With this move, Feuerbach announced an attack on all abstractions, and in particular those of Hegelianism, which was still haunted by the ghost of theology.[85] Abstraction, he asserted, involved turning away from what determined a being and from its material existence; since matter was not actual existence, it was nothing, in the sense of the nothing from which God created the world.[86] But humans were not produced by nothing, but always by something; they were materially determined; suffering preceded thinking; qualities of things were sensed insofar as they had an impact on the perceiver, and the impact preceded the thought.[87]

Humans in Feuerbach's sensualism were thus concrete and determinate. But not, in his estimation, the same as other animals. They were a species apart, insofar as they had consciousness of their determination. When the human overcame abstraction and speculation to grasp itself, it would find its own essence "undetermined, but capable of *infinite determinations,*" i.e., a being both universal and yet not abstract, in a determinate world.[88] The human species was "universal" in the sense that it could consciously comprehend the determinations of other beings. This conception of human universality lay, of course, at the heart of Marx's early Feuerbachian humanism in the 1844 manuscripts, and Marx retained a similar notion of human consciousness even in his late work, where human ability to plan and create underlay his productivism.[89] It was also an important ingredient in the so-called true socialism of Moses Hess, Hermann Kriege, and Karl Grün of the mid-1840s, later so despised by Marx and Engels.[90]

Principles of the Philosophy of the Future pointed toward a new, concrete, communicative ethics based on the relationship between I and Thou, and Feuerbach described that relationship in terms of sensual as much as linguistic exchange. Now Feuerbach stressed the limitations of thinking implied already in Descartes, using the method he had developed in *The Essence of Christianity.* The attributes of God are always the attributes of the humans seeking to define their own essential activity; a space alien, he noted, would never mistake discussion of God by humans as a description of an objective higher being, but would recognize that humans were talking about themselves.[91] For someone like Descartes, who defined his essential activity as thinking, only those aspects of thinking purified of the world would seem real: the only reality was to be found in abstractions, logical connections, and universal truths. The essence of thinking and therefore of God would be abstracted from determinations, from time and space, from matter. The problem with Hegel, Feuerbach argued, was that his turn to temporality in the end merely reduced the temporal to a moment of the ideal.[92] Idealism failed, on Feuerbach's account, to grasp the objectivity of the world; thinking, regulated solely by its own qualities, could only grasp the world as itself, as thought: it was necessarily solipsistic.

"The proof that something is," he argued, "has no other meaning than that something is not only thought of. That proof cannot, however, be derived from thought itself."[93] Knowledge required breaking out of the "unbroken continuity" of circular thinking, and it required a turn instead to the self-interruption of thought by the senses, from a circular to an elliptical model of cognition.[94] In place of thinking about things as abstractions, the human should bump into things as specific, concrete objects. Precisely the nonidentity of the thing in the world with the totality of the world was what indicated its existence, its objectivity. The object existed insofar as it was not swept up in the totalizing, "absolute" dialectic of idealism.[95] The ego was not absolutely distinguished from the world, but in an ongoing encounter with the world; it was porous, intermingling with the world, and the idealist conception of a self preexisting the world was at an end.[96]

This conception of the ego as porous led Feuerbach to stress even more strongly the importance for humanity of love and feeling. For the encounter between one human and another implied a kind of communication different from that of the idealists, one premised upon sensual interaction. The discovery of a self that was not one's own led to the discovery that one had a self in the first place; indeed, "Love means nothing other than becoming aware of this difference" between self and other, and furthermore recognizing that it is precisely the distinction, the separate existence of the object for one, rather than the other's resolution in the consciousness of the self (i.e., as imagination) that is pleasurable. "Pain is a loud protest against the identification of the subjective with the objective," i.e., against idealism; "[t]he pain of love means that that which is in the imagination is not in reality."[97] Love, both in the form of a general feeling toward other humans and in the form of sexual love, served as proof of Feuerbach's anti-idealism. Love also connected his work to the world of politics. Or rather, it seemed to align his thought against any political system that sought to limit or control the horizontal interconnections among people from above.

Love in Feuerbach took several different forms. One was realized in Jesus, whose concrete suffering out of love for the world opened up God's sacrifice and revealed the individual to be human, part of a larger whole. At the same time, though, Feuerbach stressed that corporeal love, indeed sex, was the basis of communication: "And the strongest of the impulses of Nature, is it not the sexual feeling?"[98] Sexual distinction, according to Feuerbach, was the essential basis of humanity: "The distinction of sex is not superficial, or limited to certain parts of the body; it is an essential one: it penetrates bones and marrow. The substance of man is manhood; that of woman, womanhood."[99]

> When there is no *thou*, there is no I; but the distinction between *I* and *thou*, the fundamental condition of all personality, of all consciousness, is only real, living, ardent when felt as the distinction between man and woman. The *thou* between man and woman has quite another sound than the monotonous *thou* between friends.[100]

Where love of Jesus (as representative of the concrete and material divinity of man, on Feuerbach's reading) fit among the love of lovers and the monotonous love between friends was unclear. Indeed, even though Feuerbach's writing implied a political point, his account of the I-Thou relationship was particular and concrete. Rather than implying some conscious, universal brotherhood of humans, it seemed to imply a natural order of love and unity. But being-for-another need not signify love and unity; a consciousness may also confront other consciousnesses as things to be exploited, manipulated, or otherwise overcome, for example, in the economy and in war.

Love, in other words, only provided an answer to the problem of politics at first glance. Familial love and patriotic love need not coincide. Feuerbach's doctrine of coming-to-consciousness by means of a dialectic between I and Thou could not bear the weight of a developed social or political theory.[101] But it could provide a mobilizing image. Feuerbach's formulation of the I-Thou relationship offered a radical, concrete negation of abstractions and universals and claimed to be a guide, a foreshadowing of the new world of brotherhood—in Stirner's cynical formulation, yet another abstraction. His theory combined critique, negation, with the attempt to articulate a new, positive conception of the world. It tore down Christianity and implied something else to be erected in its place: new human beings, a "new species" (*neues Geschlecht*), in the phrase of a letter from Feuerbach to Arnold

Ruge.[102] The process of creating this new world would be slow and perhaps silent, but would be nonetheless violent.[103] In short, Feuerbach's work echoed with the rhetoric of revolution. Yet he retreated to the small village of Bruckberg in Bavaria, where, excluded from the academic world by his atheist and democratic beliefs, he lived off the proceeds of his wife's inheritance, a porcelain factory.

The writings of 1842–43 marked a change in Feuerbach's work, but also the apogee of his influence. After 1842–43, Feuerbach found himself vacillating between a natural religion to be manifested in a positivist natural science and a Protestant-inflected atheism that worshipped a new, worldly man.[104] The problem was, the new man could not, according to a theory founded on the principles of immanence and sensualism, emerge out of the head of a thinker. It had to emerge from the world itself, indeed to be already part of the world. Feuerbach's truth would not reach humanity in the form of a revelation; it had to be shown to be already present, already revealed in religious texts themselves. In other words, Feuerbach's own approach led him to a different method of analysis.

His 1844 work on Luther summarized his new method, while surprisingly transforming Luther the theologian from the archreactionary from whom Feuerbach as a young philosophy student had sought to escape to a prophet of a new world. Luther, Feuerbach noted, started with God, who had all the positive attributes of "virtue, beauty, sweetness, power, health, amiability," while "man is personified depravity, contrariness, hatefulness, worthlessness, and usefulness."[105] But, Feuerbach argued, a strange thing happened in Luther's Jesus-centered work: God became manifest through a man, Jesus, and indeed existed only for humanity. "Luther was the first to let out the secret of Christian faith," namely, that God is the "omnipotent Creator for us"—in other words, by implication we are God's main concern.[106] In the end, Feuerbach argued, Luther had removed any aspect of inhumanity from God; he had implicitly revealed the secret of God in man. Any residue of a nonhuman God lived on as the terrifying, because unknown, Devil.[107] More than that, Luther's God was intended for man in the sense of being man's object. Thus, Feuerbach noted that Luther wished Jesus to be viewed as a "roast, larded capon," something that was in itself insignificant but desirable for humans. And just as the capon should be eaten, so ought the body of Christ in the Eucharist: "What is a roast in itself?" Feuerbach asked; "[t]o believe is to eat, but in eating I abolish the object in question and I change its attributes into my attributes, flesh and blood."[108] In Feuerbach's view, it was Luther's inability to make the full turn toward humanity and its potential that led him to reject the world; for Luther, everything that was good in the world was in fact realized in heaven, the alienated realization of humanity. Belief, in Luther's sense, meant a yearning to die: "The true believer thus has (naturally, if he gives heed only to the inspirations of faith) no other wish than to die . . . for 'the spirit is already in heaven through faith.'"[109]

Feuerbach's work on Luther was published under the repressive conditions of the mid-1840s, but its message was clear to anyone who had read other works by Feuerbach: Christianity was a religion of death that contained a new religion of life, a worship of humanity that was precisely a-theistic.[110] But this moment of calling for a break with Christianity—implicitly or explicitly a concomitant end to the personal rule of the monarchy and a call for the realization of human potential—remained just a moment. Feuerbach's influence peaked in 1844–45. The criticisms from Stirner and others of Feuerbach's anthropocentrism were mounting; the radical trio of Moses Hess, Friedrich Engels, and Karl Marx began to distance themselves from Feuerbach; and Feuerbach himself seemed unsure how to answer the criticisms. He responded to Stirner's insightful attack on the theological remnants in his conception of humanity by simply dismissing the arguments.[111] Feuerbach denied that he had developed in the form of the species another abstraction that took the place of God, an abstract humanity that now stood above the individual, representing an infinite potential. Instead, Feuerbach argued that the "species" was nothing more than a concrete person, a "Thou," a man who recognizes another human in the form of a woman and with her produces a child. The species was a simple, natural relationship that necessarily pointed beyond the individual—it was the individual that was an abstraction. Reproduction, Feuerbach argued, led to the idea of the species, in the form of "other people, other places, other, happier times."[112] But that argument solved nothing, since it rendered infinite potential little more than a sentimentalized hope for the future of one's children. Feuerbach's first impulse was to defuse Stirner's critique rather than to confront it. The answer Feuerbach eventually found was to turn ever more toward a materialism that abandoned all parts of the speculative tradition—as though he were confirming the critique of Marx and Engels, who accused him of determinism and ignorance of human practice. The motif of infinite human potential—i.e., of a praxis-oriented revolutionary anthropology—gave way to a new emphasis on finitude and need (although elements of humanity's "universality" by virtue of human consciousness remained).[113] "The human sense of dependence is the foundation of religion; the object of this feeling of dependence, what the human is dependent on and feels dependent on, is originally nothing other than nature. *Nature* is the *first, original object of religion*, as the history of all religions and peoples proves in abundance."[114] By nature, Feuerbach meant the world as it existed, in all its facets, as an object external to humans but perceived—immediately—by the human senses. This materialism was a radical criticism of idealism. Its translation into political terms, however, was unclear.

Feuerbach and the Revolution

Feuerbach considered his thinking a direct contribution to radical politics. Like Marx and Ruge, the radical poet Georg Herwegh, and the democrat Christian Kapp, a wealthy radical and philosopher and friend of Feuerbach since his days in Erlangen, Feuerbach expressed his hopes for revolution. But his political thought remained vague. He did not discuss at all issues such as the most efficient organization of power, the best means of representation, the proper place of law, and the limits to state power in the form of rights. He supported, to be sure, an ill-defined "revolution" against the "German-Christian state system" and for "communism."[115] Given that Feuerbach simultaneously upheld the sanctity of property, the latter seemed to mean little more than "not individualism."[116] He criticized "political idol-worship" in the form of monarchism, and asserted that materialism was a republican doctrine, insofar as the personal God paralleled the monarch.[117] Feuerbach, in short, felt part of a radical milieu, indeed felt himself to be at its center, but did not expend much energy on political thinking itself. Perhaps the sense of being aligned against the dominant culture, to be part of a countercultural current, served for Feuerbach as a claim to political relevance. The revolution would not, he informed Ruge in 1844, take place over months or years, but over centuries; the Germans, he asserted, remained "political children" still in need of education and self-knowledge.[118]

Indeed, Feuerbach's "politics" involved unfolding the true, authentic human being. It involved coming to be oneself, experiencing the immediacy of life, of matter, of friendship, of sexuality. He dropped out. Removed from the world of institutions and the state, he took to the mountains with a hammer to engage in amateur research on geological history. Resigning himself to exclusion from the academy, Feuerbach embraced life in Bruckberg. He proclaimed that "I learned logic at German university, but optics, the art of seeing, I learned for the first time in a German village." When the Revolution of 1848 came, he began to grow a beard, the symbol of German radicalism.[119]

Just as Feuerbach held back at key moments in his philosophical work, however, so too was his reaction to the revolution distanced. He was certainly in favor of a revolution of "the people" against God and king, which he expressed in an enthusiastic letter of March 3, 1848, to his publisher Otto Wigand: "[T]he French Revolution has brought forth a revolution in me as well. As soon as I can . . . I will go to Paris, without wife, without child, without books."[120] But this letter, like much of what he wrote to Wigand, should be read carefully. Feuerbach admitted to his friend Christian Kapp that he was having trouble writing—indeed that "with me all work is a chronic disease."[121] In the letter to Wigand quoted above, Feuerbach goes on to suggest that he would not finish any more volumes of his collected works: the purpose, after all, had been to "prove the historical correctness and truth of my thoughts, line by line," but "why should I continue to plague myself with this abstract, cheerless matter?"[122] For Feuerbach, the revolution offered an opportunity to escape obligations to his editor, to escape his wife, with whom he had been on difficult terms after she had learned of his obsession with the young Johanna Kapp in Heidelberg, and to escape from Bruckberg and its failing porcelain factory. Feuerbach departed for Paris at the end of March 1848 but never arrived. He stopped at Frankfurt, where the National Assembly convened on May 18. Feuerbach was not impressed by the parliament, asserting that "without blood, without loss of life, new life does not come into the world."[123]

He was certainly aware of the forces that were at play—and that were ripping the revolution apart. The later National Liberal politician Ludwig Bamberger reported a subdued evening with Feuerbach after the reports of the bloody June Days in Paris reached Frankfurt, when the republican controlled military spilled workers' blood in the streets.[124] In the heated debates of the time, though, Feuerbach remained silent, despite pleas from students, political activists, and other intellectuals on the democratic left; he was by his own account passive.[125] Feuerbach's letters are filled with slogans of the democratic revolution, but not with incisive political thought. He affirmed the "republic" and the "democratic spirit," i.e., the spirit that turned over affairs of state to the "people" and not to some particular "court or class"; at the same time, he stated that he would accept a constitutional monarchy as the necessary "preschool" for democracy, so long as such a monarchy respected press freedoms and other basic rights.[126] He denied, however, that the elected National Assembly contained the decisive figures of the revolution. The forces who would decide Germany's future were the republican and democratic figures outside of parliament.[127] He asserted that "the majority of the parliament does not have the majority of the people behind it, as it imagines; the minority is inside [the parliament], the majority outside."[128] After the occupation of Frankfurt by Prussian and Austrian troops in September, Feuerbach abandoned the city for Darmstadt, where the radical editor of the *Westphälisches Dampfboot*, Otto Lüning, had invited him. He then made his way to Heidelberg, where Christian Kapp lived after resigning from the Frankfurt Assembly in protest. There he accepted an invitation by the radical students of Heidelberg, on strike against their university, to give lectures on religion. The university opposed the lecture series, but as a slap in the face of the professors, the city's radical leadership allowed the lectures to take place in the Rathaus.[129] In Heidelberg, Feuerbach met a series of intellectuals at Kapp's house, including the physiologist Jacob Moleschott, the young poet Gottfried Keller, the poet and author of the *Deutschlandlied* Hoffmann von Fallersleben, the novelist Berthold Auerbach, Friedrich Kapp, and others.[130] Feuerbach's wife noted that giving these lectures would not coincidentally put him in Heidelberg, near the Kapp family—and Johanna, who helped him to prepare his lectures.[131] According to Keller, Feuerbach's lectures were "laborious" and "bad," but the content was inspiring and even life-changing.[132]

The lectures, which later appeared in book form as *Lectures on the Essence of Religion*, were Feuerbach's restatement of a decade of work that claimed to reveal the truth of man and the universe. His aim was grandiose: he declared that "a new era also requires a new view of the first elements and foundations of human existence; it requires—if we want to retain the word—a *new religion!*"[133] What this statement means has been the subject of debate, and some have rejected its significance altogether.[134] Certainly, Feuerbach did not aim at a philosophic religion in the sense of the Hegelians, the absolute unity of subject and substance in the world—such a notion had come to seem absurd to him. But he did aim to find a new way of thinking about the world and being in the world, a way of understanding the significance of life, the centrality of love, and the challenge of death that would provide orientation in the manner of traditional religions—even if God was abandoned in the process. Indeed, the whole point of his critique of religion was to dismantle the mediations that alienated humans from their essence, in the form of false idols, and thereby to transform worship into self-worship.

In the 1848–49 lectures, Feuerbach did not find a solution to this challenge. In the main part of the lecture, Feuerbach defended the truth that paganism expressed: that humans related to nature by way of direct, experiential dependence, need, and hunger, and that this dependence pushed humans to create gods. Nature, Feuerbach contended, was itself infinite and without ultimate origin; the universe was an infinity of matter in motion and the cause of itself.[135] Indeed, "Man with his ego or consciousness stands at the brink of a bottomless abyss; that abyss is his own unconscious being," i.e., all the "*not-I* which is distinct from me yet intimately related to me, something *other*, which is at the same time my *own* being."[136] Yet against an enlightened paganism, which rendered humans the objects of material processes, Feuerbach still maintained a grand history of progress. Christianity marked both the rejection of the world and a step forward to the revelation that "the divine being is man"—a notion that now needed to be brought back to mankind: "he is man according to man's poetic claims, desires, and thoughts, or rather man as he should be and some day will be."[137] Feuerbach called for a revolution in consciousness, to overcome the worship of God in Christianity, to transform man, now "half animal, *half angel,*" into "*men,* into *whole men,*" the final words of the lectures.[138] Even this "whole man" was, however, utterly dependent on nature.[139] The completely humanized Martin Luther remained, but was now exposed to the cold, uncaring elements. Feuerbach's revolutionary lectures called for new relations, but remained suspended between a worldly eschatology on the one hand, and passivity and dependence on nature on the other.

The lectures undeniably lack Feuerbach's complex and subtle discussion of love, community, and intersubjectivity that he had developed elsewhere. They primarily offered a materialism with vague residual metaphysics of progress. The fact that ideas are crude, however, does necessarily lessen the popular attention they receive. Feuerbach hoped that his lectures would make "political materialists" out of the sects of both philosophical and political idealism.[140] Nature, he asserted, was not a monarchy headed by a personal God, but rather a republic.[141] Natural laws apply to all of nature, just as "in a republic the only laws are those that express the will of the people."[142] Feuerbach's republicanism equated the totality of nature with the totality of the people. It remained at the level of a vague worldview, unable to address key problems of democracy, such as the constitutional procedures for reaching agreements, the necessity of political parties, and so on. It was an unpolitical doctrine of politics. It lacked the concrete, finite, complex world of intersubjectivity and self-legislation.

Feuerbach had the chance to see blood spilled soon after his lectures ended on March 2, 1849. The uprisings in Baden and Rhineland-Palatinate began in early May 1849. The students who had invited him to lecture in Heidelberg were directly involved. Alfred Michel was killed in battle, Adolf Hirsch and Alexander Spengler fled to Switzerland, Valentin May was arrested and jailed, Eduard Haas fled to France and was apparently then arrested.[143] Feuerbach by contrast returned to quiet Bruckberg to resume the life of the solitary philosopher. He later claimed that he left Heidelberg to avoid the uprising of May 1849, certain already of its outcome. In spite of his passivity during the revolution, the police targeted him: he was expelled from Leipzig in 1851 and was the object of a police search.[144]

After 1848, Feuerbach's thought seeped into a variety of radical thinkers, writers, and doctrines. His followers viewed his work as interesting for the development of a revolutionary, atheist, and materialist worldview. Keller, for example, praised the way Feuerbach's work revealed the world to be "infinitely more beautiful and deeper, life more valuable and more intensive, and death more serious"—all part of what he considered a republican worldview.[145] Feuerbach himself developed some of these materialist thoughts, but in the work he considered his most mature and important, the 1857 *Theogony*, he returned instead to the problem of how and why humans produce myth and gods. In other words, he remained concerned with religion; he did not simply leave it behind.

CHAPTER 2

Moses Hess, Love, and "True Socialism"

"**N**o religion—that is my religion."[1] Feuerbach's 1846 statement was deliberately paradoxical. On the one hand, he rejected religion insofar as it was the alienation of human qualities onto a nonhuman, transcendent entity. On the other hand, the rejection took a religious form: the substance of religion remained, now purified of religious form, as "my religion." Feuerbach did not abandon religion by rejecting it, but rather claimed to reveal its true content. That content, as the previous chapter showed, was the true human essence. It was the human "species-being," now become conscious of itself as limitless possibility (from the point of view of humanity) to sense, to know, and to act.

During the first half of the 1840s, as Moses Hess and Marx moved from radicalism to communism, Hess latched onto Feuerbach's formulation. Hess sought to transform the theoretical concept of the species-being into a practical tool for political mobilization. Along with others making a journey from radical liberalism to socialism, such as Karl Grün, the student radical Hermann Kriege, and Karl Marx himself in the *Economic and Philosophical Manuscripts*, Hess sought to fill the concept of the species-being with content that Feuerbach, always the careful philosopher, shied away from. Hess argued that the true human would be at one with other humans: he or she would be part of a harmonious species-being. Freedom and equality would be reconciled.[2] Such bold statements of unity and harmony did not appear in Feuerbach's published work, although he also did not reject them. He showed a fondness for the "true socialist" Hermann Kriege and his utopian ideas, although he expressly rejected the idea that social-political revolution was imminent.[3] Yet Feuerbach could not simply reject attempts to give his ideas a practical edge, if he wanted to preserve the radical implications of his philosophy. Precisely the question of what the true, authentic human was—and therefore what the aim of revolutionary activism was—drove the reception of Feuerbach by Hess, Dittmar, and Wagner as well, as the next chapters show.

Hess was a professional revolutionary, motivated by a sense, indeed a faith, that a harmonious and just social order was coming, a world in which humans would complete their prehistory as social animals and become fully human, in accord with both nature and the cosmos.[4] Like Feuerbach, Hess sought to break out of an increasingly implausible world of philosophical idealism, and sought instead to ground humans in the material world. His early touchstone was not Hegel but Spinoza, but like Feuerbach, Hess's early work remained within the world of critical idealism. As the context changed and a new, radical left formed, he broke with both Judaism and Christianity in the name of secular redemption. Hess sought new forms of politics connected to new revolutionary subjects. In the 1840s, Hess's revolutionary subject was a Feuerbachian "humanity" as a whole. Indeed, his reading of Feuerbach helped turn Hess from liberal to radical politics in the early 1840s. During his next phase, from about 1845–49, while Hess was working closely with Marx and like Marx seeking a way out of Feuerbach's lofty language and a return to the concrete world around him, the proletariat played the key role. Hess's late work diverged from that of the late Feuerbach's, however. While Feuerbach would concentrate after 1846 on the individual human, dependent on nature and trying to make sense of matter, Hess sought to buttress his faith in a human-centered universe, whether in his search for a reinvigorated Jewish nation as the lever of universal emancipation of mankind or in his search for a law of gravity that would determine future social organization.

The shifting focus of Hess's works (as well as his sloppy and imprecise writing) makes it difficult to identify any one of these revolutionary subjects as the fundamental to Hess's thought. Attempts to do so, the most important of which have made Jewish identity the key to Hess's entire intellectual trajectory, do not do justice to the dynamism of his thought.[5] What Hess noted in 1837 as the central problem of Judaism, its combination of a universalizing monotheism with a particularizing nationalism, did indeed mark his work over the entirety of his life, but as a more general problem of radicalism: how to combine advocacy for a specific group, such as labor, with claims to emancipate humanity as a whole. The common denominator in Hess's work lies in a restless, often dilettantish, search for a new movement, a new insight, the "new" in general, which would give meaning to the entire course of history. This was true of his vaguely conceptualized "socialism" of the early 1840s, the turn with Marx to an immanent history of the proletarian revolution, the search for the foundations of a redemptive Weltanschauung in natural phenomena, and identifying nationalism as the key to the realization of human potential. He had faith that the universe would reveal the redemptive significance of the world through signs of order and harmony—hieroglyphs of a higher order. As part of his quest for a new politics, Hess reiterated the major themes of Feuerbach. He rejected both a personal God and personal immortality, and with it a Christianity that ignored the problem of creating a worldly set of solutions to worldly problems. He sought a new form of voluntary association or organization, something like "love," that would organize society on voluntary grounds, not by the power of the state and formal law. Hess sought throughout an immanent, historical development that would lead to human emancipation. This focus on immanence led him to put much stock in love (as a way for the individual to transcend his or her individuality without such extraworldly concepts as "God") and to concentrate often on death, the limit to existence and meaning—but with different results than Feuerbach.

Born in 1812 the child of a traditional Jewish family, his father a merchant and factory owner, Hess grew up with his grandparents in the Judengasse in Bonn.[6] Like other Jews in the Rhineland, his family had experienced emancipation into a liberal capitalist society under Napoleon, only to have their rights taken away by Prussia after the Wars of Liberation. Hess's formal education took place in the context of the Jewish heder. As he wrote in a diary entry, his Talmud lessons were "beaten black and blue into me up to my fifteenth year."[7] His earliest extant letters indicate the tension he felt between the particular way of life of the Rhenish Jewish communities and "humanity" as a universal category.[8] Along with Hebrew in school, he began to learn German and French from tutors. Soon he began to educate himself, reading deeply in the writings of Rousseau, the radical Enlightenment, and postrevolutionary French Romantic thought. He identified strongly with France, even going to France three years after the Revolution of 1830 to participate in the next phase of world history. In 1834, he returned to Bonn, penniless and unsure of what he wanted to do with his life. Relations with his father, whose life revolved around mercantile activities and religion, became strained. By 1836, Hess had also lost his faith in a personal God, and by his own account landed at an atheistic, nihilistic position, which he only began to transcend as he read the work of Spinoza.[9] In 1837, he attended the university in Bonn, but only for a year; in that year as well, Hess wrote his first book, *The Holy History of Mankind by a Young Disciple of Spinoza*. The title already pointed to Hess's aim throughout his life, to find the way that the immanent, secular process of historical development connected with sacred intent. As he wrote nearly thirty years later, this "spiritual direction" (*Geistesrichtung*) played a role in all his later studies and experiences.[10] Hess explicitly viewed himself as a prophet or apostle in the mid-1830s; while he ceased to make such a mighty claim in later works, it nonetheless marked all of them.

Hess's Early Search for Worldly Redemption

Hess's earliest publications, his *Holy History of Mankind* of 1837 and his 1841 *European Triarchy*, marked by his break with traditional Judaism, do not count as revolutionary texts. They did contain radical moments, such as criticism of the new autonomy of money in the capitalist world and of the Christian Prussian state; but these were echoed by other writers of the time, including liberals and conservatives. What characterized his early work was rather the search for a universal history of mankind from the point of view of redemption. He wrote, in other words, religious texts, unlike Feuerbach's openly irreligious work of the time. Writing like an apostle,[11] Hess produced an original and highly questionable story of the development of the entirety of humanity, indeed of the cosmos, toward unity and peace. This approach broke down after 1842, as Hess confronted radical thought from France and Germany and began his association with Marx, Ruge, Grün, and others in the heady days of what he, Marx, and Engels termed "the putrescence of the absolute spirit."[12]

The Holy History of Mankind, published in 1837, reflected Hess's religious education and his Bible-centered understanding of the world. Although it bears a resemblance to the grand historical schemes of Fourier or Hegel, its prophetic tone and reliance on the Old Testament makes it much more like a religious tract of radical, prophecy-oriented Protestantism, or even of sects that went beyond Protestantism like the Church of Jesus Christ of Latter-day Saints. Had he stopped writing at this point, one would read Hess not as a Young Hegelian, but in a different tradition entirely. The Young Hegelians, with their fixation on Luther and the Jesus of the New Testament, were not in the prophetic Jewish and Christian tradition. And yet, like the Young Hegelians, Hess sought to bring grand theological narratives down to earth.[13]

Hess's grand narrative began with Adam, who was not the first human-like creature (mention is made of the Nephilim who preceded Adam), but was the first to embody "noble humanity."[14] From Adam to Jesus Christ, the Jewish nation went through stages of formation, dissolution, renewed unity and law-giving, and dissolution yet again, as it grappled with the tension between universalist monotheism and patriarchal particularism. The Jewish nation tried to unify religion and polity. In its final phase of dissolution, under Roman domination, it produced Jesus Christ, who, according to Hess's account, recognized "the One Being in general as well as in particular" and opened the way to find God in every human's soul.[15] This "eternal truth" of the second phase of his grand history was, however, now reduced to the individual soul. An initial attempt to unify Christ with political form, the late Roman Empire, collapsed when it distinguished the "real" Christian from the pagan or Jewish Christian, i.e., when it fell away from universality in its notion of citizenship.[16] Charlemagne's attempt to reunite religion and polity failed, and the result was schism, the disunity of the Reformation, and the current, divided world.[17] Christianity failed to unify the world under holy law; the tolerance that followed the religious wars was not unity but the recognition that the power of an individual state was limited.[18] Christianity's concern with the soul and its inability to unite the world led to a fallen state. Put in language that Hess did not yet employ, the secular, liberal state, founded on the principle of tolerance rather than truth, represented disunity, fallenness, and the real, massive inequalities of the Christian world.

The third phase in Hess's redemptive history began with Spinoza. Spinoza transcended both Judaism and Christianity; his philosophy (or rather religion, in Hess's interpretation) proved by reason what the religions had pointed to through fantastic images, the ultimate unity and harmony of the world; God was in the world, immanent in the world and its history, on Hess's interpretation of Spinoza.[19] The new worldview thus transcended the distinction between materialism and idealism; with it the distinction between contemplative redemption and action in the world was suspended: "The period of the Holy Spirit has arrived, the Kingdom of God, the New Jerusalem which has been the consolation of every Christian."[20] Now humanity had gradually to realize this scientific-prophetic revelation of Spinoza, and with it to recognize the holy path of humanity toward a future social harmony, where freedom and law would come together under the recognition of truth: "Man's freedom," Hess asserted, "consists not in his arbitrary will [*Willkür*], but in conscious obedience to the divine law. Obedience is the virtue of pure man."[21]

In short, Hess proclaimed the coming of a new kind of unity of God and politics—a theocracy, founded on the revelations of Spinoza, i.e., reason. And like the new forms of social organization proclaimed by radical religious communitarians in France, the U.S., and elsewhere, Hess's New Jerusalem assumed the unity and harmony of society, the end of egoism.[22] Hess condemned the "historical right" of individuals, and in particular the right of inheritance, with special vehemence. Under the Jewish Patriarchs, when an individual died he returned to his ancestors—as did his property.[23] The egoism of the present day, Hess continued, was not related to feudal institutions but rather to money. The "money-devil" had neither "fatherland nor family," i.e., it stood outside of community.[24] Not only did inequality reign, but the notion of the general good itself was destroyed: there was "no God, no holy kingdom, no religion, and no fatherland." All that remained were animal-like *Fressorgane* dedicated to devouring the world in the individual's self-interest.[25] The "End of Days" would bring a New Jerusalem founded on different principles. The elimination of inheritance would mean the end of historical rights that cemented inequality into place.[26] Other reforms would bring about a qualitatively new society: women would now receive the same education as men, free monogamous love would replace the authoritarianism of existing marriage law and arranged marriages, and the state would educate the young, breaking down the inequalities related to access to education. In short, Hess asserted, "the state will replace the family."[27] Laws, rights, formal protections of the individual would no longer determine the shape of a state, but rather the essential coherence and harmony of the whole: "Who would need a charter, an external law for the whole, when the law lives in its interior? What abuse can be carried out through a power which is restrained by nature? Which perfidy can take place in a commonwealth where everything is open and public, where free judgment is being recognized as the element of life?"[28] In this new world, "[t]rue religion, the knowledge of God revealed in the holy history, is the only foundation of state, the basic law, out of which the other laws follow."[29] A new Sparta would arise (Rousseau's radical images accompanied Hess throughout his life), one where individuals did not merely renounce economic goods, but also found joy in an ennobled life.[30]

The Holy History of Mankind occupies a unique space in the revolutionary world of Vormärz Germany. While the Young Hegelians certainly tapped into the Christian tradition in their exposition of a radical history of redeemed humanity, their Christianity centered on Luther and the New Testament, not the prophetic tradition articulated by the radical Anabaptist or Calvinist traditions. Hess, by contrast, made extensive use of both imagery and content of the prophetic tradition. He cast aside individual immortality, of course, but in the interest of a kind of natural and enduring harmony of society.[31] And in place of rights, laws, the historically developing constitutional state, Hess envisioned a new community of free associations, self-organization, of solidarity—of love, as Hess's later rhetoric would term it. But perhaps more important was that revolution would find its source not in the will of the revolutionary, but in the truth revealed by sacred history, culminating in Spinoza. Hess claimed to speak the immanent truth of the historical process that paralleled, he asserted, the history of the cosmos.[32]

The connection between radicalism and historical process set Hess apart from the Young Hegelians, even as he began his encounter with them in his next work, *The European Triarchy* of 1841. For as he noted there, while on the one hand the Young Hegelians, like Cieszkowski, echoed his call for a turn from contemplative philosophy to practice, toward the transformation of the world, on the other hand their criticism of the Bible, exemplified by Strauss's reading of the life of Jesus as profane history, "robbed the past of its sacred nature."[33] Hess grasped the tension that would arise between the reduction of humans to empirical reality and the ascension of humans to "humanity," apparently even before encountering Feuerbach's *Essence of Christianity.*[34]

For Hess, as for Feuerbach, the essence of Christianity remained necessary for human emancipation. Just as Feuerbach moved toward earthly love as a political way out after starting to dismantle the specters haunting human society, Hess viewed love as the foundation of the New Jerusalem. "God is love, teaches Christianity. Love is the soul of the totality, unifies all, love is religion in the widest sense."[35] But Christianity, with its inward-oriented love, with its life separate from the state (i.e., the political community), was inadequate; "the religion of love will reveal itself [from now] in the works of active men rather than in a didactic priesthood."[36]

Just as in *The Holy History of Mankind,* Hess rejected the liberal notion of a separation of religion and politics (indeed, at times in Hess's work one has the feeling that he would oppose separations, distinctions, of any kind). But events had forced him to reexamine his theocratic tendency from before. Frederick William IV had come to the throne of Prussia a conservative Pietist, taken with Catholic mysticism. And in Cologne a dispute continued to simmer between the Catholic Church and the Prussian state over the church's right to sanction marriages and the Catholic bishop's refusal to recognize mixed marriages between Catholics and Protestants without guarantees that the children would be raised Catholic.[37] The dispute in Cologne occasioned a concerted attack by conservatives against Hegelianism, and would push Bruno Bauer and others into a position more explicitly oppositional to the state. But this aspect of the controversy did not concern Hess; the concrete problem of how religion and political institutions were related did.

The liberal solution to the mixed marriage debate would have involved the implementation of civil marriage, sanctioned by the state and unrelated to confession. But a purely civil marriage sanctioned by a neutral state would have constituted separate rights of the individual over against the totality, exactly the kind of separation of part from whole that Hess claimed Christianity promoted. Such a solution would "break the living unity of state and church, and in this way cut the nerve of the social order, the highest power."[38] The phrasing is confusing, but underneath it lay Hess's concern that marriage not become a merely formal contract, that its content, its sacred character, be maintained. Hess claimed that the Cologne dispute was due to the Pietist "indifference" of the Prussian leaders to the Catholics and their failure to provide equal love to all subjects.[39] At the same time, he rejected the Catholic solution, which would bind state power to the whims of a particular confession.[40] Instead, the state should be religious in the sense that it promoted religion, but the religion it promoted should be universal and stand above all mere confessions.[41] This state would therefore not be neutral or indifferent to society. It would have the job of ensuring that "no doctrine pernicious to the community arises."[42] In an aside, Hess asserted that Jews, too, would have to be treated equally; the criticism of Jews for maintaining an allegiance to the Jewish "nation," he argued, was the result of rules of German society that had forced Jews away from the rest of society. The exclusion of Judaism from the state was tantamount to excluding a Christian sect from it.[43] Hess's solution was vague: a civil process that apparently approved of marriage on religious grounds, but without any specific confession's notion of marriage. Hess left unanswered the question of where, then, the state should draw the line—perhaps with Muslims or atheists? Who or what was excluded?

Hess's aim was not a liberal state.[44] A state based on rights was at best a transitional thing for Hess that provided for negative freedom but nothing more.[45] The point was to move beyond the neutral, liberal state, before such a thing even actually existed in Prussia. The new world would have to transcend German contemplative and Christian approaches to politics, Hess argued, through an orientation toward practice exemplified by the French Revolution of 1789 and British utilitarianism. Hess's arguments were vague, but they struck a chord among philosophically minded radical intellectuals tired of Hegelian contemplative attitudes as well as liberal solutions.

The Radical Deed: An Ethical Path to Revolution

Feuerbach's concepts, especially that of the "species-being," accompanied Hess's radicalization over the course of the 1840s.[46] Feuerbach's references to humanity and its great potential involved a harsh criticism of established religion and its antihuman idolatry of abstract, transcendent beings. But Feuerbach's ideas lacked a specific political meaning. Hess intended to find this meaning, to defend it and establish it as a principle of revolution. In 1842, in an article for the *Rheinische Zeitung*, Hess still defended a strong, centralized state as the "institution for educating the people" (*Volkserziehungsanstalt*); the state should still act coercively through laws to offer "protection against antisocial, egoistic tendencies," and should operate positively to promote the cultivation of the individual (*Bildung*), which he construed as true freedom.[47] But by the mid-1840s, God, state, and money were all to be smashed by a revolutionary humanity. In Hess's view, the return of full humanity to the human could only mean the reconciliation of individual with humanity as a whole, in social harmony. He assumed that the goal of a radical Feuerbachian critique was the unity of humanity, the same goal expressed in his own earlier writings.

The intellectual voyage traced in the following pages cannot be separated from Hess's remarkable work as a revolutionary activist over the 1840s. In 1841–42, he helped to found the short-lived *Rheinische Zeitung;* his financial backers, however, found him too radical to serve as its editor and appointed in his place the apparently less radical Karl Marx.[48] By the end of 1842, Hess had drawn Engels into the new "communist" camp. And as a journalist in Paris, he was a participant in the radical circles around Proudhon. He was also active in the circle of German émigré radicals around Julius Fröbel in Zurich, Karl Grün in Cologne, and Arnold Ruge, Heinrich Heine, Georg Herwegh, and Marx in Paris. Visits to the Rhineland in 1844–45 were filled with speeches on communism and attempts to organize communist associations. In Brussels in 1846, he worked with Engels and Marx on *The German Ideology,* then returned to Cologne to engage in further activism. His works of revolutionary theory, then, took place in contact with revolutionary practice, as Hess established himself as one of the leading German radicals of the Vormärz.[49]

Hess's philosophical revolution started, as in Feuerbach's case, with a critique of the idealist tradition from Descartes on. The cogito was in fact the beginning and end of Descartes's thought, he claimed; the ergo sum was secondary and largely irrelevant. Thought became an activity in itself, the ego a mathematical point freed of all admixture with the world.[50] As a result, both self and world lost content and meaning. Hess argued that the conceptual bases of idealist philosophy were utterly wrong, in his most important theoretical work of the decade, "The Philosophy of the Deed." "The ego is thus not something static or lasting, as the egoists [*Ichsager*] maintain, but rather changing, in constant motion."[51] This constant motion implied a constant interchange with the world, a constant activity appropriating, working, and expelling matter. Activity in the world was the essence of the ego; the self was part of the world, acting in the world to create itself. Thus did Hess sum up what he found so important in Feuerbach's rejection of abstraction and speculation and the turn to a notion of the "porous ego" in constant, sensual interaction with the world. Hess later would criticize Feuerbach for remaining fixed on thinking rather than turning to action.[52] Hess himself forged ahead in his attempt to connect philosophical discussion to the contemporary political struggle.

Traditional religion was his next target. "Theological consciousness" was the "big lie, the principle of all slavery (and mastery) to which our society is subjected."[53] Like Feuerbach, Hess suggested that speculative philosophy was just another variation on theology.[54] A theological consciousness assigned to God the attributes of self-conscious humanity, robbing humans of their own power. It deferred authentic community and being to somewhere beyond the existing world. It led humans to mistake their creations for their creator.[55] Most important, the Jewish and Christian traditions splintered humanity into disparate individuals at the mercy of an omnipotent God.[56] The human being of theology was an isolated beast, not yet unified with a conscious and harmonious human collective. How humanity, with all its potential, had become so alienated from its essential character still required explanation. Hess found that explanation in the actual organization of the human world, which, he asserted, reduced humans to individual, rapacious animals out for themselves, to "social animals" not in Aristotle's sense but rather in the sense of Thomas Hobbes. Religion was only comprehensible in light of the actual state of the world: "The people, which, as the Bible teaches, must work 'by the sweat of their brow' in order to prolong their wretched existence—the people, we say, *have need for* religion."[57] Religion served the same function as opium did for painful diseases: to reduce humans to "an animal lack of consciousness." But it did not have the active power to battle the disease itself.[58] As a result, body and mind were split into two parts, and freedom of mind came to exist apart from the world. Indeed, this otherworldly "freedom" was merely a reflection of worldly subordination.[59] Without social liberation, the ideal of spiritual freedom was meaningless. By the same token, however, the social freedom from want propagated by French authoritarian socialists like Cabet was impossible so long as it relied on submission to God or priests for its implementation. Hess criticized many French utopian thinkers for assuming that there should be an authoritarian "priesthood" in charge of directing the human collective; he was also not surprised when French socialists like Cabet or even Louis Blanc sacrificed freedom of the press.[60] Both the German tradition of religious criticism from Luther to Hegel and the French tradition of revolutionary social criticism from Robespierre to communism had fallen victim to a notion of transcendent religious authority, rather than turning to the essence of the human. Therefore neither could reconcile freedom and equality.[61]

The aim was to eliminate false idols, concepts, or institutions presumed to be different from, above, and transcendent of humanity. The human should return to itself; humanity should be conscious of itself, of its own powers and essence and unity. Hess's arguments helped to clarify Feuerbach's paradoxical statement that "My religion is—no religion." Religion was an alienated vision of the self, it was humanity separated from itself, objectified, unable to become conscious of itself as itself. In the new world that Feuerbach's philosophy pointed toward, in Hess's interpretation, the human knew itself immediately, in direct experience and knowledge of its own essence as ego-in-humanity. Hess's political position, then, replicated Feuerbach's call for the transformation of religion into anthropology—then took the entire discussion one step further, declaring that anthropology next had to become socialism, social practice, if the immediate unity of human with human essence, with species-being, was to be achieved.[62] The struggle for socialism was a struggle for human essence per se, for the truth of religion, for a religion that was no longer a religion but rather pure, unmediated self-worship.

The next step was to criticize the worldly basis of theological consciousness, which Hess found in money. If God was in fact "accumulated spiritual humanity," the point where all spiritual goods like love and justice flowed together outside of humanity, then money represented "accumulated human labor." In the current social world, humans carried out all work in isolation from one another; the product of labor was only accessible as private property, which was by its very nature inauthentic because it was enjoyed on the level of the individual human animal, not the human in conscious harmony with humanity.[63] Money was the creative potential of humanity now revealed in the world as something otherworldly in the sense that the "rich Jewish or Christian-Germanic money-wolf" accumulated it in his pursuit of the idol of omnipotent Mammon.[64] Money was an essential part of the world of economic competition, which required that humans be in perpetual struggle with one another rather than act in harmony.[65] This was the world of the huckster (*Krämerwelt*), of the individual separated from the species; this was the practice of egoism, and Judaism and Christianity provided merely its theory.[66] Money was the "realized essence" of a Christianity that built upon the individual who had a personal relationship to God and could enjoy personal immortality separated from and beyond the human world.[67] And worst of all, the pious world of modern Christianity forced everyone to buy into its insidious logic: "freedom" now meant a worker's freedom to sell his or her essential human powers in order to survive, slavery was now internalized under the guise of freedom. Hess condemned the English abolitionists who attacked open slavery in the name of the hypocritical, concealed world of wage slavery.[68]

Given the way Hess framed his criticism of the spiritual God, the worldly God of money, and the beastly nature of egoism, his criticism of rights comes as no surprise. The Declaration of the Rights of Man and Citizen of 1789, he argued, made sense as a gesture toward human equality; but no sooner was formal equality proclaimed than hierarchies reemerged, in particular a new aristocracy of money and education, which was a monopoly over scarce resources. The Terror of 1793 represented an early, despotic, and failed attempt to deal with the unexpected consequences of this new inequality.[69] A liberalism that merely demanded basic rights thus only addressed a part of the problem. Individual rights assumed an individual separated from the rest of humanity, just as a democracy based on the individual's right to vote served to block the real harmony of the people.[70] Rights reflected nothing less than the full scale emergence of the "social world of beasts," of individuals abstracted from their social essence: "Practical egoism was sanctioned when humans were proclaimed to be *isolated individuals*, abstract, *naked persons* to be *true* humans; when human rights were proclaimed, the rights of *independent* humans; when the *independence* of humans from each other, their *separation* and *isolation*, was declared to be the *essence of life and of freedom*, and *isolated people* identified *as free, true, natural* humans."[71] In other words, human rights sanctioned "the war of all against all."[72]

By attacking human rights, Hess of course did not intend to eliminate all freedoms, as his ongoing criticism of authoritarian communism showed. He rather sought to overcome the cleft between individual and species. In fact, the individual was to view him- or herself as part of the species, to the point of being willing to sacrifice oneself for the species.[73] Hess was unclear about what this sacrifice might be in practice, such as perhaps sacrifice in war. It was the same kind of vague republicanism that had led Feuerbach to proclaim the right of the state to carry out capital punishment. Rights as tools of the egoistic individual against the world, against humanity, were to disappear, not rights in general. In the same way, Hess proclaimed that "liberalism is the final phase of life, of politics."[74] Like Karl Grün, Hess assumed that the new human, fully conscious of self and of humanity, would no longer need the systems and procedures of the world of alienated politics, individual rights, and egoistic economic competition. "The unbound self-motivation [*Selbstbethätigung*] of the individual nature" of the egoist would come to an end.[75] The revolution was in a sense an inward matter, a return to one's essence that opened the way to discovering the world of other humans, so long obscured by God, money, and philosophical abstraction.

In short order, then, the idealist ego, Judaism, Christianity, money, capital, human rights, and by implication the *Rechtsstaat* fell victim to Hess's criticism, which revealed them to be fetishes and idols that concealed the true nature of humanity. The criticism pointed the way out of humanity's self-enslavement to what it had itself produced: God, state, and capital. The negative side of Hess's criticism was fierce and brutal; he even started to sound like the anarchist Bakunin in his praise of negation and destruction: "Every new creation is a leap, emerges out of nothingness, out of the negation of old circumstances."[76] But Hess condemned the Young Hegelians for having remained with the negative side of critique and for having failed to develop the positive side, the new synthesis. Max Stirner, he argued, wanted humans to become animals, separate from each other, denying their unity under one species and taking advantage of each other for selfish gain; in the end, he advocated the status quo. Hess accused Bruno Bauer, by contrast, of wanting humans to retreat into their own internal freedom separate from the world, becoming plantlike in their passivity.[77] Neither dealt with real, living beings. Hess conceived of the human as actor and worker.

A new conception of the human came into focus: a subject constantly in motion, constantly exchanging matter with the environment, and doing so consciously, through an act, a deed, through labor. Hess's concept of labor went far beyond the rarified form of wage labor to encompass all aspects of the human encounter with the world. Labor was the process of "working out" or of "working one's way out" into the world and then back to oneself.[78] The result was a dramatically different conception of the human that sought to overcome the distinction between labor on the one hand, and consumption or enjoyment (*Genuss*) on the other. Now the "true and only pleasure" (*Genuss*) would be found in "free activity," the free deed.[79] Free activity would no longer be "labor" in the sense of work carried out according to the demands of others in return for basic needs; it would be self-organized, self-imposed, conscious activity.[80]

Hess's conception of the self appeared to be the logical extension of Feuerbach's notion of a "porous ego" in constant interaction with the sensuous world of object. Hess anticipated some of the materialist images of the never-ending processes of life later adopted by Feuerbach and the materialists of the 1850s, Jacob Moleschott and Ludwig Büchner. But Hess's aim was different; his orientation was not just a new view of the world, but socialist emancipation. His aim was the transformation of labor itself. "Life," he proclaimed, "is the exchange of productive life activity," the constant exchange of material between self and world; exchange among humans was exchange of a specifically "*social* life activity," and necessary for the survival of the species. Therefore humans' "actual life consists only of the reciprocal exchange of their productive life activity, only in *cooperation,* only in connection with the entire social body."[81] Human cooperation and exchange was the real essence of the individual: the human was always social.

The point of Hess's critique, then, was to reclaim this humanity, to throw off the false (and self-created) chains that bound humans and to find the true essence of the species. It was time for the human animal, the "money wolf," who acted only in his or her own interest, to give way to the real, authentic human: "the world of the animal declines, and man appears."[82]

Marx, Engels, and the "true socialists" in Westphalia, including Karl
Grün and Hermann Kriege, all adopted some variety of Hess's formulation
as they sought to organize a new movement.[83] But in 1845–46, while in
close cooperation in Brussels, Hess, Marx, and Engels broke with what they
came to term "true socialism." In their argument, "true socialism" took the
following form: if we only recognize the real definition of humanity, the
true, natural and social essence of the human in practice, then we can act
in full accord with our potential, consciously, in association with others.[84]
Hess, Marx, and Engels would argue by contrast that the model of emancipation in "true socialism" was itself idealistic: to call for the discovery of
the "true" human essence in order to become free was mere ideology critique, not a confrontation with the real powers of the world.[85]

In fact, already as he was formulating the "true socialist" position in
1843–45, Hess had begun to develop a more complex, historical argument. Egoism and individualism, according to Hess, had been necessary
at an earlier stage of social organization to compel people to enter into
relations with one another. "The *social* world, *human* organization," he
asserted, "has its natural history, its genesis, its *history of creation,* as does
every other world, every other organic body."[86] The destruction inherent
in the world of individuals and competition was a necessary part of the
"history of cultivation" (*Bildungsgeschichte*) of the species. The Jews, he
asserted, had a "*world-historical* calling in the natural history of the social
world of animals to develop humanity into the *beast of prey*"; they and
the Christians had succeeded in fully converting humans into "bloodsuckers"
and "beasts of prey."[87] Like Marx, Hess turned anti-Semitism upside
down by attacking the entire Judeo-Christian tradition as both a necessary
part of the history of human redemption and a source of inhuman social
organization.[88] For only after the completion of this earlier phase of history did an economic surplus and a level of knowledge appear that would
allow humans to satisfy their basic needs and to comprehend the forces
of nature and use them for human ends. The surplus production itself,
however, became a burden in its alienated form of capital. A country like
England, Hess noted in 1845, suffered not from too few goods but from
too many. However skewed by his search for a "holy history" of redemption, Hess was offering a history of competition, increased production,
and the crisis of modernity: overproduction and poverty.[89] In Hess's view,
this absurd moment rendered necessary the next step in the emergence of
human consciousness.[90] The reappropriation for humanity of "its God, its
alienated wealth [or potential: *Vermögen*], its essence" was a historical
process leading from chaos, destruction, competition, and accumulation
to human harmony.[91]

Thus the final phase of human prehistory was the coming-to-self-consciousness of humans as part of humanity. Hess was vague on the details. But clearly now freedom and equality would be reconciled, as the species became the end rather than the means for an individual.[92] The individual's death would gain a different meaning now, as an affirmation of the life of the species, another positive moment of life.[93] In this new world, the *horror vacui* held by egoists would be vanquished by a sense of belonging in the species-being. This would be a lengthy transition, as an entire generation would have to be brought up according to the new realities of self-assertion, self-organization, and self-determination of humanity. Love would replace competition, and the unity and harmony of the species would replace the egoistic accumulation of property.[94] Now "authentically human activity," real human history could begin.[95]

According to Hess, when humanity reached harmony with itself, that would register not only in the world of humans but also in the cosmos in general. Socialism had a cosmic significance. As he wrote in 1845, "The human is the highest and therefore final being of the earth; the best always comes last. All beings of our planet have already been formed and are engaged in their *second* kind of development. The human being is not yet formed and therefore still in its process of emergence, in the *first* kind of development."[96] Indeed, the totality of cosmic history consisted of a series of contradictions and conflicts, out of which arose order and harmony, of the planets as well as of humanity. "Just as our planet has had a developmental history full of natural revolutions, elementary struggles and storms," so humanity had to undergo struggles before its "perfected organization" took shape.[97] True, harmonious society, true love, was the culmination of a cosmic history that still bore traces of the Holy History Hess had described in 1837.

Imputing order and direction to the universe was hardly an incidental or marginal part of the socialist tradition. Indeed, Fourier's entire theory revolved around a cosmological conception; who can forget his strange account of the mating of the northern and southern hemispheres of the Earth to produce seas of lemonade for humanity?[98] Cosmological ruminations and teleological thinking provided the answer to one essential criticism of socialist thought, namely, why anyone should assume that there has to be an immanent tendency toward harmony and organization in the human world at all, given abundant empirical proof to the contrary. If one espoused the "principle of hope," it was difficult to dispense with a moral teleology.[99] To ground socialism on such cosmological assumptions was more than Feuerbach, or Marx, could countenance. It is evident, then, that Hess's adaptation of Feuerbach in *Red Catechism for the German People* of 1849–50, "the social revolution is my religion," contained a religious conception that actually diverged from Feuerbach.[100] In 1846 Feuerbach bluntly criticized those who took the human as the teleological endpoint of the universe: if nature had its origin and goal in humanity, then it was once again conceptualized as subordinate to a higher being, rather than an objective entity existing in itself: "Shame on you for your belief that the world was created, *made* for humans, shame on you for your belief that it was *created, made at all.*"[101] Though Hess would have argued that the entire process of development was immanent rather than transcendent, against a personal God who created the universe, nonetheless what Feuerbach called the "human arrogance" of this teleological assumption remained.[102]

Hess never came to terms with these arguments by Feuerbach. Indeed, by 1846, he and Marx claimed to have broken with Feuerbach and with the "true socialism" that they had helped to develop (and that arguably haunted both writers for the rest of their lives). For Hess, Feuerbach was now a "mere" thinker, not a revolutionary, and the tireless activists Karl Grün and Hermann Kriege were fuzzy-minded idealists.[103]

Both Marx and Hess criticized the implicit elitism and authoritarianism of French utopian socialism. Hess asked, for example, how Proudhon could proclaim equality and at the same time speak of God the Father and His children, using exactly the language "exploited by kings and clerics" to ensure their mastery. But education required educators, organization organizers; how could they avoid the hierarchical distinction between mental and manual labor that both had earlier criticized? Marx, in his *Economic and Philosophical Manuscripts,* claimed that insofar as the individual producers themselves made labor social, and did not hand the power to command labor over to "society" as an abstraction or to socialist technocrats, the new world would spontaneously form.[104] The problem of education could not be so easily set aside, however. The "conscious self-creation" that both he and Marx proclaimed as the goal of communism[105] required, for Hess, a transformation of consciousness as well. Hess focused on education or upbringing (*Erziehung*) which he called theoretical as opposed to practical reform.[106] The historical process toward the new world would not occur by itself. Children would have to be raised to be active and oriented toward people. A kind of spiritual education would be required, parallel to what the Christians had offered in past centuries, to overcome possessive individualism. The new consciousness would therefore affirm the death of the individual as part of life as a whole.[107] Alongside this "education and human cultivation," the "organization of labor" would be required.[108] The end result would be a different kind of society, based on the unity of the species: "The organic form of the *togetherness* of species and individual is the spiritual property of the species, the individual consciousness of the human essence, which becomes living property of individuals or body of the species and the individual means of life, insofar as it is developed, formed, effected in the individual. The development or effect of consciousness in each individual is education."[109] An education, in short, that would give humans back their true god—their alienated essence, indeed their "nature."[110]

Marx rightly criticized the vagueness and idealism of Hess's reliance on education to bring about the new society, and Hess accepted much of this criticism. In a letter to Marx of July 28, 1846, Hess agreed with the need to break with the "German ideology," and asserted that it was now necessary to ground the revolutionary movement on "historical and economic presuppositions," a position Hess held to the end of his life.[111] But Marx's critique did not do justice to the issue. When Marx asked "who educates the educators?" in his "Theses on Feuerbach," he was, like Hess, pointing out the authoritarian implications of the French socialist project of bringing people to socialism by ethical socialization. But he was also shutting down discussion of an important aspect of the revolutionary process: not mere advocacy of change on the basis of the direction of history, but the question of how to bring it about. Marx sought the point in the historical continuum where history and criticism, history and theory, would coincide and lead to the revolutionary deed, and claimed to find it in the proletariat.[112] This may have appeared a convincing, hard-headed approach to social change that tapped into contemporary discussions of fate of the working class. Yet Marx's approach seems more fragile in retrospect than Hess's, more subject to disappointment in reality and indeed more eschatological in orientation, given the total and yet vague demands placed on revolution. At least Hess's notion of empathy and sentiment could explain why members of the petty bourgeoisie like Hess and Marx found their way to socialism. Marx's assertion that some intellectuals managed to grasp the totality of the historical process correctly and therefore became socialists is far more demanding an explanation, and far less convincing.[113]

Hess's relationship with Marx suffered mortal blows from Marx's authoritarian tendencies within the German communist community in Brussels, even as they remained close in political and social thought.[114] Like Marx, Hess used a caustic tone, in, for instance, what he wrote for the *German Ideology* and in his critique of "The Last Philosophers" Feuerbach, Stirner, and Bauer.[115] Hess also adopted Marx's understanding of economics, derived from the British classical economists. In October and November 1847, Hess published a series of articles under the title "Consequences of a Revolution of the Proletariat" in the *Deutsche Brüsseler-Zeitung*, which had become an organ of the new Federation of Communists around Marx and Engels. Hess's articles reflected the Federation's discussions of a platform for a communist party, and foreshadowed *The Communist Manifesto,* which appeared a few months later. Not only were Hess's specific proposals similar to those of the *Communist Manifesto* (a progressive tax, an end to inheritance, a national educational system), but Hess also asserted that the precondition of an authentic, social revolution would be a proletariat reduced to selling its labor as a commodity. Even the image of communism as a frightening "specter" for the bourgeoisie appeared in the essay.[116] Hess called for the organization of the proletariat for revolution in the face of a rotten bourgeoisie. Marx apparently managed to halt the publication of the articles, believing that a bourgeois-democratic revolution, rather than a proletarian one, was imminent. At issue, however, was not merely political strategy but also his and Engels's status; as Silberner points out, their break with Hess occurred in part because Hess never fully capitulated to them.[117]

Hess also retained aspects of his own original worldview, even in the heady days of the Revolution of 1848. As already noted, his revolutionary pamphlet *Red Catechism for the German People* made use of religious forms and proclaimed that "the social revolution is my religion."[118] In it, Hess described at length a compulsory, national system of state education for all children and youth, organized around science, art, and industry. The education would combine the formation of youth into "armies of laborers" who would build for society with martial arts from boyhood on.[119] The old image of a revolutionary republic modeled on Sparta returned.

A new Sparta failed to materialize in 1848–49. Hess greeted the February Revolution in Paris with great optimism: "If the French republic and the rule of the Proletariat survives but a single year, we will perhaps be living in a communist republic already in the year 1850."[120] On March 3, 1848, Hess's friend Andreas Gottschalk led a workers' procession to the town hall of Cologne, to demand a people's militia, equal and universal voting rights, freedom of the press, and freedom of speech, along with measures to support the poor and workers of the city. The meeting quickly became tense, and Prussian soldiers intervened—itself a provocation in the Catholic and Rhenish city. Gottschalk was arrested along with other leaders of the protest.[121] Hess hastened back to Cologne in early April, where he was soon involved in the new workers' association organized by Gottschalk and Friedrich and Mathilde Anneke; Hess welcomed the "pleasant anarchy" (*gemütliche Anarchie*) of associations and meetings. He was nonetheless soon disappointed in several respects. First, he sought to refound the *Rheinische Zeitung* as a revolutionary socialist newspaper; Marx and Engels outmaneuvered him, and themselves founded the *Neue Rheinische Zeitung* as a radical democratic newspaper, reflecting Marx's belief that the proletariat was ready for nothing more than supporting a bourgeois revolution in Germany. As a result, the left was split in Cologne between Marx and Engels, who had its major organ, and Hess, Gottschalk, and the Annekes. Liberals and democrats were also divided and the radical democrats were riven by the rivalries on the far left. The local elections of early May 1848 resulted in a great victory for political Catholicism. The revolution in Cologne thus split into three separate factions, each critical of Prussian rule but also hostile to each other.[122] Hess, dismayed by the machinations of Marx and Engels, abandoned Cologne and made his way to Paris, where he remained until April 1849, working as a journalist, participating in debates of German radicals, and witnessing the revolution's failure at first hand.[123] Already in May 1848 he foresaw a conflict between the workers and the middle class; a few weeks later, he reported on the June Days, when working-class Paris was transformed from a "battlefield" into a "slaughterhouse": "There can be no doubt that the poor working people will in the end succumb. Possibly tomorrow order will reign in Paris."[124]

The Feuerbachian decade thus ended in disappointment. References to Feuerbach's philosophy dropped out of Hess's writing. And yet, the basic critique of God, state, and money remained, as well as an implicit notion that socialism involved the harmony of humanity. Hess found the solution to the problem of why one should assume harmonious development in the first place: "love" was a principle somehow embedded in the cosmos. He now put this problem at the center of his theoretical writing.

The Revolution and the Cosmos

"Love" was the key to much of Hess's political writing in the 1840s, either explicitly before 1846 or implicitly in the notion of "society" as a kind of religion thereafter. Love had a specific meaning for Hess. It was not merely romantic love and certainly not lust. It stood rather for "life" in general, "the whole creation, the whole universe, which is eternal, infinite, immeasurable—like love."[125] Love was a kind of principle of eternal creation on all levels: social and biological as well as chemical and cosmic. Love was transformation and yet also part of a harmonious unity. The notion of love as dynamic and transformative shaped Hess's other conceptions of a new order that would bring human history to its final resolution. Love as a natural process was not unlike digestion, another image of harmonious order for Hess. Unalienated labor, for example, involved the constant transformation of the world, yet in a socially organized manner. Even eating revealed such an order: "What the mouth admits as means of nourishment, it does not hold tightly in its jaws as its 'inalienable property.' Instead, after it has digested or eaten [the food], it delivers it up to the stomach. This digests or consumes it in its way and delivers it up to the blood. The blood forwards it on to the various organic domains, which need it for *their* activity, and so on, until it finally passes back again to the elements, which for their part are absorbed, consumed, digested, that is, used for organic productions, by the various organic domains."[126] Hess meant literally this parallel between eating and other processes in the universe: social production, cell reproduction, and the development of the cosmos were all part of one system. After the failure of the Revolution of 1848, Hess sought meaning, embodied in the processes of love, digestion, and death, in the cosmos as a whole. He was armed with the weapons of the midcentury materialist, the telescope and the microscope. Hess was part of the transformation to a new, definitively post-Hegelian age of scientific thinking, along with other advocates of a new scientific *Weltanschauung* like Ernst Haeckel and Ludwig Büchner. The scientific-materialist age did not mark a complete break with the past, but did display an important shift in rhetoric as the old Hegelian language came to seem implausible.

Hess spent most of the rest of his life in Parisian exile, living off the meager proceeds from the inheritance left by his father. After his father died in 1851, Hess married Sibylle Pesch, his lover since the mid-1840s, who was a Catholic and possibly a former prostitute. Hess's father had disapproved of her, both because she was not Jewish and because of her alleged moral failings.[127] Hess did not give up his revolutionary aspirations. Nor did he find his way to an early socialist Zionism immediately. Most of his "revolutionary" work in the last decades of his life took place in the natural sciences, where Hess sought empirical evidence to support his notion of a tendency toward harmony, unity, and socialism immanent to the universe.[128] Following the work of Jakob Moleschott in particular, but also the late Feuerbach, Hess called for empirical science and philosophy to come together in rejecting the idealist German tradition of natural philosophy.[129] Also like the new materialists of the 1850s, but unlike Feuerbach (as Chapter 5 below discusses), Hess sought to discover a coherence in the material universe that would reveal the coming new order of humanity.

Matter and spirit, Hess asserted, were both infinite and in constant motion.[130] There was no heavenly universe somewhere beyond matter. Hess remained loyal to Spinoza's notion of the total immanence of the world. But within the world there were certain immanent laws that stood at the heart of all history, natural and human. All aspects of the universe, from the cosmos to the individual cell to human society, were organized by means of a "rotary motion," a tendency toward circularity with centripetal as well as centrifugal aspects. A kind of "circulation" (*Kreislauf*) was to be found at all levels, involving for example evaporation and condensation, energy and matter, dynamics and statics, analysis and synthesis, production and consumption, division of labor and accumulation of condensed labor.[131] Gravity made circulation possible: gravity mediated finite matter and infinity to produce organized life, gravity provided the impulse toward the circulating equilibrium that created the individual.[132] Indeed, gravitational equilibrium in the realm of spirit permitted knowledge of all of world history, Hess asserted.[133] In a sense, then, the entire universe was "socialist" in its tendency toward equilibrium and harmony: "Socialism is the basic law of the universe."[134] Hess's universe was not constructed by a series of meaningless laws, but by an underlying law. Cosmic history was not subordinate to meaningless fate, as in the ancient world, but had a single, universal meaning; it was inflected by Christianity, even as it overcame Christianity in a Spinozian unity of matter and spirit.[135] Unlike the cosmic and organic unities, Hess claimed, the social world had not yet reached its "sabbath," when a "grand central kingdom of humanity forms like a spiritual sun," around which all of society would orbit.[136]

Speculation based on empirical observation about the organization of the universe formed an important part of German radical discussion in the decades after 1848.[137] Hess was not alone in his ruminations. Indeed, he published in the most important journals for such speculation, including *Das Jahrhundert,* where leaders of the radical materialist movement such as Karl Vogt, Ludwig Büchner, and Jakob Moleschott also published; *Die Natur,* edited by the scientific popularizer Otto Ule; and *Der Gedanke.*[138] Hess stood out from these other thinkers in his concern for social organization. Unlike the others, he had a dynamic, genetic notion of social development heavily influenced by Marx. Hess was thus better able to defend his scientific colleagues from the allegations of relativism and amoralism.

In 1856, a woman named Mathilde Reichardt published a book of letters concerned with Feuerbach-influenced materialist thinking and addressed to the physiologist Jakob Moleschott.[139] Reichardt's book created a stir by rejecting the category of morality, and along with it a series of moral institutions, including marriage, as alien to the material world. A young, single, and intelligent woman asserted proudly that her materialist ethics liberated her from the constraints of traditional institutions: this was not the message that the moralistic, materialist republicans wanted to present to the population or to the repressive German states of the 1850s. Hess provided one of the only serious and convincing responses to Reichardt from the camp of the republican scientists. Reichardt, he claimed, repeated the arguments of Stirner by operating with an abstract, dehistoricized individual rather than the individual as he or she actively, concretely appeared in history. Ethics, Hess argued, do not derive directly from "nature," conceptualized as a set of static laws, but rather develop as part of a general social development. The point of the scientific critique of religion was not to abandon religion and to be left face to face with a cold, nonhuman universe, but rather to find the connections, the gravitational tendencies toward harmony, that characterized society. Marx as well as Moleschott was necessary for this positive critique of religion, Hess asserted. Only by combining Marx's description of society with the physiological and physical theories of Moleschott, only by taking seriously society on its own terms alongside cosmic and organic life, could unreflected religion be transformed into full consciousness of the self in society. Ethics were still necessary, but not on a metaphysical basis. They derived rather from society and economy, from the "mode of reproduction."[140]

The unity that Hess proclaimed was revolutionary, as he intimated even in the censored world of post-1848 reaction. Hess attacked all forms of speculation, as he had before 1848. Philosophical speculation about nature, which produced nothing for society, should be superseded by science; speculative (financial) capital should give way to direct social organization. Both forms of speculation needed to be replaced by an alliance of proletariat and scientist. While speculation was necessary for an embryonic society, once it was born, once it began to find its own center of gravity and self-organization, society would have to wean itself from the two forms of speculation—just as a child had to wean itself from its mother.[141]

Though he called for a combination of Moleschott and Marx, Hess's conception of world history followed a different course than either. Hess continued to concentrate on the progress of human consciousness, as Judaism achieved a breakthrough to a limited monotheism, Christianity proclaimed universality, Spinoza overcame Christianity, and the Revolution of 1789 opened the way to an ultimate history of harmony and redemption. In short, Hess retained the sacred historical schema of his 1837, *The Holy History of Mankind,* but organized it more clearly as the development of humanity from religion to science. Against Reichardt, Hess argued that the new, postreligious worldview would not amount to a return to polytheism, with its relativistic, warring deities, but would be a higher version of monotheism based on the true principles of rotation and gravitation.

In the same decade after 1848, when Hess was formulating his account of cosmic history, Marx looked at society: "[I]f we did not find latent in society as it is the material conditions of production and the corresponding relationships of exchange prerequisite for a classless society, all attempts to explode it would be quixotic."[142] Marx's careful writing avoided the speculative flights that appeared even in Hess's "empirical," scientific writings. Though also a dialectical materialist, Marx tended to avoid the nonhuman realm, concentrating instead on the conscious and goal-directed acts that characterized the human world (and therefore socialism). But the differences should not obscure the similarities: both Hess and Marx sought laws of motion immanent to the world that would lead to socialism; both compared social and biological forms in their search for the bigger patterns in history (note Marx's famous description of the commodity as the "economic cell-form" of capitalism and of his history as the "natural history" of capitalism).[143] When Engels immersed himself in the natural sciences a few decades later, he was also seeking to address the question of how to conceptualize socialism as part of the unified natural world.

But a unified natural world also involved death, which raised the problem of whether life had any ultimate meaning at all. Hess's approach to natural science made death central to the process of eternal circulation. Even solar systems burnt out, but this burning out was part of the eternal circulation of energy and matter that would eventually, through gravity, lead to the formation of a new solar system. The new worlds forming out of the nebulous gases of decadent, old orders were the "arsonists who come into contact with the old, extinct, and petrified during their development, and who present to us the sublime drama of a heavenly revolution. Death and resurrection, solidification and dissolution, are the means of eternal reproduction."[144] The cycle redeemed the dying individual: death was to be suspended in an eternal process of creation. Hess offered the individual little more than an aesthetic comprehension of the universe to resolve the problem of death.

Feuerbach, through his own critique of philosophical abstraction, had come to question whether any consciousness, no matter how "high," could release the individual from existential angst. Hess grasped Feuerbach's point, hidden deep within the complex stories of the *Theogony*, and protested. If the human's wishes and therefore religion reflected hunger, homesickness, and illness in the world, then that belief would come to an end when man either had the means to happiness or at least conceptualized the conditions for a happy life and strove for them on a scientific basis.[145] Feuerbach's error, according to Hess, was to fail to take the next step of science, to go beyond egoism as he had gone beyond religion. A second Luther, Feuerbach nonetheless remained wedded to the religious world even as he destroyed its logic.[146] Hess's argument on the one hand reflected his earlier critique of Stirner; but on the other hand Feuerbach was not Stirner, and his basic point remained unanswered. The individual was what bore consciousness, and that individual was also conscious of his or her own death. All the assertions of a grand, eternal, cyclical process to the contrary, being was finite for the individual. Hess's description of galactic revolutions offered but little solace to an individual in the world.[147]

Hess needed to connect the individual in society to the entire universe if his ambitious conception was to work. Such a connection would prove the presence of intelligent design. This he found in "race," a biological fact, in his estimation, that moved above and beyond the organic to social organization and eventually to a harmonious humanity.[148] Hess's attempt to develop a new, quasi-religious worldview based on natural science was therefore an important factor in his turn back to Judaism—now conceptualized in secularized, national and racial form.[149]

Rome and Jerusalem

Hess's work shows his continuous search for a coherent, unified story of social development as part of the immanent laws of the universe. A popularized Spinoza also runs like a red thread through Hess's work. In light of Hess's search for material forces that propelled history forward, for signs in the empirical world of an order to the universe, the turn to Jewish nationalism and racial thought in the last 15 years of Hess's life cannot be surprising. What surprises one in *Rome and Jerusalem* is rather the personal tone and the sentimental, even melodramatic images that mark the text. He had used sentimental and melodramatic images in his agitational writings: his "Communist Credo" of 1844, for example, proclaimed a "religion of love and humanity" and spoke of the mutual love between a boy and a girl as the basis of the family in communism.[150] Yet, in *Rome and Jerusalem,* which took the form of a collection of letters, this sentimentalism was different. He now wrote in the first person of his own mother, the sad Jewish girl whom he addressed in the letters, his religion, and his upbringing. He wrote of his deep sorrow for his mother, who, he claimed, had until recently appeared to him almost every night in his dreams.[151] Jewish women, he claimed, had a particular, deep love for children that was constitutive of the unity of the Jewish nation, connected to the "highest love" of God. Every Jewish son, Hess asserted, perhaps on the basis of revelation, was a potential messiah, every mother a *mater dolorosa* (an odd phrase that reminds one of the mourning Mary).[152] Hess remembered his grandfather fondly as well, a pious man, crying over the destruction of Jerusalem, immersing himself in religious studies, awaiting the "End of Days," which Hess interpreted (presumably not wholly in accord with his grandfather's thoughts) as "the period when the development and education of humanity will reach their highest point."[153] And he affirmed the forms (though not necessarily the content) of Judaism, forms that asserted the unity of the Jewish nation over against the "meaningless nihilism" of Enlightenment and reformist critiques of Jewish rituals.[154] Hess portrayed himself as a natural part of the Jewish

nation, as though there was no question about his authenticity in this matter. Sentimentality served a kind of naturalizing argumentative function: the
sentimental is the authentic, unquestionable truth in a particular individual,
resistant to logical or empirical testing. Sentimentality allowed Hess to present the experience of a minority in the same way that German nationalists
or French republicans presented their own self-evident sense of national
belonging.

Hess's own life did not conform to these sentimental images. Whether
he really saw his mother every night in a dream is questionable;[155] he certainly did not marry a woman from the Jewish community, although he
asserted that women were at its heart, but rather Sibylle, who was apparently
involved in a number of scandalous affairs. Indeed, in 1860, as Hess was
composing *Rome and Jerusalem,* he and Sibylle separated for several years.[156]
Hess stated that the Jewish nation deplores a childless union, but he himself
produced no children.[157] Finally, his fond reminiscences of his Jewish
upbringing in 1862 contrast sharply with the diary entry cited at the start
of this chapter, where he recalled being beaten black and blue over his
Talmud lesson. Indeed, Hess spent many years as a revolutionary rejecting
the conservative forms of Judaism, which he had experienced in Bonn, as
well as Christianity. It is not surprising that a revolutionary would aim at
crushing the old world of mere forms.

One can easily comprehend how Hess found his way to Jewish patriotism, not only in the context of the revival of revolutionary nationalism in
1848–49 and in the late 1850s, but also in reaction to the ubiquitous anti-
Jewish attitudes among his fellow radicals.[158] Even the most self-critical
such as Feuerbach resorted to stereotypes about Jewish egoism, as noted in
Chapter 1. Far more disturbing, however, were the statements from Hess's
own fellow radicals. A liberal radical like Arnold Ruge did not hesitate for
a moment to use anti-Semitic images as he attacked Hess, whom he referred
to as the "communist rabbi" and accused of smuggling cigarettes.[159] A leading radical like Mikhail Bakunin was explicit in his hatred of the "trium-
phant reign of the Yids," and Fourier declared the Jews the "secret enemy
of all nations."[160] Even his own publisher, the radical Otto Wigand, stated
that *Rome and Jerusalem* "goes against my entire purely human nature"[161]
In Hess's view, Protestant, nationalist Germany—including the radicals
there—had failed to accept religious and ethnic difference. Hess articulated
this difference in terms of race, not culture. Hess's willingness to accept
racial arguments, to try to turn them around into affirmations of a Jewish
race, coherent in both physiognomy and culture through the ages, indicated
a rage as well as an intellectual weakness in his position. He asserted that
"[t]he Jewish race is one of the primary races of mankind that has preserved

its integrity"—i.e., a race that originated separate from other races, whose continuity may be seen in the shape of noses and curly hair in ancient representations and therefore was created thus; this assertion was pseudo-science at best, and puts Hess among the same caliber of thinkers as Karl Vogt and even Arthur Gobineau (with whom Zlocisti compares him).[162] The argument of some of Hess's Zionist readers that *Rome and Jerusalem* marks his authentic position, the position to which his work had been striving throughout his life, misses the continuity in Hess's orientation toward natural history.[163] Even Waxman, in his influential translation of *Rome and Jerusalem,* leaves out Hess's reflections on germs and cell development, apparently because he found them too extraneous to the "real" argument. In fact, Hess's conception of a natural history of the cosmos, then the world, and only thirdly humanity underlay his affirmation of Jewish nationalism. Here, as in Hess's earlier works, the point of the book was less its content than its practical aim: the attempt to mobilize for a radical transformation of the world. Here, too, Hess was concerned with the basic issues that governed his earlier works: the rejection of personal immortality, and the affirmation of death as the creation of new life; the description of love as a form of immediate human solidarity beyond market or legal relations; and most important the search for a lever that would speed up the progress toward a revolution to realize this new vision of love and humanity in the world.

The contradictions within Hess's Zionism were clearest where Hess sought to affirm Jewish forms of cultural practice. "No ancient custom or usage should be changed," Hess asserted, "no Hebrew prayer should be shortened or read in German translation," since these forms were the source of Jewish nationality despite the history of the Jews' dispersal across the world.[164] Hess claimed that the Reform attempt to adapt Judaism to a modern, liberal worldview sucked the marrow out of Judaism, leaving only its skeleton.[165] Yet Hess also claimed that these forms would enter into flux as soon as the nation re-formed as a nation, as soon as Jewish law began to develop according to the needs of the people: written law and fixed forms had only been necessary to deal with the challenge of diaspora.[166] At issue is not the validity of his claims, but rather what Hess was trying to do with them: namely, to call for a naturally given group to form in order for it to engage in historical progress. In short, Hess did not advocate a strict, formal orthodoxy; the form served only to support a political search for a lever to move world history forward.[167] Hess's ambivalence about orthodoxy emerged clearly in his discussion of sacrificial rites, which had been criticized for their cruelty. Hess first denied that such sacrificial cults could be part of a true historical religion, "which breathes only love for humanity and the knowledge of God"; then he stated that the real historical reality of national unity would eliminate such practices from Judaism.[168]

All the talk of Jewish traditions, of Jewish forms, of the Jewish religion, then, seemed to be reduced to a political proposition: the Jews formed a physiological race different from other races in Europe, especially in Germany, and that it should assert itself in history again. The point was not merely to devise a pragmatic response to the continued oppression and prejudice against Jews but to further the progress of the world. And Hess hoped to have discovered a true basis for this conception in the world. The Jewish nation overcame the "sickly atomistic conception" of personal immortality of Christianity, with all of its depoliticizing implications;[169] and the collective that Hess had sought, bound together by love not law, by inner will not external coercion, seemed to be manifest in the Jewish nation. Furthermore, the notion of a nation implied a unit that survived over time and allowed Hess to assert the unity of living and dead among the Jews: "And therefore do I love also death," he stated, and argued that only the Jews had risen to that spiritual height of honoring death and continued life.[170] In Judaism Hess found the essence of the revolution he had sought from his earliest days as a revolutionary. Hess found, in his mind, the key to history, both human and natural, and the proof of a grand, intelligent design, of an entity that would redeem the universe.[171] By the end of the century, however, Hess's descriptions of the spontaneous generation of higher beings, including originary races, seemed at the least quaint. Waxman, possibly in embarrassment, declared the long note 7 to *Rome and Jerusalem* "abstruse" and leaves it out of his translation, which otherwise presents Hess as a modern-day Jewish prophet.[172]

For Hess, personal mortality was redeemed by the persistence of the race, a superindividual unity; love above mere forms was embedded in the properly formed racial, national community; and the revolutionary transformation of the world—in Hess's terms the final stage of social development that would complete the cosmos—came from the proper alignments of these truths at a propitious moment. In other words, some external configuration was needed so that the Jewish race could reorganize itself as a nation, so that the redemption of the world could begin. Just as his socialist ally in Germany, Ferdinand Lassalle, found that moment in 1863 with the possibility of a new, strong, imperial Prussia under the leadership of Otto von Bismarck, Hess found that moment in the strong leadership of the French nation by Napoleon III, an "iron dictatorship of kingship" to which the French people have submitted, Hess asserted, only because "the Emperor is true to his revolutionary descent."[173] French colonies, he asserted, would now link Europe and Asia; the Suez Canal would rebuild civilization in the land of Zion; France's grand emancipatory tradition of 1789 combined with the ethical potential of the Jewish people would lead to a peaceful world that also resisted the leveling aspects of modern civilization; and the Jewish nation could finally become "the educators of the wild Arabian hordes and the African peoples."[174] Imperialism and racially oriented nationalism, then, would be the motors of a progressive history; against Marx, Hess asserted that "the race struggle is the primary one, and the class struggle secondary."[175]

And yet, despite his turn to nationalism and his sympathies with Napoleon III's imperialism, Hess remained a committed socialist. One year after *Rome and Jerusalem*, Hess published *The Rights of Labor*, with its radical call for a unity of all working people against the powers of reaction and capital.[176] Hess's revolutionary instincts stopped him from following Lassalle's party toward a Bismarck-dominated, Caesarist social monarchy following Lassalle's death. In 1867, he condemned any attempt to unify Germany on the foundation of a "feudal-legitimist, Prusso-Russian absolutism."[177] Hess's aim was never simply power and social comfort, but a transformation of society in the direction of "true" popular sovereignty, i.e., the autonomous self-rule of an emancipated, self-conscious humanity. Unlike Lassalle, he feared both Bismarck and the possibility of another failed revolution. As he stated in a letter to Lassalle, he had no faith that the German proletariat could ever accomplish a successful socialist revolution.[178] Likewise, Hess's aim was not the primacy of one race, but rather the redemption of all races through a grand, world-historical, revolutionary overturning of the liberal, critical, individualistic, materialistic society developing around him. On his reading, the redemptive message of the "Semitic race," revealed through Jewish mythology, implied redemption of humanity as a whole. Appointing one race the redeemer of humanity in general, of course, undermined the universalist message of Hess's thought.[179] Although he clearly believed in scientific racism, his work still sought the revolutionary subject, and once again, the particular elements of that subject did not fully jibe with its appropriate, "messianic" task. "The masses are never moved to progress by mere abstract conception," he proclaimed; "the springs of action lie far deeper than even the socialist revolutionaries think," namely, in attaining "national independence" on a "common, native soil."[180] Hess was not merely a pioneer of Zionist thinking, but also of that entire, grand schema for world revolution by the wretched of the earth—a movement that has, paradoxically, often taken up anti-Semitic positions in the Middle East and elsewhere.

A professional revolutionary is not interested in accurate scholarship of the past, but in grasping emergent, transformative movements toward the future based on the true potential of humanity. The revolutionary seeks not mere facts but powerful ideas whose truth lies in their ability to transform the world, and thereby to prove their scientific basis. Hess's work on Zionism formed in the same context as his experiments with other forms of socialist politics and his quest for the key to the universe in natural science. This complexity is what makes Hess interesting, even where his particular arguments are thin. In a series of letters written to Alexander Herzen following the failed Revolution of 1848, Hess wrote: "I am more of an apostle than a philosopher."[181] In this sense, he seems closer to Fourier than to the late Feuerbach: to Fourier's insistence that the universe had some meaning embodied in its overall history, that such meaning was embodied in the hieroglyphics of nature in Fourier's words.[182] He would never rest content with contemplation of the given; real history was not accessible to the contemplative, philosophical observer, Hess maintained, but remained a closed book, a "dark, mystical region."[183] That desire to announce the impending transformation of the world, the coming of a new harmony, provides the continuity in Hess's thought. The emergent, transformative element in the world changed over time, from humanity in general to the proletariat, from the scientist to the nation of the Jews, but in all cases the real historical subject brought the good news of a coming new order.

Feuerbach was sympathetic to Hess's goal of liberating the true potential of humanity. The search for meaning in the universe was also ever-present in his work. He would have been less sympathetic to Hess's belief that the universe was oriented toward producing a harmonious humanity as its highest expression of order. Hess's forays into natural science in fact aimed at more than a momentary distraction, and more than Feuerbach's affirmation of the external world of the senses. Hess believed that his investigations would reveal the connections among cosmic, organic, and social history, the meaningful totality that he claimed Spinoza had revealed.[184] Little material is available on Hess's personal life, but even there he seems to have been oriented toward meaningful totalities, whether in the form of Masonic teachings or in his interest in holistic healing methods.[185] "Love" was but another expression of this unity; "love" and "science" went hand in hand, since both expressed the principle of natural, dynamic order. Not a liberal order of contracts and individuals and profits, but an order founded on unmediated, direct connections among people; not a liberal morality of individual commandments, not a set of laws decreed by the higher state, but the order of a dynamic community. Hess's Zionism never displaced his socialism, and he remained active in the early phase of the formation of the Social Democratic Party in Germany at the same time as he sought funding for the colonization of Palestine in the late 1860s.[186] Hess died in Paris in 1875. His body was buried in the Jewish cemetery in Deutz, a suburb of

Cologne; his gravestone bears the words "Father of German Social Democracy." In 1961, Hess's body was disinterred and then reinterred in the Kinnereth Cemetery in Israel, along with the remains of other socialist Zionists.

Feuerbach may well have sympathized with Hess's politics—after all, he did join the Social Democratic Workers' Party near the end of his life. But already in 1846, Feuerbach had rejected the assumption that humans were the pinnacle of natural history, that there was some teleology in nature tending toward the perfection of humanity.[187] Indeed, "love" for Feuerbach could only be comprehended as a human affect, not as some universal, objective principle of order: "Love from the standpoint of a non-human or superhuman, non-sensual, non-suffering God or being is an obvious deception; for if humanness falls away, love falls away with it."[188] For *this* Feuerbach, a religion that was no religion seemed to be little more than a value-free positivism that conceptualized the human as a determinate part of a material universe. As speculative and often fantastic as Hess's explorations of the cosmos may seem, they revealed a problem in Feuerbach's concept of the species-being: that it risked having no political point whatsoever. If Hess's search for cosmic order was of no value, then one might well be left with the human as a finite being floating in a universe devoid of meaning. To avoid the prospect of nihilism or mere individualism, at the very least the concept of humanity had to link up with some inner-worldly tendency toward the realization of order. Hess and Marx sought these tendencies in the proletariat. The feminist Louise Dittmar would seek them in the discovery of a non-Christian, secular worldview.

CHAPTER 3

Louise Dittmar, Myth, and Marriage

Feuerbach's message of infinite human potential and his critique of theology and institutions reached the leading feminists of the 1840s. His message had an impact on the thinking of Mathilde Franziska Anneke, the radical Rhinelander who would later become known as an American suffragist and associate of Susan B. Anthony; Malwida von Meysenbug, revolutionary intellectual and later friend of Nietzsche; Louise Otto-Peters, who was the central figure in the refounding of German feminism in the 1860s; and the novelist and essayist Fanny Lewald. The individualistic, cigar-smoking poet Louise Aston did not mention Feuerbach, but then again she was in the circle around Max Stirner and Edgar Bauer in Berlin that explicitly rejected him.[1] But none more than the Darmstadt autodidact and radical democrat Louise Dittmar (1807–84) sought to develop his philosophy systematically and seriously, in a series of books written from 1845–49. Her feminism was wrapped up in an attempt to lay the groundwork for a new Feuerbachian "religion" of revolution.

Feuerbach's radicalism implied a call for a qualitatively new approach to life. The full implications became clear in Dittmar's work, as she turned from negative critique to a positive call for revolutionizing the life of women and humanity in general, after the destruction of oppressive institutions like marriage. Her early work, probably written between 1843–45, was critical, even sarcastic; it took on existing institutions, from bureaucracies to universities, accusing them of promoting mediocrity and servile thinking. By 1846 at the latest, Dittmar had immersed herself in Feuerbach's writings, and her own writing began to move from criticism to action. A conception of God that robbed humanity of its potential underlay the stagnating institutions of church and state, she argued. The alienation of human potential in the form of God was historically necessary as a way to bring humans a consciousness of the world, but that at some point humanity had to grab its nature back. Like the German Catholics, with whom she had contact, Dittmar conceived of a religion of humanity, a religion that focused not on the objectified God but on the perfectibility of humans.[2] Out of her critique of institutions, she thus derived a positive argument for a new worldview and a new, substantive, human-oriented politics of the German nation (by which she meant a people rather than a state). Like the French socialists, whose work she engaged throughout her brief literary career, Dittmar saw the place of women as central to the transformation of society. Like the German socialists Karl Grün, Hermann Kriege, and Moses Hess, she proclaimed the importance of love for the new world. However, hers was no romantic utopianism; she rejected French attempts to build "castles in the sky," to plan the new society in advance.[3] The basis of the new society, which she began to describe in the revolutionary year of 1848, would indeed be "love," but her notion of "love" was shaped by the austere ethics of neoclassicism and the economic and technological progress that would make a new world possible. Dittmar's feminism was an idealism based on the rejection of God, an advocacy of long-term loving relationships between man and woman based on the rejection of the patriarchal family, and a call for emancipating women and men rooted in the concrete possibilities of the age of steam power.

The rediscovery of Dittmar's work since the 1980s has focused on her brilliant and scathing criticism of institutions of male domination, like marriage. More than the other feminists of her day, she rejected the notion that women had an essential nature different from that of men; the institutions of domination therefore demanded enlightened criticism, not romantic transformation. But along with her critique went an attempt to rework religious motifs for a postreligious age. Commentators have either ignored these parts of her work or set them aside as unfortunate lapses in judgment.[4] Viewed in the context of the Feuerbach-influenced radicals, however, her considerations of different kinds of religions help explain the problem she set for herself. She aimed, namely, at replacing the Christian teleology culminating in harmony after the end of history with a view that affirmed conflict, conflagration, and redemption. She envisioned the rebirth of the human out of the violence of a Nordic worldview at one point; at another she imagined the violent imposition of ideals on the world. These two notions—one of inevitable conflict and the other of the forced realization of human ideals—were in tension in her work. But either way, radical change was the result of a human decision about the nature of his or her "gods," in the form of a Weltanschauung or specific ideal. Dittmar provided several different such conclusions, which are not all in accord with one another; what links them is the attempt to find a new, postreligious religion.

Dittmar's writing represents apparently the only concerted attempt by a feminist of the time to enter into the discourses of religion and philosophy on the terms set by the men in those fields. She made use of neither novels nor personal journals to put her views down, choosing instead to write political and philosophical tracts. Her first works appeared anonymously, one even suggesting that the writer was a man.[5] Although the content of her work treated issues relevant to feminism, from marriage and housework to education and equal opportunity in the professions, Dittmar did not seek to adopt a specifically "female" style; her writing was, in Georg Simmel's phrase, "objective" in the sense that it engaged in already-existing, "externalized" forms of discourse like philosophy, theology, and political theory—exactly what Simmel, reflecting on the later, difference-oriented feminism of the German Empire, would consider specifically "male" forms of thinking.[6] She demanded that her ideas be taken seriously as ideas, not as the ideas of a woman. She stands out, then, as a German woman radical, outspoken, clear, and open in her critique—and, as Ruth-Ellen Boettcher Joeres has noted, unique in her context.[7] But even more, her work ranged across a variety of disciplines; had she remained an anonymous writer, it would have been hard to connect the different texts. The explicitly feminist critique of the institution of marriage does not necessarily fit with the stoic image of sacrificing oneself for an ideal, nor does it fully square with Dittmar's positive reception of German mythology, especially the affirmation of conflict in Valhalla and the notion of a final *Götterdämmerung* that would open a new future. Feuerbach's ideas, in particular his notion that the truth of religion lay in humanity itself, provide the red thread running through her work.

Traces of her life may be found in her work, but no more than traces. With the destruction of her papers in World War II, other direct sources on her life have vanished. There are no known pictures of her, or even descriptions of her appearance by contemporaries. Careful work by several historians has uncovered details about her family and context.[8] Her Lutheran father was a lifelong public servant involved in finance and accounting in the court city of Darmstadt; her Calvinist mother came from a similar social background in Kassel. Dittmar was the seventh of ten children, and the youngest daughter, which both made her responsible for her aging parents' household and made a marriage extremely difficult, given the lack of a dowry. "From my earliest youth," she wrote in 1849, "I found nothing more painful than the contempt and scorn for my sex." Ill-treatment of "even the lowest woman" and the arrogance of "often quite ungifted men . . . would have made my life unbearable to me, had I not fought against it with all the power of my soul."[9] Her mother died in 1840, a year after her father's death; as Christine Nagel has noted, Dittmar probably spent the next eight years running the household of her unmarried brothers.[10] Her scathing, unromantic description of housework no doubt owed much to her personal experiences.

But drudgery was only one side of her life. Her family was connected, socially and by marriage, with the radical community in and around Darmstadt. Dittmar's brother Georg Hermann was a friend of the radical student Georg Büchner; as a participant in the ill-conceived plan to ignite a revolution in Frankfurt in 1833, Georg Hermann Dittmar was forced to flee into Alsatian exile.[11] Dittmar's brother Karl Anton married the daughter of Karl Leske, whose publishing house printed works by Karl Grün and Karl Marx during the 1840s.[12] Two other brothers emigrated to Texas, perhaps involved with the formation of socialist communities in New Braunfels or San Antonio.[13] Details about Dittmar's life in Darmstadt, her education, her role in the community are hard to find, but she must have had many opportunities to read, hear about, and discuss political and philosophical issues of the day in the salons of the educated middle class. These salons afforded her the opportunity to present her own ideas; Nagel, again, has pointed out how her first works, which consisted of relatively short, focused chapters as well as occasional inside jokes, probably came out of these presentations.[14] What also appears in these first works is criticism of the texture of both women's and men's everyday life in German society.

Dittmar's adoption of the Feuerbachian critique of theology led in her case, paradoxically, to a reaffirmation of mythical thinking. The turn against religion entailed its reconceptualization and even reinvigoration. In a way, the revolutionary Feuerbachian's central problem became clear in Dittmar's work: is a religion possible that conceives of the death of its gods as well as the realization of its ideals?

Critique, Crisis, and the Way Forward: Dittmar's First Publications

In 1845, Dittmar published two books, *Bekannte Geheimnisse* (*Well-Known Secrets*) and *Skizzen und Briefe* (*Sketches and Letters*); the first had probably been written several years previously.[15] Though both writings contained sharp, sarcastic comments, *Bekannte Geheimnisse* was more merciless in its critique and lacked that connection to a secularized religiosity that marked all of Dittmar's later writings. Taken together, these two works set the stage for Dittmar's later radicalism, and reveal the connection between Feuerbachian radicalism and the critique of everyday culture, especially the mediocre and self-satisfied Juste Milieu a.k.a. Justus Michel (a reference to the sleepy and apolitical "German Michel," the object of derision and satire at midcentury).[16] It was Feuerbach's *Essence of Christianity*, she would later remark, that gave her the courage to battle all imposed authority. The occasional cynicism of her earlier writings was less prominent in her writings during the revolution. For that reason, perhaps, she stated in 1849 that she would not, at that point, write what she had in earlier works. Their critical attitude had nevertheless been a necessary step, she claimed, in her intellectual development.[17]

Bekannte Geheimnisse is full of inside jokes and images that clearly had meaning for her audience, but not for us; its scornful tone, however, is clear. Other works of the time that made use of the "German Michel" targeted the sleepy, apolitical, and lethargic German people. For example, an anonymous pamphlet of 1843 penned by Wilhelm Schulz focused on the German people's willingness to be stepped on by the aggressive French and their own monarchs and nobility.[18] The writings of Schulz, a friend of the Darmstadt radical Georg Büchner and an early German follower of Proudhon, whose ideas would influence Marx, must have been known to Dittmar.[19] Her story echoes some of Schulz's criticisms: she suggested, for example, that German liberalism was irresolute and incapable of principled actions.[20] But other criticisms have more to do with irresolute, "bourgeois" behavior in society: the much-criticized "juste milieu" of Louis-Philippe's France. Juste was born, for example, into a world with few shadows, for "where there is not much light, there are not many shadows"; his godparents baptized him in the river Styx, where he learned indifference; he received rights as a citizen under the principle that "order is the first virtue of the citizen" (*Ruhe ist die erste Bürgertugend*). And, Dittmar continued, Juste had a kind of speech impediment in his childhood that kept him from saying what he was missing.[21] The examples from the book could be multiplied: with a sarcasm equal to any of her day, Dittmar took on the good subjects of the German states—including her family and the milieu in which she lived.

One must assume that those who heard her speak from these notes laughed with her and at themselves, but at some level the insinuations must have hit home. What, for example, would her brothers have thought of the advice given by Juste Milieu's father? "My son, an official post is a bread basket; man is a stomach; his powers are his arms, which he needs to reach into the bread basket, and the university is the theory of this science."[22] By implication, the purpose of seeking an administrative office was primarily a rent-seeking activity: that the first career Juste Milieu's father recommends is theology, since rural clerics rarely die of hunger. The stupid Juste Milieu, however, expresses his surprise that the priest's words are such "bad comedy" and that they only reach "female ears," and that the women cry—and he is therefore removed from theology.[23] Dittmar's sharp prose skewered both the little bureaucrats of established religion and the behavior of women who believed clerics. Dittmar's feminism was not one that would tolerate the actions of foolish women; like the British feminist Mary Wollstonecraft, arguably the most important figure in the modern feminist tradition, her aim was to transform women as part of their emancipation.

Dittmar's criticism shifted to the treatment of women near the end of the book—but notably here, too, women were involved in their own repression, as Juste Milieu's mother wails about the fate of families who cannot get rid of daughters and advises him to find a woman from a good, Mandarin family: a "zero" (*ein Null*), like herself.[24] Juste Milieu seeks a wife (following a fable of an ape-dealer who packages apes in the form of "kitchen plant," "salon plant," and the like); he "simply demanded a simple, modest, virtuous, sweet, pleasing, domestic, educated, reasonable, talented, lovely, rich wife, whose whole heart he would fill entirely, who would hang on his every word with undying love and loyalty, and who would think of nothing else but him."[25] And he is lucky enough to find a bride who believes this of herself.

The world Dittmar painted was one of utter hypocrisy. Her readers must have been struck by the last lines of the work, which called Juste Milieu "a humorist who ridiculed himself but couldn't take ridicule long."[26] For herein lay Dittmar's secret: her criticism hurt, targeting all that was worthwhile around her, from learning to writing, from religion to philosophy, from marriage to occupation. Two years later, in her first signed publication, Dittmar remarked that "since my earliest youth existence seemed to me nothing but torture; I saw nothing in it other than raw, untamable drives that battled each other blindly. Life nauseated me and only death seemed to provide redemption."[27] This viewpoint permeates *Bekannte Geheimnisse,* despite the humor; one is reminded of Feuerbach's bitter jokes about religion at the end of his 1830 work on immortality, also published anonymously. It is hard to imagine Dittmar writing light novels like those of Fanny Lewald. Sometimes genre is not a strategic decision, but is determined by one's entire personality.

A shift in style emerges in *Skizzen und Briefe,* related perhaps to a growing sense of independence on Dittmar's part. That work brings up all the major themes of Dittmar's later work, including religion and philosophy, labor and socialism, and the status of women. These short sketches plunged Dittmar into contemporary discussions, and reveal a person already conversant with the German and French radicalism—perhaps not surprising, given her contacts with Leske, whose publishing house had just released works on socialism and Feuerbach. Most important, though, the sketches opened up a new perspective on the world for Dittmar. Now she began to elaborate her politics of self-sacrifice and submission to the higher ideal of humanity. The book made four moves that set out Dittmar's project for the coming years: first, to find the essence of religion in humanity; second, to describe how that essence became hidden from humanity through the alienation of religion; third, to gesture toward a new world that would realize the ideal of an unalienated humanity; and fourth, to demand that the harmony of humanity involve equality for women.

First, she addressed the question of what religion actually is. She insisted that religion and philosophy actually addressed the same phenomenon, namely, the "drive living in every human for what is higher." She notably did not use the term "highest being" or "God," but instead the comparative form, which already suggested what was strived for existed in relation to what is. Religion and philosophy operated, though, on different levels: religion worked on the level of feeling, while philosophy made use of consciously articulated concepts. The knowledge of religion gradually rose with the development of people and peoples toward higher knowledge: "As the religious feeling emanates from man, so it returns to him, as the highest and only authority over him."[28] The notion that religion's truth was the higher nature of humanity, which humanity as it developed would eventually recognize and bring back to itself, corresponded to one important aspect of Feuerbach's own thinking in *The Essence of Christianity,* where God's attributes provided the key to understanding the attributes of humanity; so did the critique of ideology implicit in Dittmar's assertion that the errors of religion were the product of a lower level of human development, or even "oriental" stagnation (echoing a concept more important to the other Young Hegelians than to Feuerbach).[29]

Dittmar's first move to relate religion to philosophy involved, then, reducing both to human striving. Her second argument concerned the way religion concealed this truth of humanity from humans. At times in *Skizzen und Briefe,* Dittmar formulated her aphorisms in the second person. She was arguing with someone who claimed that her equation of religion and philosophy was an error—someone later revealed to be herself.[30] Her discussion of predestination also made use of the second person: "I recall having defended another assertion besides my faith in education against you."[31] Dittmar argued that the doctrine of predestination (perhaps conveyed by her Calvinist mother) was morally pernicious, since it made humans feel helpless in the face of necessity, and robbed them of the freedom of thought and action. The argument had a religious basis, in the virtue represented by Jesus Christ, the freedom of belief: to deny this freedom, Dittmar argued, was to fall back into idolatry. Dittmar echoed Feuerbach, whose Lutheranism shines through in his denial that God could possibly have a qualitatively different character from the human (a position not in accord with Calvinism).[32] And her position, she stated, was not born of reason, but of necessity, of a drive that existed within her toward a higher virtue, a higher ideal, in this case the freedom of belief. The aphorism concluded with a consideration of how the original religious impulse, one of freedom, was turned on its head, as religious authorities were established who denied religious freedom. Once again, the Feuerbachian motif appeared, in which the liberating impulse of religion was transformed into its opposite, enslavement. The second move in her larger argument points, then, to both an inherent striving for a higher ideal and its alienation in the form of a reified, idolatrous religion. Just like Feuerbach, she found that faith destroyed the truth of religion; it replaced the omnipotent "I-Thou" with the solipsistic "I."[33]

The third stage of Dittmar's argument involved a turn to the actual content of this ideal, in the future, harmonious order of society. By 1845 at the latest, Dittmar was in contact with Karl Grün, who had made a name for himself as a radical socialist and follower of Proudhon and Feuerbach, and with Moses Hess, whose work she admired; as noted, she was probably also aware of the work of Wilhelm Schulz, who by 1843 had come under the influence of Proudhon.[34] Following Hess, Dittmar described socialism as a system in which production and consumption, labor and pleasure, were one: "only what I freely do, in the highest sense of the term by *my free will,* is *my* labor, just as it is also my only true pleasure."[35] Socialism in this sense, stated Dittmar, had as its task precisely humanity; it was human unity, "the higher development of the human, free unfolding, the recognition of the purely human, secured circumstances, a higher culture."[36] Dittmar did not understand socialism merely as a state of mind, however; it was only possible once basic life needs were met, just as philosophy was only possible on a higher level above mere emotion. The problem lay in the organization of current society, which impeded harmony. It was a system of isolation (*Isolirungssystem*), which promoted egoism and selfishness, and which furthermore permitted people to starve in an age of overproduction.[37]

In these first three moves in her thought, Dittmar recapitulates the argumentation of the socialists of the first half of the 1840s, who thought that they had discovered a path from Feuerbach to socialism, and she did so with a clarity that Hess and Grün lacked.[38] A fourth move, toward feminism, however, took her beyond them. Harmony meant equal education, equal participation; if the two hands playing an instrument are not in accord, the result can only be discord. But nothing was more determined by prejudice and assumption than the state of women. The unequal education of men and women hindered the "higher thought" of harmony.[39] So long as women were denied their basic freedom, their freedom to think and act, Dittmar proclaimed, they could not freely determine what their own nature was; and men's freedom (i.e., nature) would only become clear when women were free.[40]

Socialists of the 1840s often called for women's rights, but they were not often explicit about what they meant. Only a few, such as Karl Grün, went beyond a platitude to demand that women cease having the status of slaves sold into marriage.[41] Dittmar placed the condition of women in the center of the discussion, and connected it up with both Feuerbachian radicalism and the existing social system. The French novelist George Sand, she proclaimed, was more heroic than even the German Catholic leader Johannes Ronge insofar as she challenged the barriers to women that had existed for millennia.[42] That was a strong statement, especially in Darmstadt, where Ronge's new movement "away from Rome" had made of him a popular nationalist hero.[43] In her early, anonymous texts, she already demanded an equal voice where social theory and politics were under discussion. And already Feuerbach was the most important figure. The Feuerbachian critique of theology and his turn toward the concrete human were her starting points—and her end points, too, insofar as the ultimate ideal of humanity was not yet determined. In *Skizzen und Briefe* Dittmar began to lay out a project that would take her out of the grey world of Juste Milieu, where, as she put it, there were no shadows or contrasts, because there was no light. Cynicism and sarcasm were not enough: Dittmar sought ideals to strive for.

Feuerbach and Human Striving

The new project involved entering the "male" world of philosophy, and Dittmar's next publications approached Feuerbach directly. They displayed a socialism and a feminism that demanded not merely words but the heroic deed; the "emancipation of the human spirit," she exclaimed, derived not from the isolated individual, but always from *"Ich und Du,"* echoing both Hess and Feuerbach.[44] Her works of this phase were still anonymous. She signed her 1846 *Der Mensch und sein Gott in und ausser dem Christenthum* (Man and His God, Within and Outside of Christianity) "Von einem Weltlichen" (by a worldly man); her work on Lessing and Feuerbach of the next year was unsigned. In both of these works, her writing took on a new, more confident tone. She no longer wrote short aphorisms or anecdotes; now she wrote a sustained, clear argument about God, religion, humanity, and social change—clearer indeed than contemporary works of "true socialism" by Hess and Grün, and different in form from anything else written by the women of her day.

Dittmar now drew upon Feuerbach of 1841, with his combination of an attack on abstraction and an affirmation of human potential. His works of 1843–44, which completed his break with idealism, were not as important to her, nor to the German Catholics with whom she was in contact.

Their Feuerbach was the earlier one, who argued that religion was a human product and the projection of human characteristics onto nature, and who called for a reversal of this project so that humans could recognize themselves. The project of self-recognition would lead to self-determination, according to human nature and not the dictates of an alien God whose very alienation made "unnatural" phenomena like slavery and war possible.[45] In *Der Mensch und sein Gott,* Dittmar put these moments into a historical process, and in doing so laid the foundation for her rejection of revelation as a source of knowledge in her later work on Lessing and Feuerbach—a full break with revealed religion.[46] She sought a replacement for religion that would find another way of conceptualizing human emancipation and self-realization—in Feuerbach's phrase, a new religion that was no religion.

Dittmar realized, even as she wrote it, that it was not enough to say "Humanity is the goal of all of our strivings."[47] Humans had oriented themselves toward gods conceptualized as existing outside of them, and this act of alienation had to be explained. Dittmar explained the process of the species' development through the example of an individual. As a boy gradually became conscious of external powers, he imputed them to a personalized agent standing outside of the world: the forces of nature took on the attributes of gods, as a way of explaining their effects. This was the first "revelation"—though in Dittmar's account it was not a revelation by an outside power, but a self-objectification that enabled humans to perceive themselves in the world. As Dittmar pointed out in her careful examination of Lessing in 1847, once one had a rational conception of how religion formed, then revelation itself became unnecessary. Not only could reason reconstruct the formation of religious conceptions, but reason could explain them—and thereby explain away the personal God.[48] It was perfectly possible to imagine Moses as a thinking, better informed man who found a way to move his wild people in the right direction—without the need for revelation.[49]

People's conception of these gods directly determined how they lived.[50] Once again, the anti-Jewish motif of German radicalism asserted itself. Judaism, as a form of religion relying on externally imposed laws, oppressed and exploited the people, leaving them weak and helpless before an external God, and ultimately denying the reality of the world in the face of God. The result was eventually a complete degeneration of humanity.[51] Christianity represented the next step, as the reality of humanity was revealed in love, in the "improvement" (*Veredelung*) of humanity. But this notion of perfectibility still contradicted the Christian orientation toward heaven.[52] Despite the attempts of the heretical Arianist tradition to view Jesus as a perfected human being, not as God, the antihumanist side of Christianity won out and the "Jewish ghost" reasserted itself.[53] Even the Lutheran Reformation, on Dittmar's account, was unable to affirm earthly, human reason over blind faith, as Luther's commitment to a literal interpretation of the Eucharist as Jesus's body shows. Here again, Dittmar claimed, the "spirit [*Gemüth*] of the old Jehovah," the "inheritance of Judaism in Christianity," reasserted itself.[54] Christianity was in a sense impossible, seeking to unite love with the principle of a separate, alien God.

In fact, however, the problem for Dittmar was no longer how to attack religion, but rather how to recreate it in the face of modern materialism. Religion was irrelevant in the modern world, the world of calculation and the stock market. Like Hess and Grün, Dittmar saw a new world where money had become God; materialism and the hypocritical religion that accompanied it deprived humans of freedom. The religion of the present had to take another form entirely, one that could confront the decadence of the modern world, with its strife between people, classes, and states—all of the marks of disharmony noted by both French socialists and German radicals.[55] The only way to recover humanity was to return to the actual content of religion.

It was up to reason to lead the way back to the original positive notions of Christianity, which were fraternity, community, and reciprocity.[56] Reason and conviction had to replace faith and to reveal a deeper truth of human perfectability: "Religion must therefore yield to the conviction of the perfectibility of the human race, i.e. of the development of its own essence," not in another world but in the present world. A doctrine of salvation (*Heilslehre*) should be replaced by actual healing (*Heilung*). The son, now grown and himself a father, was in a position to teach his children by reason and love rather than by the old, authoritarian means.[57] Religion would remain, but now in an enlightened form. It would not, as the Christian religion did, demand of Jews that they convert: that contradicted the universality of Christianity. Instead, the new religion would be truly universal: "Our church is the world, our religion is reason, our Christendom is humanity, our credo freedom, our worship service the truth."[58] God was not just the heart, love; God was now the deed in the world;[59] and the content of that God was, as Feuerbach had noted, the quintessence of humanity itself, the perfection of the whole toward which each individual strove.[60] Dittmar grasped Feuerbach as the founder of a new "church," one open, universal, and true in the sense of oriented toward nature and toward humanity. He was an idealist, but his idealism was immanent to the human. Dittmar's use of Feuerbach to proclaim a new religion of humanity fit together with the socialists like Hess and Grün, but also with the German Catholics around Ronge and some of the democrats in the south like Julius Fröbel.[61]

As radical politics intensified just before the Revolution of 1848, Dittmar suddenly found opportunities to appear in public as a politicized woman and to address a wider audience. Only a few years before, in 1843, Louise Otto had given up her masculine pseudonym and begun to sign her own name to political articles published in Saxony. In contact with radicals like Robert Blum and Ronge, Otto had brought feminism into public discussion.[62] Dittmar's opening came under similar circumstances. The radical preacher of the Free Religious movement Carl Scholl and the democratic lawyer Gustav von Struve, a German Catholic, founded the Montag-Verein in nearby Mannheim in March 1847 to provide a venue for radical lectures, and they invited Dittmar as one of their first speakers.[63] With these connections, Dittmar was in the center of southwest German radicalism. Scholl, who would later deliver the eulogy at Feuerbach's funeral, was involved in the creation of a new ecumenical movement that would unite disillusioned Catholics, Protestants, and Jews; Struve would be involved in Hecker's failed armed uprising in Baden in April 1848. Dittmar was in substantive agreement with their programs. Like Dittmar, these movements sought to go beyond established religion, and to replace it with a doctrine of human striving for perfection. The lectures in Mannheim were the initial deeds that would help translate this goal into practice—exactly what Dittmar was looking for.

The foreword to the lectures contains an unusually personal statement from Dittmar. Of particular interest is her discussion of religion, after two years of intense thought on the subject. She admitted in the foreword that she had been at best blasé about religion until recently; she had viewed it as little more than unjust and oppressive, and "my nature stands in opposition to injustice [Unrecht], not in pious toleration of what is apparently unavoidable." But now, after addressing an audience of German Catholics and the Free Religious dissenters, she announced that true religion took a completely different form, one of spiritual independence: it was "nothing other than the freedom of the spirit, the eternal development of humanity through its liberation from spiritual limits."[64] The point was to put these spiritual aims directly into a concrete context, which is what the lectures themselves did.

Moral categories alone, Dittmar asserted, were insufficient. The pagans and Jews, she claimed, made virtue, i.e., a devotion of the self to the community or people, the primary moral value: the individual should put the goal of the collective over his or her own. Christians by contrast put the individual at the center, but the individual's goal was deferred to a future world.[65] In both cases, human yearning for happiness made up the emotional content of religion; in neither case did religion satisfy that yearning.

That yearning had to become fully human if humans were to enter into a harmonious relationship with the world. And that fully human yearning was for Dittmar concrete and material: the "first, crude letter in the alphabet of living life" was not virtue or love, but subsistence, nourishment.[66] First food, then morality.

The reformation of religion in the spirit of democratic renewal required focus on economic and social facts. Only satisfaction of basic needs, a basic level of wealth, permitted humans to gain a sense of respect for themselves, a *Selbstgefühl*, which, Dittmar argued, was the prerequisite for all further ethics: "Without wealth [*Wohlstand*] there is no freedom, without freedom no ethics and without ethics all of life is based on anarchy," i.e., it consists of disorder.[67] Certainly, ethical life involved the "harmonious union of all human demands";[68] but these could not be gained by demanding virtue or love in a world of degradation and poverty. Indeed, a world of hunger was a world where humans remained at the level of animals, unable to develop a sense of self (*Selbstgefühl*). It was therefore a world in which religion consisted of the subordination of the self to a despotic god.[69] Repressive religions reflected hungry conditions. Christianity may have superseded paganism and Judaism, on Dittmar's account, by its affirmation of the individual spirit; the Reformation may have succeeded in asserting the connection between the concrete human and his or her ideals, in place of decadent Catholic indulgences; but Protestantism still proclaimed that ideas were free while leaving real people in chains, and rested content with "alluring utopias, unreachable islands of beatitude."[70] In short, material reality and ideal remained separated.

And it was never more true than under the "unchecked rule of capital."[71] The current economic system saw scarcity in the midst of overproduction, Dittmar proclaimed, sharpening her earlier socialist criticism of an economic order based on chance and caprice. Under such conditions it was useless to wring one's hands and hope for a messiah. For in fact the conditions for change were at hand. Industry, commerce, new machines, railways, the steamship: all made humans lords of the whole world—and yet society was in a state of decadence, its power serving to destroy humans, not realize humanity. The contrast between science and ignorance, material wealth and human poverty, "between this *flying through the air* and this *crawling on the ground*," was a necessary step in humanity's becoming conscious of its next task and developing its own sense of self in striving for a new order.[72] These amounted to arguments for a socialist republic; more than that, a dialectic developed between material conditions and the possibility of a new society, a concrete utopianism, that connected Dittmar directly to the socialist thought of her time.

But remarks in the foreword and afterword to the lectures added a new complication, that of the oppression of women.

The place of women illustrated the systematic and unconsidered relegation of an entire group of humans to a degraded status characteristic of the present system. Unlike other feminists of the time, Dittmar did not merely question but flatly rejected a natural bond between women and domestic tasks. Dittmar described her own position as "hostile to domesticity" (*Häuslichkeit*), and she even viewed household labor as inappropriate for women.[73] The problem for women, she stated, was how they could grasp their own condition and demand rights for themselves. The prejudices against women were in large part the result of social conditions that women faced. It was a lie, she wrote, that women were incapable of perceiving the debasement and disregard to which they were subjected. She herself had from the earliest days, she claimed, suffered from a painful sympathy for the mistreatment of the lowest women: "[M]y feelings were so deeply injured that I felt disdain for myself and for my own sex," she wrote. Overcoming her own self-hatred, as well as her dislike of religion and anger at men for oppressing women, constituted something like a divine revelation for her.[74] Now women's work no longer seemed part of the natural order.

The *Vier Zeitfragen* left many questions unanswered. Its real value lay in the new formulation of criticism that Dittmar developed there, which would structure her most important work from the revolutionary period itself. First, her method was to start with what actually existed, with concrete description of conditions of labor or nutrition in the present, and only then to move to the "higher" values of love and virtue; in taking material conditions as her starting point, she was moving closer to Marx (of whose work she seems to have been unaware). Second, she sought elements of change from within what she observed, such as technology. Finally, she retained a notion of the "spirit" that strived toward a higher, better world of perfected humanity. At first glance, this spiritual moment appears to go against the antispiritual tendencies of Feuerbach. In fact, Feuerbach's philosophy also contained a positive, utopian moment of striving toward the human notions of perfection embodied in human gods. Feuerbach's writings retained a religious form with some reservations; Dittmar retained it more openly. If God was the projection of human ideals, now human ideals would be recognized as such—and a human might act resolutely, in the world, for their realization. The result would be a new religion of humanity, with secular and material goals but spiritual, religious forms: "He who is seized by an uplifting idea knows neither limit nor sacrifice," she wrote, and described such self-sacrifice as "martyrdom."[75] Under her pen, Feuerbach's call for a new religion took form.[76]

Dittmar and the Revolution

When the revolution came, Dittmar followed the events with passion. Like Louise Otto, she sought to be a "patriotic poetess" of the nation.[77] Her verse took a position in favor of Hecker and his short-lived armed uprising in Baden of late spring 1848 against moderates like Heinrich von Gagern.[78] To Hecker, the law and order that Gagern defended was neither, since the system robbed the people of their freedom. Dittmar's poetry endorsed the politics of the radical deed of the "martyr for freedom," even if the result was violence. In her "Germania (German National Anthem)," Dittmar called on the German men to fight for a new world:

> Out to battle, German men!
> Out to battle, break the chains.
> Topple the hypocrites and the tyrants
> A new breed [*Geschlecht*] emerges from freedom.[79]

She demanded a radical cure:

> Go forth, Storm, and seize 'round you greedy flames,
> Unchained be the power of the wild lion!
> What that power crushes let be boldly sacrificed,
> The altar of freedom demands the courage of sacrifice!
> Go forth, go forth, close not the temple of peace,
> Until our enemies flee the palladium.[80]

Dittmar clearly believed that the violence of the existing order justified revolutionary violence. The time had come for the deed.

But what kind of revolutionary deeds were possible for women? In *Vier Zeitfragen,* Dittmar wrote that it was a deed and not merely verbiage for a woman to give a public, political lecture.[81] She herself gave a series of lectures in Darmstadt, Mannheim, Mainz, and perhaps elsewhere during the revolution.[82] Sometime in the first months of revolution Dittmar contacted Ludwig Feuerbach in search of support for a new journal aimed at the education of women. Feuerbach first mentioned her in a letter of August 8, 1848, to Otto Wigand, recommending that Wigand publish her journal.[83] A week later, during which time he probably read her works on religion, Feuerbach sent another letter in praise of her work:

> She is more critical than productive, more of a reflective than a poetic nature. She has not a brilliant, but a thinking mind. But she distinguishes herself from all other women who are writing insofar as no other has seen through

the essence of Christianity and of religion so thoroughly. If you read how she discovers the contradictions in Lessing's work on the education of human-kind, to be sure on the basis of my thoughts but also in her own way and independently, you will be astounded at how this lady puts our philosophers and theologians to shame through the freedom of her mind.[84]

He must have sent a letter of high praise to Dittmar herself, who responded with a long, passionate poem entitled "For Ludwig Feuerbach," which praised him for revealing the "inner kernel of truth" that lay behind God, namely, "the freedom of nature." Germans would make real this truth: "German People! . . .Your learning time is over, the people are ripe for the deed." The revolutionary deed would sweep away the decadent world of the present:

> If the "Judas of all times" is felled, "Traitor-Gold" decays,
> And the true Stone of the Wise, pure "human worth," arises,
> And humanity is arisen, leaves all trace of the animal behind,
> Unites the "highest being" and follows the freedom of nature.[85]

The essence of Germany would redeem humanity. The entire poem, she asserted to him, consisted "as a whole only of the consequences of your doctrine."[86] Wigand apparently hesitated to publish Dittmar's journal (which was to contain more prosaic material than her poetry). Feuerbach became even more insistent after receiving Dittmar's poem, criticizing Wigand for failing to provide a publishing home for "Dittmar, who has more logic in her head and courage in her body than most of our professors and national representatives."[87]

Dittmar probably met Feuerbach in September and October 1848, when he stayed for a time in Darmstadt. By this time her writing evinces a resolute and mature thinker. She was now convinced of the value of her project of combining German nationalism, socialism, and feminism. During the revolu-tion, she produced her most important texts, including a work on Nordic religion, probably written just before the revolution and moving beyond her previous discussions of religion; her manifesto on marriage and revolution, *The Essence of Marriage;* and her essay on Charlotte Corday, Marat's assassin. These three works are connected systematically. The first provided the outline of a new, Germanic Weltanschauung of redemption that affirmed conflict and action and rejected the passivity of Christianity and other "oriental" religions. The second outlined a critique of a specific legal institution and the historical conditions under which it could be smashed. And the third described the ethics of the deed in practice. The latter two works were written during the revolution itself, and first published as part of her short-lived journal *Die sociale Reform,* reprinted as a separate monograph by Otto Wigand.[88]

As the poem to Feuerbach shows, Dittmar attacked the notion of a God who was "dictator of the heavenly kingdom, who only demands, punishes, and threatens."[89] She was outspoken in her rejection of the religious traditions around her—but, like Feuerbach, she was interested in the truth of religion once it was correctly understood. That meant comprehending religion as a creation of humans, as a product of human potential. In the poem to Feuerbach, she referred to the half-truth of the pagan world, which raised nature into a goddess of fate, and the half-truth of Jesus, who left behind him inequality and injustice in the world. Only one people, that poem asserted, had found the "spirit of truth" in itself, in its own freedom: the ancient Germans. But the German people had forgotten the necessity of the deed, she wrote, echoing Moses Hess's and other Vormärz radicals' praise of the radical deed. Dittmar did not intend these statements to be mere flourishes of the pen. Her work on Nordic religions suggests that she saw in a specific Germanic culture a new worldview that could redeem the world of its "oriental" passivity.[90]

Her essay on Nordic religions applied Feuerbach's arguments about the nature of religion, stating that the highest beings imagined by religion were the ideals and strivings of the society that created that religion: "[M]ythogical images are the hieroglyphs of the highest truths, whose deciphering offers us deep insights into the relationships of nature and spirit."[91] The notion of a hieroglyph pointed to a Feuerbachian analysis of religion: one had not merely to refute but to understand the truth behind an ideological representation. Religion did not merely serve to conceal material interests, in Dittmar's view (though there could be no doubt from her writings that Dittmer also thought contemporary religion served to justify tyranny, whether of rulers, of capitalists, or of men in the household). Rather, religion represented some kind of true conception of the entire world.

One kind of conception came from the Orient, specifically from Indian mythology. This was the "egg of all religions," and culminated in harmony and unity—and in the suppression of individual freedom. Indian and Christian mythologies were variations on this theme, and they culminated in Chinese stagnation, fatalism, and despotism.[92] The conception of "oriental religions" as stagnant and unfree was hardly new, but Dittmar's inclusion of Christianity among them would have surprised almost everyone (except perhaps Schopenhauer and later Nietzsche). Dittmar wanted to use Feuerbach's approach to introduce her own alternative to oriental religions, which would bring redemption down to earth: Germanic myths.

Discussion of ancient Nordic and Germanic tales had reached its high point at midcentury, as nationalism coincided with the search for non-Christian conceptions of the universe. From the Brothers Grimm to Louise

Otto, who in 1845 wrote the libretto for a five-act opera to be performed over two evenings, they sought a new expression of the nation and its yearnings.[93] Dittmar lent to these discussions her own idiosyncratic style, combining historical speculation with Feuerbachian philosophy. The ancient Germans, she asserted, had an approach to the world that was utterly different from the Christian one, a new "world-egg" that would offer humanity the possibility of rebirth.[94] Their gods were like living spirits in the world. The good ones, the Æsir, were the "alive, effective forces in nature and in ethical existence." As such, they reflected "unconsciously" the image of the Germans themselves. The Jötnar, or giants, were the enemies of the Æsir and the Germans, and therefore their opposite, both physically and morally: "spiritless, false, lying, sensual, and raw."[95] The elves (*Alfen*) likewise came in two forms: light-elves or black-elves, angels of light or demons of the dark.[96] Their world, like the world of Faust and Mephistopheles, was forever in struggle instead of oriented toward final peace and harmony. For the Germans, Dittmar asserted, the prime mover was chaos, a kind of perpetual force embodied in Odin. This principle of change and motion inhered in things, rather than being a momentary lapse to be overcome in the final moment of harmony. In the beginning was not the word, but energy (*Kraft*); history was not oriented toward resolution but toward a perpetual struggle for the development of the world.[97] Dittmar did not return to the ancient sagas to find a faith to replace Christianity, but rather to find a different, conflict-affirming, immanent conception of the world.

The new principle was not world-weariness, but joy in life; it was not a yearning for resolution, but a yearning to purify the world of the Jötnar. "Energy and proportionality [*Mass*]," i.e., originary forces of nature, made up "the deep idea of world conquest," they were "the soul of development," the "self-creation of freedom."[98] That was why the ancient Germans did not seek to rest in peace, but desired instead Valhalla, eternal struggle and eternal life. Woman found an ideal in the Valkyrie, always young and beautiful and accompanying the heroes into battle (unlike the medieval Christian image of the woman as a witch to be burnt at the stake, in a society that claimed to honor beauty while it destroyed the female sex).[99] What were heroes and Valkyries struggling for?

> Here as well the world comes to an end after its goal is reached, after the Jötnar are exterminated by the Æsir. In a long prophesied conflagration of the world heaven and earth collapse. The universe burns, around the World Tree Yggdrasil the flames blaze, the earth sinks into the sea. Gods and men are annihilated.

The image of the end of the world is, however, redemptive; out of the ashes arises a new world; the result is a new life, a new human, a qualitatively higher form of existence based on "a *higher unity* of spirit and nature."[100]

In the end, Dittmar argued, there were two basic conceptions of the world. In one, the world was created by God and at the disposal of God; it was useful to God and nothing more, and therefore was in itself of no value.[101] Here Dittmar invoked one of Feuerbach's most important themes, that of the nihilism inherent in the conception of a personal deity's capricious creation of the world, a creation that rendered the world itself meaningless since it was no more than the effect of the real essence, God.[102] In the other conception, there was inherent meaning in worldly phenomena, the world had a goal in itself (*Selbstzweck*), and the goal of humans was self-consciousness and self-determination. Here, too, nature was an object to be manipulated—but with the key distinction that the manipulation would occur within the world and become the "full property" of humanity, which would find a kind of symbiotic relationship with what it manipulated.[103]

For Dittmar, as for Feuerbach, to think about religion and mythology was to think about politics (although Feuerbach's practical sense of politics was more limited than Dittmar's). Mythology functioned as a self-image of humanity; if they were correctly read, the hieroglyphics of myth offered a way into the forces that motivated human activity. They also offered hints about the course of world history. Constitutions, German unity, rights, and measures to relieve social ills were not the only things, or even the most important things, at stake in 1848. At issue was the coming battle between the Æsir and the Jötnar, the epic struggle between good and evil. At issue was the destruction of the world around her, the "twilight of the idols" (*Götterdämmerung*), and the rebirth of humanity, now self-determining.[104] At issue, as she would write in a different context, was the development of a new "religion of the future." The new religion would fuse the aesthetic experience of religion with the practical, worldly aims of politics. The fiery political speeches that Dittmar apparently witnessed in the Frankfurt National Assembly in 1848–49 were indicative of the new world to come. The religious imagery of the church provided an affective background for speakers caught up in their ideals, who spoke not only to other delegates but also to the audience watching from the wings. What happened at the Paulskirche, in Dittmar's estimation, foreshadowed a new kind of church, a new kind of religious culture, a new, true anthropology beyond the lies of theology. It combined the lyrical, the domestic, and the epic in a new, total form of political-aesthetic experience that would lead to a world beyond even the freedom of the ancient Greeks.[105] A revolution was at hand.

Within two years, Dittmar wrote in 1849, one might expect an end to the inefficient cooking of private households, stock market pyramid schemes, divorce proceedings, and the artificial barriers of all guilds.[106]

The Essence of Marriage

Dittmar's manifesto on marriage was part of her proclamation of the dawn of a new age. The title indicated that her model was Feuerbach's *Wesen des Christenthums*. The work did not mention the Æsir, the Jötnar, or the *Götterdämmerung*, but one can glimpse moments in it of Bakunin-like joy in destroying the old to make way for the new. *The Essence of Marriage* is a carefully structured manifesto of revolution. Like *The Communist Manifesto*, it combined philosophical critique of false idols, an analysis of real conditions, and a program that is both utopian, pointing toward a reality that does not yet exist, and concrete, in the sense that the new reality is based on trends in the existing world. Unlike *The Communist Manifesto*, *The Essence of Marriage* does not designate a specific group that will carry out the revolution; where indeed might Dittmar have found within the set of problems that she analyzed the emergent social group that Marx did in the proletariat? Dittmar's turn to humanity did not exhibit what Marx would disparagingly refer to as utopian socialism's "fantastic emotionalism" and sentimentality.[107] Rather, it revealed an authentic problem for a thinker who took seriously the radical demand that women were human, deserving to be emancipated from their institutional chains and allowed to develop their full potential, at a time when virtually no one, not even women themselves, supported that demand. The communists could focus their hopes on the newly emerging proletariat; Dittmar focused hers on enlightenment from religion, on technology, and on a new, quasi-religious, ethical belief in humanity.

The book's first move followed Feuerbach: Dittmar divided the institution of marriage into two parts, its form, conceived of as false and doctrinaire like theology, and its content, which expressed a truly human ideal. The form was a long-term contract between a man and a woman, devised according to strict rules set by the state; the content was love. Love was a kind of "force of attraction," which existed as a basic law throughout nature, as both Goethe and natural science showed.[108] Love, then, was the cause of marriage, and happiness its aim, but neither, the book argued, was the case in fact. The social and economic conditions of marriage, combined with its institutional form, contradicted both its natural cause and aim.[109] Feuerbach's criticism of theology and the church in defense of the underlying truths of religion now took on a concrete, revolutionary form.

First, though, Dittmar had to be more precise about what she meant by love. Feuerbach was vague in his discussion of the matter, slipping between sex, dialogical communication between a man and a woman, and dialogue within a human community. Dittmar did not have this option, because precisely the vagueness in the term "love" opened up the possibilities for repression of women that she opposed. The liberals adhered to just such a notion of love, as Dittmar pointed out with respect to the article on sexual relations in the *Staats-Lexicon* by Karl von Rotteck and Carl Theodor Welcker, one of the most important statements of liberal political thought in the decades before the revolution.[110] They asserted that the family was the natural, ethical basis of society, but they saw the needs of men and women within the family as fundamentally different. Women needed love; men were driven by pride. And if women were deprived of love, they tended toward insanity. The entire argument led to a model of marriage in which women had to be legally subordinate to those who kept them sane—and those outside of marriage would serve the needs of men as prostitutes.[111]

Existing marriage law made these circumstances necessary. It created monarchical relations at the local level, granting the man rights over the family and especially the woman that resembled those of a capricious monarch over his subjects.[112] Furthermore, marriage was an economic necessity on the part of women: they needed to enter into a legally defined relationship of subjection in order to survive. The state created the rules to enter this marriage, even banning some marriages, and also set the rules for exiting a marriage. As a result, the "natural right" of entering into a loving relationship—"natural" in the same way that bodies gravitated toward each other in the universe, as she noted elsewhere—was crushed by the artificiality of a contract that smashed the "personal rights" of women to realize their own sense of love and created in their place a "police state of love."[113] Married women lived in a "prison" (*Zwangsanstalt*) where they served at the pleasure of men, satisfying men's sexual needs and engaging in the daily "pointless, inorganic bustle" of housework, a "treadmill" that deadened the mind.[114] Indeed, the work of women, in which stitch replaced stitch, chore replaced chore, was like the unproductive labor of the speculator on the stock market producing money from money, or the scribbler exchanging word for word: thoughtless, inorganic, a matter of mere form and process, not substance.[115] The political institution of marriage created all this misery. The state intervened in rights, for example by requiring public divorce proceedings that humiliated women; now it was time for the state to protect the rights of women, not wives, against the man in marriage and the world outside of marriage. The way to do this was to ensure their economic independence.[116] The state should provide schools for women to receive training in medicine and other fields, child care for mothers, and the opportunity for women to travel and edify themselves with examples of art and science.[117] Only by removing the state from marriage and guaranteeing that neither partner was forced to enter into servitude could humanity be liberated from the chains of empty contract and money.

Dittmar left no doubt that revolution was her aim. It was time for women to rise up and to "rip the veil from the image of truth," to reveal the doubts in their heart and to curse the "huckster-souls, the hagglers, the usurers, the sellers of souls" and their dirty morals.[118] Now all relations, religious, political and social, were called into question and on the verge of collapse.[119] Referring to the arguments of Rotteck, Welcker, and other liberals, Dittmar wrote: "One says that the implementation of social projects will destroy family life. May the family life of today be eradicated root and branch!"[120] Only then would love reign. "Love," Dittmar wrote, "is the combustion point of life: all the rays gather together in it, all light streams out of it." As such, love was the reflection of nature itself—and nature itself had to be free, to operate separate from the state.[121] Neither did she want love reduced to animal drives, which she condemned here and elsewhere. She split love into two components, sensual and ethical—a move that is implicit in Feuerbach, although he did not articulate it in these terms. On the one hand, love had to do with the drive for life, which seems to mean the drive for reproduction; on the other, it had to do with the drive for perfection (*Vervollkommnungstrieb*), for the creation of a truly natural life, "not pagan-Greek, but a human life fully soulful."[122] This higher love was ethical, in the sense that it oriented oneself toward the spiritual or mental goals of the individual as part of humanity; the more developed a soul was in this sense, the more it "rules love, i.e. seeks to bring it into accord with oneself. . . . Thus love, as the most powerful driving force of the soul, becomes the first creator of human nature."[123]

"With the realization of love a second history of creation begins, the history of the creation of the human soul."[124] At first sight, this argument seemed to lead toward the suppression of sensuality by higher ethics. But this was not Dittmar's intention: she asserted that suppression had been historically necessary, as part of the process of the ethical education of mankind, but that it had resulted in the perverse situation where women were expected to be sensually warm or cold depending on externally given rules, whether religious or ethical or legal. With the reduction of sex to the rawest form of nature under conditions of repression, such as when women were reduced to a form of property in marriage, went a tendency of women themselves to reject the senses as "a mark of barbarism" and "to rob ourselves" of "a means to our mental development" (*Vergeistigung*). In short, in one of Dittmar's most striking phrases, "[c]ontempt for woman, her social oppression, is related most closely to the contempt for and oppression of the senses."[125] The senses were to be liberated, but not as purely sensual relations. The whole point of Dittmar's argument was that a liberated consciousness of humanity and of its goals and needs, freed from political and economic conditions that hindered individual freedom, would lead to a higher notion of the senses. Dittmar's revolution, like the revolutions of Marx and Hess, would involve the transformation of the very way humans interacted with their world. Women would recognize their highest ideal, fidelity: "A female being aware of herself, of her nature, when she is fully in command of her actions, can *never* bind herself to a man other than with the idea of fidelity." Indeed, the liberated woman who no longer had to sell herself into a marriage out of economic necessity would be "the natural representative of ethics, of spiritual love," and of the realization of real fidelity, i.e., lasting love between one man and one woman.[126] In a sense, the revolution would transform sex—in the direction of freely willed, steady, monogamous relations, clearly distinguished from those of animals.[127] A radical woman would not give herself up completely in passionate embrace of a radical man, but would retain, even develop, her consciousness. Dittmar's notion of radical female love was therefore quite different from the notion of women's radical, voluntary submission that Carola Lipp has found in radical men's writing of the time.[128] A tension does remain in Dittmar, which will reappear in Wagner's account of Siegfried and Brünnhilde discussed in the next chapter: whether the "highest spiritual development" of women was truly in accord with the aims and desires of the liberated man.

But whence would come change? The working class was not in the same situation as women. Marx could point to the growing centralization of production and presence of working men in radical organization, while women were systematically isolated from one another, locked up in the prison of the private household. If the prospect of revolution was other than a chimera, the shiny utopia that Dittmar had criticized in her earlier work, then somehow historical development had to enable that change.[129] She found it in steam power, in technology, which both enabled and required the building of bridges and canals, the flattening of forests and redirection of streams, the development of new forms of industry and new towns. The next step was for steam power to emancipate the household as well, to revolutionize food preparation, for example, to render women's work as archaic as the work methods of the Silesian weavers.[130] "Happiness, wealth, freedom, and life" depended on technological progress, and technology would lead to the revolution: "[T]he spirit of steam power reveals itself in politics."

Indeed, the revolution had already begun although many were unaware of it: "Houses and palaces collapse, entire cities are overwhelmed by the molten lava of revolution."[131]

Idealism, Violence, and Death

It is impossible to miss the return of the *Götterdämmerung* in these words of Dittmar. While her proposals for reform sounded reasonable—end to state intervention in marriage and divorce, state support for children, equal rights for women, and so on—they were embedded in a larger, more violent image of change. She embraced violence as a vital part of revolution, as her 1849 description of Charlotte Corday's assassination of Marat shows. The French Revolution was itself the "world on fire" (*Weltbrand*): "The sun plunged down to wrap this world in eternal darkness, and as it collapsed cracking into fiery gorges, the earth split, a sea of blood enveloped the fiery flames, and ruin cooled itself in the glowing sea of blood."[132] The *Götterdämmerung,* the twilight of the idols of aristocracy and clergy, was the context for Corday's revolutionary deed in defense of freedom.

Descriptions of Corday took many forms in the half century after her death. Carlyle painted her as a victim of fanaticism, dreaming not of love and life but of "[d]eath well-earned"; her German admirer Adam Lux, soon himself to be executed in the Terror, saw in her a new Brutus; Jean Paul painted a picture of a saint; the press at the time asked whether she was in love.[133] Dittmar rejected the notion that she was merely in love—that was impossible, it would make her into nothing more than a "dependent being incapable of autonomous thought."[134] No, she was a woman "in the grip of grand ideas," and as such was at one with her very being, which she now had either to assert or to destroy.[135] These were the grand ideas of classical republicanism: virtue and universal rights. The Jacobin tyrants like Marat were smashing those rights; Corday therefore carried out the radical deed of defending them. Like Brutus or Cato, her love for freedom became an ideal, even a crime.[136]

Like Jean Paul, Dittmar focused centrally on the problem of political violence in the name of an ideal. The act was in itself a contradiction, both a grand, heroic deed and murder. At one point in the essay, Dittmar suggested a way out: "[S]he did not want to murder, she wanted only to destroy a monster."[137] But she immediately dropped this argument to make clear the contradiction of taking an inhuman action in the name of humanity. Only the context could explain the action: "What a Marat created, inhumanity as humanity, had to awaken a Charlotte as well: the figure of a downtrodden humanity coming to its own aid." But the action itself had to remain contradictory, since the situation was: Corday was no "angel of assassination," but rather a "manifestation of the contradiction" between the morality demanded by laws and the actual guarantees of that morality that law afforded.[138]

Dittmar's account made of Corday a woman who participated fully in the heroic and tragic contradictions of republicanism, and was willing to commit the ultimate sin against her universal values in the name of those values, dooming herself in the process. She was not controlled by merely sensual love; she was not a "dehumanized" woman like the "furies of the guillotine"; she was one of those "for whom it is a necessity to destroy themselves in order to live."[139] Was Corday a fanatic? Yes, Dittmar argued, by the standards of a "profane utilitarianism"; she did not take action according to the mundane standards of utility, however, but rather according to the sublime goal of "the full dignity of mankind," and that was the point of her life.[140]

The essay on Corday makes a woman into a radical republican who does not act out of womanly love or material interest. Dittmar's Corday took action in the name of a higher ideal that she felt to be sublime and true. But did that distinguish her from Marat himself? Where was the limit to violence? Indeed, what was the revolution? The criticism of Dittmar in Louise Otto's journal *Frauen-Zeitung,* that Dittmar was a reactionary who made Corday into a martyr and gave aid and comfort to the aristocrats, misses the mark. The real problem is that Dittmar rendered a complex story too simple in her attempt to create a mythical hero of the revolution.[141] Dittmar's work shows little sign of grasping the complexity of 1848. In this, she was not unlike Feuerbach himself, who reportedly said in 1848, "I am waiting for the revolution, but I don't see it yet!"[142]

Dittmar was out of step with most of the feminists of her day. She was not a moderate, but a radical democrat; she spent very little time on the different moral sensibilities of women, and offered no romantic defense for women's special responsibility for children in the present day. She had indeed read her Fourier well. The response from other women radicals was limited and generally negative. Kathinka Zitz-Halein referred to Dittmar's lectures as attempt to deprive women of all femininity and to make them into hermaphrodites; Johanna Fröbel similarly asked whether Dittmar's striving for revolution in fact contradicted the nature of women, their physical weakness.[143] Their responses underline Dittmar's unique place in the revolution, as an advocate of women's liberation oriented toward a republican virtue for women that was not premised on maternity.

Dittmar's revolution aimed at life itself. She hoped for a popular movement that would sweep away the contradictions of a Christianity that saw death as the truth of life and true life possible only in death.[144] Revolutionary humanity would seek to redeem humanity itself, now conceived as a harmonious unity; the revolution had a "presentiment of what was becoming" (*Vorempfindung des Werdenden*) that pointed toward a higher idea, "the ideal of life in the correspondence of all its parts."[145] Her revolution also aimed at the complete fulfillment of each individual within the community as an entity with its own dignity and self-created goals, its own *Selbstzweck;* echoing Julius Fröbel, she proclaimed liberation of both individual and society.[146]

The alternative to this redemption of life was bleak. Dittmar says that the alternative Corday faced to taking action in accord with her higher ideals was an "empty vegetation" (*leeres Fortvegetiren*). Dittmar meant a life that had no deeper meaning, where fate seemed to rule. In another context, Dittmar would have called this orientalism, a "noxious fatalism." In a sense the essay seems to describe her own predicament: what would happen when two years passed and nothing changed? As a woman without wealth, she had limited ability to emigrate, little access to a public in a reactionary age, and was probably shut out of social networks given her radical activities. She was in the provinces, and faced the empty choice of "planless hoping or hopeless plans," as she wrote in one of her few extant letters.[147] From 1852 until her death three decades later in 1884, she apparently published nothing and participated little if at all in public events. While her neighbor Louise Büchner was involved in refounding the German women's movement in the 1860s, Dittmar's name was notably absent, and no reference is made to her work in those—or any other—circles.[148] One wonders whether she revisited the opposition she developed in her work on Nordic mythology, especially her notion of the ideal of oriental religion: "Here the only true solution is to be found in death, in the destruction of the self."[149]

CHAPTER 4

Richard Wagner, Love, and Death

In the spring of 1849, as Ludwig Feuerbach returned to his provincial home in Bavaria, the stage was set for the final, violent confrontation of the revolution across Germany. After King Frederick William IV of Prussia rejected the Frankfurt National Assembly's offer of a crown of a united Germany on April 28, 1849, the individual German monarchs considered the revolution over. Local radicals disagreed and turned to violence across Germany. In Dresden, in the Kingdom of Saxony, radicals took to the barricades, where Prussian troops confronted them in battle from May 5–9, killing over 250.[1]

One of the revolutionaries was the composer Richard Wagner. Although he was a musical director (*Kapellmeister*) of the Royal Saxon Court, Wagner—in debt, dissatisfied with his own work, and annoyed with what he considered a frivolous public that ignored him—threw himself into the violent revolution, in association with his radical friend August Röckel and his new acquaintance Mikhail Bakunin. He attended secret meetings, collected weapons and ammunition, possibly sought to arrange for the import of hand grenades, and kept watch in the tower of the city walls. Röckel and Bakunin were arrested, while Wagner escaped—pursued, however, by posters issued by the Saxon government seeking his arrest.[2] Fleeing first to Paris, Wagner ended up in Switzerland and remained in exile for the next 12 years.

Once on the road to exile, Wagner began to revise the story of his participation in the revolution.[3] By the time he composed his autobiography in 1870, Wagner had transformed himself into a disillusioned, skeptical observer, a man whose true nature was unpolitical, an isolated aesthetic genius standing above the fray.[4] His later account reduced the hundreds of pages of prose on politics and theater he produced at the time to purely aesthetic contemplation. The years of the revolution were a period of vulgarized Feuerbachian radicalism for Wagner; his work was especially influenced by the notion of a "purely human" being who would emerge after the end of religion and politics. But Wagner's later account reduced the influence to little more than a superficial aping of Feuerbachian language.[5] By the 1870s it was far more useful to be a Schopenhauerian conservative than a fiery anarchist and to advocate the renunciation of the world in pseudo-Christian phrases rather than to call for the overthrow of worldly elites, especially for the purpose of impressing Wagner's chief sponsor, the young Bavarian king, Ludwig II.

But the program Wagner set for himself during his period of Feuerbachian radicalism in 1848–51 remained intact to the end of his life. First, he sought to express the essence of mankind via myth, which he conceptualized as a direct "poetic force" of the people. He understood the people (*Volk*) as an organic, integrated whole rather than merely a collection of individuals; the people initially grasped the world immediately and without analysis or understanding, and expressed its nature in a fantastic form that in fact revealed their own true nature.[6] Second, Wagner intended to overthrow existing opera by restructuring its form and content, to express better the eternal, natural truths of myth. His aim was to change music and to overthrow the bourgeois social relations that supported opera in the nineteenth century. These first two parts of his program came together in his attempt to create a new, totalizing and politicizing "music drama" that countered the inauthentic world of liberal modernity. In other words, he called for a new, authentic combination of music and drama, where a revolution in form would accompany revolutionary content. He aimed to create a new myth that revealed the real, eternal human world in the language of the people, to provide the structure of meaning for a new, human society. Wagner remained a radical as he turned to myth in his later operatic work.[7]

Wagner's turn to myth, like Dittmar's, seems at first glance to contradict Feuerbach's project. The Feuerbach of most scholarship over the past 100 years is first and foremost a critic of myth as ideology. That Feuerbach showed how God, state, and king, indeed "sacred" institutions in general, were human constructions. The divine becomes the human in a simple, emancipatory reversal. Now the human world may begin; now myth should no longer be necessary. Certainly, that was how Marx and Engels's "scientific socialism" made use of Feuerbach. Marx fixed his attention on the problem of religious forms in the world, turning the critique of the Judeo-Christian God to capital. Under the rule of capital, everyday relations among people took on the form of commodity relations; commodity relations followed their own logic of exchange value rather than real need, and capital, as a self-regulating system operating above the heads of capitalist and worker alike, determined the direction of society. Marx turned to images from polytheism to describe the rule of industry. He described giant factories as "Cyclopean," replicating human actions but now on a superhuman scale: humans created their own race of gods who then ruled over them.[8] Capital was a historical process that created out of the many different forms of economy, polity, and society one global system. Revolution, where society grasped control of itself, was the solution to the alienation of capitalism. In a Feuerbachian tone, Marx argued that "[a]ll mythology subdues, dominates and fashions the forces of nature in the imagination and through the imagination; it therefore disappears when real domination over these forces is established."[9]

Yet Marx's use of Feuerbach was not the only possible one. Feuerbach himself—and Wagner—took a different path. While Marx put human mastery over nature at the center of his theory, Feuerbach turned away from that fantasy after the mid-1840s. Humans were dependent on nature, and nature was essentially alien to humanity; myth and religion became essential aspects of human existence in the face of nature. Feuerbach, like Wagner, became more rather than less concerned with myth after the failure of the Revolution of 1848, a matter explored further in the next chapter.

Both Feuerbach and Wagner had vague notions of what revolution actually was in 1848–49. Neither was concerned with the practical problems of rights, institutions, and political representation; both had instead a notion of revolution that would release a redeemed human essence. Their revolution itself took on mythic form, in the sense that it became part of a meaningful, violent narrative of the transformation of humanity—something more like prophecy than theory. Like Hess and Dittmar, Wagner and Feuerbach saw the need for a radical deed that would transform the world. They showed at times, for example, an admiration for Karl Sand, the deranged student whose assassination of the establishment dramatist August Kotzebue in 1819 precipitated harsh repression of the democratic and nationalist forces in Germany. In one of his earliest letters, composed when he was 16 years old, Feuerbach wrote to his mother from Mannheim: "We went to the church-yard and saw the place where the good Sand lies buried, which is completely flat and covered up with grass. We ripped out much grass, and send you some, because you, too, were fond of the German youth."[10] In 1867, while enjoying the patronage of the Bavarian monarch, Wagner praised the terrorist Sand's "deed," which derived, he thought, from the right "instinct" that Kotzebue "was the corrupter of German youth, the betrayer of the German Volk."[11] By 1867, Wagner had turned to the right, as had radical nationalism, but the image of the redemptive deed remained strong. Wagner's fantasies of a fiery end to the false world of the gods found a parallel as well in the words of Feuerbach's followers. The émigré Alwin Sörgel announced that a river in central Texas near San Marcos had been named after Feuerbach—or literally "fiery stream."[12] Louise Dittmar ended her 1848 discussion of Nordic mythology with an image of a terrible *Götterdämmerung*, a fiery end of the old world from which a new one would be born.[13] The poet Theodor Held proclaimed that "The heavens are in flames! / And waves of flames cast / A throne to the ground / 'Save yourself, oh Lord, by a miracle!' / Piously pray the believers / But your Lord and Master, Christians / Died in the Fiery Brook."[14] And Feuerbach himself referred to his work as "fiery brook," "the purgatory of the present times."[15]

After 1848–49, the revolution as a general concept remained in thoughts of Feuerbach and Wagner, but now in the sense of transcending fake, inauthentic life in the present, and in ever more powerful, emotionally loaded ways. This was not a political notion of revolution. It did not focus on rights, institutions, and representations, but on overcoming everyday interests and partisan emotion through a new way of living that would amount to a higher order of human life. Rather than hoping for the moment when political parties could represent interests, they hoped to overcome parties and the world of the masses. They called for welcoming death as an ever-present entity. Rather than viewing it as the gateway to a better world of personal immortality, they promised authentic life over against the inauthentic world they lived in, and they intuited that myth contained a deeper expression of humanity. Wagner and Feuerbach operated in a secular, post-Christian world—even in Wagner's later years, when he claimed that his work represented a return to Christianity.

Wagner's intellectual link to Feuerbach was less oriented toward Feuerbach's precise writings than those of Hess and Dittmar. His connection was, rather, at the level of images and emotions. The one book by Feuerbach recommended by Wagner to his friends was the 1830 work on death and immortality, with its many poems and images related to death.[16] Feuerbach served in Wagner's writing as a marker of radicalism seeking to renew humanity. Wagner dedicated his essay "The Artwork of the Future" to Feuerbach, the author of "The Philosophy of the Future," not because he had grasped the intricacies of Feuerbach's philosophical turn from 1842–44, but because he had grasped its general aim to discard outdated and implausible metaphysical systems in the name of a new, immediate, authentic humanity. Feuerbach himself had little more than a passing acquaintance with Wagner's contributions in music and drama.[17] But the two were embedded in a common intellectual milieu. The German poet Georg Herwegh, editor of the classic work of Vormärz radicalism *Einundzwanzig Bogen aus der Schweiz* and a follower and friend of Feuerbach since the early 1840s, was close to Wagner during the latter's exile in Zurich, for example; neither Herwegh nor Wagner could return to Germany after the revolution, of course, but in a glowing letter Wagner invited Feuerbach to Zurich in 1851.[18] (Cosima Wagner would later destroy much of Wagner's correspondence with Herwegh.)[19] The young Swiss writer Gottfried Keller, whom Feuerbach's lectures in Heidelberg had radicalized and who, like Feuerbach, would fall in love with Johanna Kapp, was a frequent guest at Wagner's home in Zurich. A character modeled on Feuerbach appears in Keller's classic novel *Green Henry*.[20] The radical publisher Otto Wigand published Wagner's *Art and Revolution* as well as most of Feuerbach's mature work.

As with so much of the rest of that group, Feuerbach and Wagner sought to go beyond "mere" liberalism. They sought a transformed world, not a merely rationalized world, through democratic revolution. For both, exploration of myth was part of their radical activity—but with important differences. Feuerbach's analysis took myth apart, in order to show how it expressed an essential need of humans, but also enslaved them. For Wagner, the creation of new myth was part of the creation of a new world, or at least a rejection of the old. But this distinction was not absolute: Feuerbach saw the need to create myth as a human endeavor, and Wagner's music dramas cast doubt on the very myths he was building up. But unlike Wagner, Feuerbach never transformed his contradictions into a destructive, racist nationalism. Wagner pulled together romantic, nationalist, and materialist strands of thought that presented an early apologia for violence on the far right. In at least some respects, Adorno was correct to call him a "bourgeois terrorist."[21]

The Politics of Myth in the Revolutionary Wagner

Richard Wagner's work after 1848 attacked both religion and politics as impediments to the realization of the "purely human" (*das Reinmenschliche*). Wagner, like Feuerbach, turned to myth to express this critique. But he did so as a poet, not as a philologian. He sought not to analyze myth but to use it to represent the absolute, true human essence obscured by material conditions of life. For Wagner, the revolution was not about understanding the past but about shaping the future. The political use of myth is the link between Wagner's first revolutionary ventures in 1848–49 and his operatic theory developed over the 1850s.

Wagner's first foray into revolutionary politics in summer 1848 was a speech before the republican Vaterlandsverein of Dresden. In flowery terms he called for universal suffrage, a single representative assembly, a people's militia in place of the standing army, and the elimination of the aristocracy. He embedded these classic republican demands in a romanticized notion of monarchism: a loving monarch, a republican king, would arise to redeem the people from its fallen state. Wagner combined that monarchist conservatism with radical populism and even the hope for a new German world empire in the new world.[22] He was not alone in doing so. The workers' leader Andreas Gottschalk made a similar demand in Cologne on March 3, 1848, and Feuerbach called for a head of state who would represent all of humanity in 1843 (later such monarchist sentiments disappeared from his writings).[23] The notion of social kingship also found expression in the 1860s, as radical leaders like Hess and Lassalle flirted with supporting Napoleon III or Bismarck, hoping that a strong, charismatic leader would push aside the power of aristocrats and plutocrats. Notwithstanding Wagner's praise for monarchism, his employer, the king of Saxony, took the speech as a challenge to his own authority, and Wagner paid the price at court. Over the second part of 1848, he withdrew into his aesthetic work. But with the radicalization of the revolution in early 1849, he returned to politics.

In spring 1849, Wagner made the acquaintance of Mikhail Bakunin, to whom he was introduced by his radical friend August Röckel. Wagner's thoughts and actions became ever more radical in March and April 1849, as the revolution entered its death throes. He now framed the struggle as one of "man" against "established society."[24] The problem, according to Wagner, was not society per se, but a specific kind of society that allowed for the development only of the individual, on the basis of individual rights. This society, he asserted, denied humanity its ability to fulfill its potential. Like Marx and Moses Hess, Wagner seemed to think that established society was in need of revolution because it was too liberal.[25] In an anonymous article from April 8, 1849, published less than a month before the Dresden uprising in Röckel's increasingly radical paper, Wagner moved even closer to the radicalism of Bakunin. He praised the violent revolution as the "ever-rejuvenating mother of mankind," attacked the domination of the rich over the poor, and decried the bureaucratic state that "between the piles of documents and contracts" pressed "hearts of live humanity like dried plants."[26] Wagner called for the victory of life over death, the end of domination by wealth and property (i.e., the dead), and the end of monarchical rule.[27] Most important, he called for the people to recognize their humanity, rise up and revolt, and reclaim their humanity for themselves. "The living revolution, God become man," would thereby declare "the new gospel of happiness."[28] Wagner was no political philosopher, and no doubt never worked his way through contemporary political thinking in a systematic way, but he captured as few others did the radical political implications of Feuerbach's work, especially his call for immediate, authentic human relations.[29]

As soon as he fled into exile, Wagner threw himself into a series of prose works that laid out his aesthetic and political project: "Art and Revolution" and "The Artwork of the Future" from 1849, and "A Communication to

My Friends" and *Opera and Drama* from 1851. To these should be added "Judaism in Music" of 1850—a foundational piece of posttraditional anti-Semitism that would have horrible repercussions over the years to come. Its distinction between authentic and inauthentic art was at the heart of Wagner's theory.[30] Wagner wrote these hundreds of pages with speed and passion. Despite his disavowal of revolution in a letter to his wife, Minna, written on the way into exile, these were in fact revolutionary works.[31] They provided a record of a kind of radical thinking that made its way into Wagner's later work. Starting with an aesthetic rejection of culture as commodified fashion, Wagner came to attack both state and religion as inauthentic, oppressive entities, and from there to reconceptualize the production of new myths as part of the radical transformation of humanity.

Scorn for the "corruption of taste and frivolity" of the modern age filled these pages, especially as it expressed itself in modern opera, influenced by French and Italian fashion.[32] Opera, Wagner claimed, had sacrificed dramatic plot and poetry to pretty melodies, which changed with the "tyranny" of fashion. Since composers sought to craft a hummable line, they were far more interested in melody than content.[33] Opera thus aimed at the masses (*Massen*), at modern, superficial individuals, not at the authentic, organic, integrated people or nation (*Volk*) with its direct notions of the world; and it manipulated the masses, just as the state did when it represented their unity in the form of a uniformed, standing army, when it declared a mechanical militarization to be the "emancipation of the masses."[34] These masses were not, for Wagner, first and foremost the lower classes; the frivolous upper classes were a quintessential part of the world of the masses, and they had made art into nothing more than commerce and luxury the ruler of the world.[35] Wagner's anti-Semitism became apparent here in his attack on what he coded as the superficial, parasitical, and artificial elements of modern culture. He directly attacked the Jewish-German composer Giacomo Meyerbeer, whom he had previously admired—and who had himself aided Wagner at an earlier stage of his career.[36] At issue was the language of the organic *Volk,* and Jews like the composer Felix Mendelssohn and implicitly Meyerbeer, Wagner claimed, could never speak genuine German because of their Jewish ancestry: they could only speak a kind of fashionable jargon, a language learned rather than a mother tongue.[37] As a result, Wagner asserted, Meyerbeer could only produce decadent fashionable opera. He could never speak the authentic language that would give opera a revolutionary function.

The inauthentic, the superficial, and the fashionable revealed a deeper political decadence. Just as in music the means of expression, the music, became the end, while the end, the expression itself, became a mere means, so in politics the means, embodied in the state, came to stand over its end, the people.[38] It reflected a world where a separate "political state" stood above and apart from the people, and where religion in the form of Christianity sought to control the state—a world where state and religion, armed with artificial myths of origin, conspired to wring the spontaneity and authenticity out of social relations.[39] Feuerbach-inspired phrases about the purely human pervaded Wagner's theoretical works at his point, including Feuerbach's notion of the authentic human essence, his praise of its promethean quality, and his critique of God and State (which Bakunin reinforced in lengthy discussions with Wagner).[40] And, as Bruce Lincoln has pointed out, the distinction between the "egoistic" nature of Jewish myth and the redemption of the world through love in Feuerbach's *The Essence of Christianity* may have also influenced Wagner.[41]

Wagner experimented with several ways to represent that absolute, authentic humanity during the revolution. His fragment on Achilles from 1849, soon abandoned, reflected the early Feuerbach, where humanity itself served as a quasi-divine creative force. Achilles' secret lay in his desire for revenge. In his pursuit of a worldly goal, he abandoned the gods and rose above them. In the words of Wagner, the new Achilles was "the perfection of God," the "conclusion of creation."[42] Achilles was a Greek hero, however, and not German; perhaps that is why Wagner, despite his own lifelong fascination with Greek myth, abandoned the sketch in search of something closer to Germany. Wagner turned to history for inspiration as well. He worked with the story of the medieval emperor Frederich Barbarossa, whose return to redeem Germany was foretold; Wagner also experimented with the story of Jesus Christ.[43] But he soon found that works of history, especially the story of Barbarossa, required him to lay out the detailed relations of the time and so lose touch with the absolutely human. History could not represent the real human, and so was not the proper source for developing a new representation of the world that would revolutionize human relations. It could not be the object of the new music drama. Instead, myth had to be the focus. Myth allowed the unity of dramatic action to be comprehended immediately and at once. History was not the proper source for developing a new, proper representation of the world that would revolutionize human relations. The past was not at stake, with all its complex relations that limited the freedom of humans; at stake was a new myth of a humanity completely at home in the world without the interference of God or state.[44] Wagner sought a new myth of origins that would not justify arbitrary authority or possession, but would rather open up the unconscious striving of the *Volk* for freedom.[45]

The poet in Wagner's revolutionary theory thus did more than represent the world. The poet created the myth of the world, gave sense to the world, formed the meaning that would organize the true, free world of humanity. The myth gave access, not to specific contexts, but to universal truths that the *Volk* grasped in its encounter with the world.[46] The *Volk* was the source of the primal melodies of nature; the poet, to be successful, had to interpret the world in a way that connected his vision to the *Volk*.[47] Poetic creation was thus rooted both in fantasy and in a kind of sensualist epistemology: the true poet engaged in the cognitive process first by gathering data that were presented to the brain in the form of a mass of perceptions, and then by making sense of the information by recommunicating it in necessarily inadequate concepts.[48] The poet bridged the gap between data and concept by way of fantasy, which was for Wagner a necessary part of human culture. Without fantasy, the infinite complexity of the world could not be grasped by humans at all. The authentic poet was able to connect this fantasy with the feelings and perceptions of the *Volk*, in a process that Wagner described as a "miracle." By "miracle," Wagner did not mean an extraworldly act of God; like Feuerbach, he criticized the notion that a God pulled strings against the laws of nature. Wagner connected this notion of the miracle with the artificial effects that appeared in what he viewed as frivolous operas, such as those of Meyerbeer, where wondrous events simply took place without deeper cause, replicating the earlier model of a mechanical deus ex machina. Instead, the miracle was a revelation of meaning that was reduced, only gradually, to human proportions. It first took the form of stories about the gods, then of stories about heroes, and finally of stories about the true, sense-oriented, pure man.[49] Tragedy was nothing other than the "artistic perfection of myth," and myth the "poem of a view of life held in common," the pure truth beyond the artificial conventions of state and religion.[50] Tragedy conveyed a message of the emancipation of humanity from artificial constraints. The pure truth of *Antigone,* for example, did not lie in the contradiction of political and familial loyalties, but rather in the higher truth of humanity that led to the destruction of mere institutions. That higher truth pointed to free love, beyond the dictates of religious morality, state law, or family custom: the love between man and woman that escaped social conventions, which Wagner found in the story of Oedipus and Jocasta. Whatever the significance of incest to Wagner personally, its function in his dramas was political, to reveal the institutional and customary barriers to human love.[51]

The poet for Wagner was the male principle embodied; the poet begat meaning, while music was a woman, passively receiving and germinating the seed.[52] The task was to combine the two in a complementary and complete relationship, not unlike the romantic ideal of a complementary and complete combination of man and woman that appeared in Feuerbach's writings. Wagner used these images over and over again, asserting that the eye was an essentially male sensory organ, distinguishing bodies, the ear essentially female, receiving feeling.[53] His obsession with sexual identity at times descended into a mildly pornographic version of musical theory, for example where the dramatic content was a rowboat and the music a still lake in the mountains: "With every movement driving forwards, the oar cuts deep into the ringing surface of water; raised out, it lets the wetness clinging to it flow back again in drops of melody."[54] The point of the sexual images was to stress a different kind of composition, one that combined work and feeling, and raised both up to a higher, total language. Music provided the feeling that conditioned the immediacy of the poet's message: the unspeakable anticipation or foreboding, the recollection that shaped the sense of the individual. Music in the new music drama was to have a meaning, and not just be the frivolous decoration that Wagner saw in Meyerbeer.[55]

Wagner's demand for the total work of art, the *Gesamtkunstwerk,* thus derived from a theoretical demand to pull together different representational forms for a fuller artwork, and from his grand, world-historical pretensions. Greek tragedy had originally formed a coherent whole, a spontaneous, collective form of art, characterized by the participation of the community as a chorus and the celebration of the body. Greek tragedy expressed the deepest and noblest character of the Greek *Volk's* consciousness. But Greek tragedy had fallen apart, Wagner argued, both because of the entry of sophistic irony and Aristophanes's comedy, and because Greek society was divided between the citizens and the laboring classes, who had the status of slaves. Class struggle doomed antiquity.[56] Christianity reacted to Rome's decadence by rejecting the world and creating a new cult of death.[57] The new work of art after Christianity would reconstruct not just opera, but the entire social and political world. The relationship between audience and performance would change. True art would abandon logic and reason for feeling, which would represent the society's own, spontaneous self-consciousness as a fully human society; it would necessarily aim at the annihilation of the state.[58] And the language had to be correct; it had to be the language of the people rather than the language of the frivolous and the Jewish. Wagner therefore sought an original language, an original poetry of the German *Volk* (as opposed to the masses who made up the individual subjects in the German lands)—the *Volk* who had poured "healthy blood" into the "sickly veins" of the Roman world—and claimed to find it in alliteration or *Stabreim,* which stressed the roots of words and thus their root connections. *Stabreim*, he asserted, provided direct access to the creative source of the *Volk*, to what feeling necessitated, to the purely human, to the mythic. The vowel, expressing the principle of female feeling, received its essential modification through the active, formative force of the male consonant.[59] Tragic drama would be reborn in the revolutionary world, as dreary industrial production itself became art, and as tragedies, now liberated from mere conventions and manners, again served as the "festivals of humanity," where "the free, strong, and beautiful human celebrates the ecstasies and the pains of his love, and, worthy and sublime, consummates the great love offering of his death."[60] This celebration of death would be by no means Christian: personal immortality played no role in Wagner's thought. Rather, a man's death was the final "renunciation of his personal egoism," in which he ascended to the universal realm of humanity precisely through the community's celebration of his deeds and the representation of his death in dramatic form.[61]

To express the mythic world of true art, Wagner sought a new artistic form beyond opera that combined the necessary plot and words of drama with the complex emotions of music, and that expressed temporality—recollection as well as foreboding. The new drama would have to be grasped as an organic unity whose actions were necessary within it, not accidental; the actions should not be the mere miraculous "effects" that Wagner criticized in Meyerbeer's work.[62] In the liberal world of the strong state, in which the individual was separated from society and the artist was forced to live from the cost of admission paid by the ordinary bourgeois, redemption could come only from the true artist, who sketched the world of the not-yet-present, pure human for a theatrical presentation open free of charge to the public.[63] The artwork would necessarily be authored by an artistic cooperative (*Genossenschaft*), combined with the single goal of creating living, sensual drama. The human would become part of nature, nature part of the human, and the artwork therefore an "immediate act of life."[64]

Wagner saw the creation of myth as an essential human activity, even though he apparently had a materialist, atheistic worldview in 1848–51. At that point the differences between his Weltanschauung and Feuerbach's were minimal. Both rejected institutionalized myths that supported the power of death—property, law, class, money—over life. But as Wagner began to discuss the creation of myths, and to lay out a program for his own attempt to create myth, his use of myth began to diverge from Feuerbach's. For all Feuerbach's respect for myth, after all, he still saw Homer, for example, as a rationalist who replaced the dark mystique of myth with the "sunlight of the truth of nature."[65] Although Feuerbach saw the process of creating myth as essential to humanity, he never followed

Wagner in leaping to the other side: to propagate myth itself as a project, with the poetic genius serving as a kind of naturalized leader of the people.[66] That was precisely Wagner's project.

How to End the World? *The Ring of the Nibelung*

Like so many other German nationalists seeking a new foundation myth for the movement, Wagner explored Germanic and Nordic mythology in the 1840s.[67] In 1844, Friedrich Theodor Vischer recommended that the ancient stories be used as the basis for a new national opera. Already in 1845 the feminist Louise Otto had drafted a libretto, in which Chriemhilde avenged the death of Siegfried through the bloody murder of her brother Gunther and her vassal Hagen.[68] And Louise Dittmar, as the previous chapter showed, immersed herself in the sagas in search of a different conception of the world suitable for the revolution. Wagner's libretto for the Ring cycle took shape in the middle of revolution. He completed the first sketch of the Nibelung story in October 1848, several months after his first, ambivalent foray into revolutionary public writing. He wrote the first version of "Siegfried's Death," the poem that later became *The Twilight of the Gods,* over the next month. The second version, completed in January or February 1849, already indicated his difficulty in bringing his story to an end.[69] The manuscript took its final form of "The Twilight of the Gods" in 1852, after Wagner had written his theoretical texts; by this time, he had already decided to expand the project from one opera to three, with a prelude, to be performed over four nights—but only after the revolution.[70]

The great interpretations of Wagner's *Ring* have taken opposite positions on the relationship between the work and its political context. In the influential interpretation of George Bernard Shaw as well as Adorno's more subtle reading, Wagner's *Ring* was a drama about the idea of revolution; the gods were little more than ordinary bourgeois, building their estates on the labor of the masses with ill-gotten capital.[71] The British opera critic Ernest Newman, however, who had an unsurpassed knowledge of Wagner's music, expressed his influential opinion that text and context were disconnected. He even asserted that it would be better for later viewers of *The Ring* had Wagner never published the theoretical works of 1849–52. Newman conceded that Wagner himself believed in the political and social significance of his work, but Newman maintained that the work far exceeded that author's intent.[72] For Newman, the content of *The Ring* was nothing less than the meaning and value of the world, expressed in mythic form.[73] The two interpretations are not as far apart as they seem, since for Wagner—as for Feuerbach—the revolution was about both existing social relations and the meaning of the world as a whole.

The central problem of cultural history, of how to relate text and context, is especially difficult with Wagner's magnum opus, given its sheer size, complexity, and frequent obscurity. *The Ring* resounds differently in different cultural-historical contexts.[74] The goal of the following reading is to work out the revolutionary, "Feuerbachian" themes in the work, and to see how the different endings Wagner proposed for *The Ring* help to illuminate nineteenth-century radicalism. The plot of *The Ring* is intricate and complex, which makes the problem of context even more difficult; it contains traces of earlier drafts never fully resolved into new drafts, a problem typical of a work composed over many years. As Shaw noted, in terms echoed by other close observers including Nietzsche and Adorno, it is often difficult to see how one particular aspect of the work is essential to the work's overall structure. Wagner had "little success in melting down the mass of material into lyric," Adorno noted, and such coherence as it does possess is largely due to an illusion created by the music and staging of *The Ring* itself.[75] The underlying themes and images, and the affect granted them through musical, gestural, and linguistic hints, matter at least as much as the plot itself. Three themes are central to the present discussion. First, contracts and obligations, along with broken promises and betrayals, run through the entire work, entangling all characters, whether gods or nearly human heroes, in a web of guilt. Second, these have at their root "gold," which Wagner both drew from the original Nibelung saga and associated with usury, Jews, and his own excessive indebtedness.[76] Finally, the theme of love that goes beyond the complex, guilty relations of the everyday runs through the whole: a love that those who want gold renounce, a love that violates the ban on incest, a love that renders divine interference in the world meaningless. Brünnhilde's self-immolation at the end of the entire sequence somehow reflected on all these themes. The question is how.

"The Twilight of the Gods," the last of the four works, tells the story of the hero Siegfried's death at the hands of the half-dwarf Hagen, in conspiracy with the Valkyrie Brünnhilde, whom Siegfried has spurned. Siegfried, the son of twins born of the god Wotan and a mortal, has actually been deluded by a special potion; upon his death Brünnhilde suddenly understands all. She now undertakes to burn the hero Siegfried, and to share the "holiest honor" of immolation by burning herself as well. Tossing the ring back to the Rhine Maidens, she and her horse plunge themselves into the fire, which grows to burn down Valhalla. The age of the gods is over; the last heroes have been burnt; as Hagen plunges into the Rhine to recover the ring, he is drowned. All that are left are men and women, who watch "with great emotion" (*in höchster Ergriffenheit*), as a series of motifs, including that of "love," resound.[77]

Wagner's *Ring* was massive in its length and its self-importance. Its ending was supposed to pull the grand story of the entire universe together. The gods' self-inflicted fate, their contracts as well as their extralegal acts, led to the creation of a race of heroes, whose eventual death and suicide would redeem the world. Wagner was himself aware how unclear the story was. It was especially difficult to combine the glorious role of the redeeming hero with the fateful death of the gods.

In his first ending, in *Siegfrieds Tod* of November 1848, the deaths of the heroes served to relieve the gods of guilt, to release the workers (the Nibelungen) from their bondage to the rule of gold, and to indicate the advent of clear, paternalistic, monotheistic rule: "Only one shall rule: All-father! Glorious! Thou!" One deity remains; the conflict between gods (Fricka and Wotan) ends. This conclusion mirrored Wagner's call for a redemptive monarch and the elimination of the aristocracy, in his political speech of summer 1848. To reinforce the message, the common folk, the "vassals and women," enter into the first version as a classical chorus that calls on Wotan, the "father of all," to "bless the flames" and join in a "bliss without end."[78]

Wagner found this ending inadequate almost immediately. Already in 1849, he had crossed it out, and by early 1851, Brünnhilde's speech began to look quite different. Now she announced to the gods that Siegfried had redeemed their guilt and fear—but that their redemption would take the form of death.[79] Newman and others have noted the contradiction that Erda had earlier warned Wotan to give up the Ring or face the death of the gods—and yet here the Ring is returned and the gods die![80] But why did Wagner come to demand the end of the gods as part of the story of redemption in the first place? The experience of the revolution and the encounter with Bakunin had intervened; both involved, not reasserting existing patriarchal power and ideals, but overturning traditional institutions. In this context, reaffirming God's power would have gone against the entire emancipatory project.

In a third attempt from 1852, Wagner gave Brünnhilde lines that announced the triumph of love over bourgeois relations: "Not goods, not gold, nor godly splendor; not house, not land, nor lordly pomp; not the cheating covenant of cheerless contracts, not the harsh laws of lying custom: rapture in pleasure and pain comes—from love alone."[81] But these words do not find their way into the final version; as Wagner noted a few years later, it was not clear what that "love" was of which Brünnhilde spoke.[82] The ending seemed too vague.

Yet another ending is implied in Wotan's statement "I want just one thing more / The end," echoed in a draft of Brünnhilde's final speech where she talks of seeing the end of the world. The affirmation of death was already part of Wagner's conception; in 1854, he wrote to Röckel that love is first possible when people learn to die without fear.[83] But now the affirmation of death seemed to break with the affirmation of love. In a version of 1856, Brünnhilde spelled the logic out completely: now all-knowing, she will close the "gates of eternal becoming" (apparently a reference to repeated reincarnation until a soul reaches nirvana) and enter the realm that is free of all wishes and illusions.[84] Wagner himself stressed that point at the time of his initial encounter with Schopenhauer in the mid-1850s, telling Franz Liszt, the Austro-Hungarian composer and pianist, that the permanent nothingness of death constituted the only salvation possible, and Röckel that a completely different conception had overtaken him after he had begun the piece, namely the "nothingness" of the world.[85] If the aim of the total series was death and an accompanying nirvana, however, then one must ask whether the whole thing was indeed necessary and not just an excuse for Wotan to escape his life.[86] Love was simply an ephemeral moment of fate in the 1856 version.

Wagner's final version avoided each of these endings; at the same time, it seemed to rule out none of them except the reenthronement of a chastised, monotheistic god. First, Brünnhilde accuses the gods of an eternal guilt: their actions led this guiltless Siegfried to death, and their curse was thus inescapable. Second, Brünnhilde herself has as a result grown wise, able to understand the gods both from within and from outside—able to be devastatingly critical. Third, she must burn herself in order to remove the curse from the Ring before it returns to the Rhine Maidens. Finally, she herself casts the flame that will burn Valhalla down, knowing that she has done so. Wagner struck the final words of the 1856 version referring to the end of eternal becoming, adding to the obscurity, at the urging of Cosima.[87] The end contains a remainder: the people milling about in an emotional state unspecified by Wagner, while the motifs imply redeeming love.[88] If the "people" here are a version of the Greek chorus, then they seem to be left at sea by the end, rather than released into a higher knowledge, a stronger community identity, or a new world.

The endings are all dissatisfying. The moment beyond death is where the message becomes least clear: what does the death of gods and heroes mean for the emotionally distraught masses? This can be restated as a Feuerbachian problem: once gods have been demolished and myths reduced to mankind, then the question of what is to be done by humans appears. Does the triumph of love mean the end of contract, prohibitions on incest and adultery, and marriage? Does it mean the end of property, and if so how? Does love redeem the world? Does the liberation of the world redeem love? Or do both love and the world come to an end, leaving an empty spot devoid of any meaning? Either the revolution begins to take on eschatological overtones, or it becomes ever less clear that revolution has any deeper significance at all.

At issue is the "mythic" nature of the drama. Wagner's notion of myth was not the same as the often incomprehensible turns of plot and endless struggles that one encounters in the Germanic and Nordic sagas. Instead, Wagner had a point to make about the course of history and the "redemption"—however vague that notion becomes—of mankind.[89] The new myth was to *do* something, such as point to a new world. The modern mythmaker was interested in creation, not stabilization. Criticism of the existing world certainly played an important role in the work: as the curse of the Rhinegold exposed the deep abyss separating contract and ethics on the one hand from love and morality on the other and revealed the dismal reality beneath Valhalla's shiny architecture of power. Yet Wagner hoped to go one step further. He wanted to point toward a different future. But none seemed adequate to the grandeur of the work. The reestablishment of the one God, now purified of his worldly contracts and gold, was too unbelievable, and too trite. The simple departure of the gods, or their immolation, was more satisfying, perhaps, but left the future empty. A Schopenhauerian reflection on the lack of meaning in the universe suggested the uselessness of the totality—and Wagner in any case sought to "correct" Schopenhauer's viewpoints in this regard to make way for a redeeming love, the direct opposite of Schopenhauer's argument.[90] What has been described as the Hegelian moment of full self-consciousness on Brünnhilde's part makes somewhat more sense, but also made the work too didactic.[91]

Wagner himself did not solve the puzzle. His doctrine of myth as a kind of truth produced by fantasy that was present to the people in an almost instinctual way, felt rather than intellectually known, let him off the hook.[92] Wagner's ultimate intent, however, is not the issue here. The issue is rather the dilemma Wagner faced as someone who held both that myth was necessary for creating a new polis and that myth had to be taken apart as ideology. The *Ring* commemorated a fundamental problem in radical thought itself: an utterly finite world, personal mortality, and the destruction of all idols left the concept of the infinite potential of mankind empty. Wagner's solution was to leave vague the overarching meaning of his drama.[93] That immediate grasp of reality that he attributed to Greek myth could work only through emotional, indistinct messages. Wagner thereby contributed to the legitimization of myth as a counter to critical reasoning;

Wagner's project drew upon Feuerbach's concern with the human truths embedded in religion, but contradicted the Enlightenment strand at the center of Feuerbach's thought.

The Two Nights of *Tristan*

In the face of personal crisis, Wagner interrupted work on the *Ring* in 1857 to devote himself to *Tristan and Isolde*. While the *Ring* addressed the broad sweep of universal history, *Tristan* marked a turn inward to the individual psyche. The complex psychological moments of *Tristan and Isolde* replaced the often flat and simplistic characters of the *Ring*. Events in Wagner's personal life, in particular his infatuation with Mathilde Wesendonck, his discovery of Schopenhauer, and his disappointment with the outcome of the revolution, influenced the work.[94] But the problems *Tristan and Isolde* treats are not reducible to a love affair, to a philosopher's argument (especially since Wagner read philosophers mostly for confirmation of his own ideas), or to political events.[95] They revolved around a dilemma present in both *Tristan and Isolde* and the *Ring*.

Wagner oscillated between two opposed conclusions in both *Tristan and Isolde* and the *Ring*. One stressed emancipation through a return to the material world that had been freed of the idols of religion, politics, and convention and now was open to free love and human society. The other highlighted redemption, but of a nihilist sort: as a release from life in order to merge with the cosmos. Wagner expressed this idea in a letter to his friend Franz Liszt, writing that since he had "never in life felt the real bliss of love," he would erect *Tristan and Isolde* as a monument to love, but "with the 'black flag' which flutters at the end, I shall then cover myself over, in order—to die."[96] In *Tristan and Isolde*, Tristan is drawn to both; he both affirms the finite world of the pure human and yearns for connection to the infinite world of the cosmic totality. Wagner's audience seized on one or the other: his admirers praised the work for its representation of rapture in the dissolution of the self, while detractors denounced the "unremitting materialism" and sexual suggestiveness of the piece.[97] Both assessments seem correct. The complexity of *Tristan and Isolde* lies in the play of opposites between ecstasy and normal life. Sexual ecstasy, associated with the night, is at one point the refutation of the lies of everyday life experienced in the day, which Wagner associates with rationality, institutions, and morality; at another point, however, sexuality falls back into precisely that logic of the day. As a work of musical drama, *Tristan and Isolde* could hardly be more different from *The Ring*, with its virtual elimination of outward action; indeed, it challenged the very notion of the

opera.[98] But like *The Ring*, it reflected upon the problem of what emancipation, what revolution actually was.

Wagner hoped that his works would be more than mere entertainment,
that they would spur serious consideration of big topics like love, death,
and revolution. Suicide posed the problem of free will for both Feuerbach
and Wagner—neither of whom accepted idealist notions of freedom. The
human in the world existed, acted, within the world, within the world of
matter. Human will was embodied, not disembodied. An abstract free will
was therefore not part of their account of humanity. In some ways, especially in the language used, Wagner's concern with self-willed death paralleled Feuerbach's own later work on the subject. But Wagner and
Feuerbach depicted the suicidal person very differently. Feuerbach's suicide was active, resolute, and conscious of his or her environment and its
failure to correspond to his or her nature. A Feuerbachian example may
be found in Siegfried's father, Siegmund, in the *Valkyrie,* who renounces
eternal life among the heroes of Valhalla for the love of Sieglinde. As
Adorno notes, Siegmund was unusual in Wagner's oeuvre; Wagner's other
heroes may will their own deaths, but they die passively, giving up in face
of the world.[99]

A brief examination of Feuerbach's comments on suicide, written during
the last active decade of his life, brings out the differences between the two.
For Feuerbach, suicide was not so much proof of free will as it was an action
taken because life could not be lived in accord with one's *particular* nature.
For some people, a life without love was impossible; for a warrior like
Achilles, by contrast, life without weapons was impossible. The suicidal
person was not rejecting a happy world of nature, but rather a world of
suffering and unhappy nature; suicide was a matter of "poison against poison." In a passage that could have been formulated by Wagner, Feuerbach
wrote: "What life's day pronounces, in a hospitable and affirmative manner,
namely that a human rejoices only by virtue of the sun of the sweet
moment, death's night says as well, only in a negative, hostile manner."[100]
For Feuerbach, the images of day and night contained a mythical moment
implying the wish and hope for a better life: "What humans are for only a
moment, only at night, only in their dreams, happy, free, supra-natural
beings bound to no barriers of naturalism or materialism—that is what the
gods are all the time, by the bright light of day."[101] Gods, in other words,
were humans in a dreamworld that allowed human wishes to be fulfilled.
But humans could only conceive of this world in which they would be fully
at home at night, when they left their own world of the day behind. Night,
the dreamworld, became the antidote to the poison of the day. Just as religion, then, was a protest against conditions limiting humans in the world,

so suicide was not merely the negation of a world that negated the self, but also a protest against conditions and institutions that contradicted human essence. Suicide in Feuerbach contained a moment of resistance, an affirmation of the world as it ought to be and not simply a rejection of the world in itself.

The one who dies in *Tristan and Isolde* did confront conditions of life that made the life of day a hell, and that made the night of dissolution seem an opening to a new day beyond any barriers. Wagner's work concentrated on the intense psychological processes of an individual, and as a result developed the modalities of a will to death better than did Feuerbach in his abstract discussion. But beyond that single individual, Wagner's contexts for suicide were distant and unfocused, intended to suggest a universal, abstract truth about the value of life. Wagner's discussion of "suicide" was in this respect actually more abstract than Feuerbach's. The meaning of self-willed death in Wagner was unclear: the yearning for death could signify a revolt against specific conditions and institutions of life; or it could be the yearning to lose oneself permanently in love and never have to return to everyday life; or it could be the yearning just for the loss of self. In the case of Feuerbach, suicide was a willed, conscious decision; for Wagner, sometimes it was (as in Brünnhilde's case), but sometimes (as in Tristan's), the character was overwhelmed by a feeling of ecstasy and passively accepted the end of life rather than acting decisively. The mortal cut in Tristan's case came from outside of the self. Wagner offered in place of Feuerbach's conscious and in a sense life-affirming notion of "learning to die" a half-conscious, primarily aesthetic, and even decadent conception of suicide.

The first example of self-willed death in *Tristan and Isolde* (in this case a failed attempt) occurs in the first act. Two characters face irresolvable contradictions in their daytime life. Isolde, the most beautiful noble lady of Ireland, is being transported to Cornwall against her will by Tristan, to be made wife of King Mark, Tristan's lord. Isolde reveals that she knew Tristan had killed her fiancé, Morold. Tristan, himself wounded in that battle with Morold, had come to Isolde to be healed—and after looking into his eyes, Isolde nursed him back to health.[102] Isolde should have killed Tristan, but she did not; her honor is therefore disgraced. She shames Tristan into admitting that he has dishonored her, and presents him with a choice: to honor his pledge to King Mark or to honor her, an impossible choice. Both characters are enmeshed in an insoluble predicament, and both drink a death potion: "for evil poisons an antidote" (literally an "antipoison": "*Für böse Gifte/Gegengift*"). But Isolde's servant has replaced the poison with a love potion. So they end the journey lusting madly after each other. The conscious decision for death gives way to semiconscious ecstasy, the "utmost rapture of love" (*höchste Liebeslust*).

The madness continues after their arrival in Cornwall. Tristan, King Mark's vassal, and Isolde, King Mark's wife, meet secretly at night to avoid the legal, conventional obligations of the day. The images of day and night thus reappear, but not in Feuerbach's sense, where "night" was a conscious decision to exit a world that did not accommodate a human's true nature. Night in Wagner was instead a semiconscious world of passions impossible during the day. The lovers' dialogue is marked by physicality and sensuality. It was not Feuerbach's ideal dialogue between a self and another self that created self-knowledge, knowledge of the world, and community. It is a fragmented dialogue on love that consists of parallel or at most intertwined monologues. It was probably in this sense that Thomas Mann called *Tristan and Isolde* "a thoroughly obscene work."[103] At the end Tristan and Isolde affirm death as a way to prevent the return of day with all its complications. They are not entering into a conscious compact; rather, they feel their way toward parallel positions on life. Their physical, sensual dialogue resounds with unanswered questions. Isolde, for example, asks what happens to the "and" that connects the two in love: "would death not destroy the bonds of love?" Tristan answers that with death the two will be inseparable, without an end, without awaking, without fear (*So starben wir, / um ungetrennt / ewig einig, ohne End', / ohn' Erwachen / ohn' Erbangen*). The distinction between *Ich* and *Du* disappears for eternity in the moment of climax/death.[104] Tristan's arguments do not fully answer Isolde's probing questions, and Isolde reverts to critical reflection almost in spite of herself.

In the final act, Tristan is dying from a sword wound inflicted by another: death comes about through the actions of someone else. At first, he strives for life—exactly the opposite of a suicidal person, despite his earlier statements that the conventions of the day had made his life meaningless. Remembering Isolde keeps him from dying and drives him anew toward the light of day. Isolde herself has become the deceiving light of day. When she arrives, he pulls off his bandage and bleeds to death. She is now left alone, wishing that he had given her one more hour of his life: "Remain awake with me for just one hour!" (*Nur eine Stunde bleibe mir wach!*) She collapses on top of him, whether still alive or dead the libretto does not say.[105] (And from the point of view of Tristan, now dead, her status is utterly irrelevant.)

Tristan and Isolde can be seen as a story of romantic, revolutionary protest against the false world of the day. Love, the true, authentic relationship between two humans, is made impossible by the complex of institutions that create lord and vassal, the state and law, and obligations of honor.

Against the day stand the immediate relations of the night: an embodied and equal encounter between two selves that is the main focus of the work. The action of day takes place mostly offstage, while the reality is the night of love.[106] Death is not only the admission of defeat in the face of day; it is also a romantic protest against what the day cannot permit, and in favor of free love over against marriage. The elimination of the self is a small price to pay for the affirmation of love, the basic human feeling. Isolde refers to the spirit of love (Frau Minne) as the regent world's becoming (*Weltwerden*), and of life and death. Under the protection of Frau Minne, Isolde defies the day; she seems to affirm a different kind of day, one of humanity liberated from oppressive institutions.

Yet *Tristan and Isolde* also tells a much darker story. Tristan seems to ask Isolde to enter into a suicide pact so that their love may remain: to avenge the suffering of love, he calls upon her to "extinguish insolent day." But he also gives a different explanation of this death: to escape as an individual into the universe (*Weltall*). His desire for the dissolution of the self is not the same as an affirmation of love. Indeed, love has no necessary role in it.[107] On this view, Tristan's "night" is an escape from both day and night—and also from Isolde. Self-willed death may seem to preserve love for all time, but it also offers escape from the unquenchable striving for sexual union—love itself was the problem to be solved by death.[108] The love potion in the work, which would seem superfluous for two lovers, as Thomas Mann noted, was a drug that could give the user a sense of separation from the world of day, leading a loyal vassal like Tristan to ask, in a stupor: "Which king?" It is the chemical that releases Tristan from normal obligations, just as the potion in *The Twilight of the Idols* released Siegfried from any normal obligation to Brünnhilde and allowed him to rape her in the guise of Gunther. The drug allows the hero to act without restraint, and hastens the yearned-for destruction of the world.[109] Tristan's obscure statement that he brewed the drug himself implies that it was no more than his fate from the time of his birth—it is the will of the world, in Schopenhauerian terms. The violence that an individual feels fate has directed against him he now redirects against the world, seeking to negate it—even if only from his individual standpoint. This interpretation takes on added power in the final act, where, as noted, the mortally wounded Tristan describes Isolde as light drawing him away from dark: a light that is "deceiving, bright and golden," pulling him back from Death's "bliss." Tristan's death is that of an individual who seeks relief from it all. The death has been labeled, unconvincingly, "redemption," but it is in fact mere negation (and passive: the hero removes the bandage, allowing the wound to bleed). Tristan's death leaves Isolde without emotional satisfaction. The glowing love of Tristan and Isolde is itself mythical in this ultimately dark drama.

Feuerbach's work at no point evinced Wagner's drive to reject the world.[110] Suicide for Feuerbach was not "redemption" in any sense other than relief from a life not worth living. Wagner's *Tristan and Isolde* may redeem the individual soul, which Feuerbach seemed to lose sight of in his turn to physiological materialism. But at the cost of emptying it of content, of making of personal immortality an impersonal dissolution of self, nirvana.

Myth and Revolution

Thomas Mann noted that God is never invoked in *Tristan and Isolde*: the world of Wagner's myth is a fully human world.[111] In a sense, the same can be said of *The Ring*, despite the presence of gods as characters. The gods who play a role in the story are anything but Christian or even ancient gods: they are greedy businessmen, petty housewives, and sneaky tricksters. As the giant Fasolt tells the gods, "what you are, you are through contract." And Erda herself states, "Everything that is, comes to an end": the gods are mere mortals. The heroes are no longer half-gods, but are instead human beings in "the most natural and joyful fullness" of their "sensually animated manifestation."[112] Even the ostensibly religious themes that played such a central role in Wagner's later works have a this-worldly aspect. Wagner's *Parsifal*, for example, despite Cosima Wagner's attempts to fit it into a Christian view of the world, was, as Joachim Köhler and others have argued, about this world, and not least about Wagner's own lusts. Once again, sexual desire is at the heart of the work. Once again, redemption comes through renunciation, in this case Parsifal's ability to steel himself against the seductions of Kundry. And once again, there is a basic ambiguity in the story. Either it is about finally "redeeming the redeemer" of this fallen, artificial, "Jewish" world and opening the way to a new community of the Grail with the death of the wandering Jew, or it is a final renunciation of the world, expressing the despair of sexual desire—with frustration goes the will to deny the will and renounce the world. In either case, the characters are of this world, and the drama is about humanity.[113]

In his later writings, Feuerbach found that in Homer the gods are already like men. Wagner also knew his Homer well. He and Feuerbach both operated in a field in which myths had lost their transcendent status and were reduced to the level of earthly matter. Myth as a part of human essence posed a problem for Feuerbach in his late works because he was simultaneously intent on dismantling myth as ideology. Feuerbach's solution took in the form of a kind of "anticipatory consciousness," as Ernst Bloch would have put it. Myth was a human process of wish-fulfillment, a process by which humans created entities that went beyond the merely human, but also bore out fundamental truths of humanity, including the ideals for which humans strove. Feuerbach's theory of myth combined the notion that creating myth was essential with the notion that myth was ideology and had to be dismantled. This tension contains the value of Feuerbach's work for both ethical and political theory.

Wagner's ambiguous and even contradictory "lessons" in *The Ring* and *Tristan and Isolde* reflect that paradox of myth-creation and myth-destruction. The mythical redemption of the world in love revealed itself in Wagner's works as the desire for death; the mythical images of a world freed from the superficialities of honor, contract, obligation, and debt, the social-revolutionary side of Wagner, gave way to a renunciation of the world in general. The latter was precisely the nihilism that Feuerbach loathed in the Judeo-Christian notion of the absolute power of God over the world, which reduced the value of the world in itself to nothing. In fact, Wagner saw just this sense of meaninglessness as a truth of Christianity that "narrow-minded Judaism" had obscured.[114] Both Feuerbach and Wagner considered the truth of sexual love fundamental to human existence; Wagner yearned for its transcendence, ultimately in death. Both *The Ring* and *Tristan and Isolde* do the work of myth in Wagner's sense, of getting to the heart of the "truly human." But what they find there is either paradox or an empty space. Unlike Feuerbach, who rejected transcendence in favor of the concrete wishes of the human in the world, Wagner posited the destruction of self and world as a way to transcend the world. He thereby fell back into the Christian metaphysics and nihilism that Feuerbach deplored. Nietzsche's later criticism that a "condemnation of life by the living" is impossible, since "one would have to be situated *outside* life" to judge its value, points to the way Wagner retained a traditional metaphysics in his works.[115]

Is it such a jump from Wagner's nihilism to the proto-Fascism expounded by so many of his followers? The rejection of the world in his work was violent, as was the world itself, which was subject to fate, to naturelike processes of destruction. The final immolation of Brünnhilde on the pyre she builds along the Rhine is not just an expression of tragedy, but also of desire. Wagner hoped at one point to see all of Paris burn down as the start of the revolution; at another to show the entire *Ring* in a theater on the banks of the Rhine, which would itself burn down after the final scene.[116] The characters populating his social and political worldview also took on mythic dimensions. The Jew in the later Wagner was an obsession, truly a quasi-mythical image of sly evil that pulled strings behind the scenes and deviously controlled the heroic German.[117] The German, meanwhile, was a race in need of purification by incestuous breeding. Here redemption was a ritual purification of the body from impure substances, and fit with Wagner's increasingly irrational positions on, for example, vegetarianism: from a position advocating compassion for animals, he developed a strange theory about how ingesting nonhuman blood would lead to a "corruption of blood" that could undermine the "white race."[118] There are many strands in Wagner. The decision by Siegmund to give up eternal life in Valhalla to remain with Sieglinde, for example, showed a moment of compassion in which the individual moved beyond egoism—including the egoism involved in the destruction of the ego—to an affirmation of both self and other, and of life. Siegmund is an isolated case, a miniature moment of "sense and sweetness," in Nietzsche's terms, marked by republican pathos and a willingness to give up fame for an immediate sense of love and justice.[119] But another, important strand involved unrestrained violence and irrationalism in politics that found an appreciative audience on the far right. Essential to the mythic formulation of politics was its basis, not in reason or careful observation, but in an "unconscious feeling," an "involuntary repellence," an "instinctive dislike" of the enemy—all notions supposedly rooted in the *Volk* and thus not subject to refutation.[120] Just as his rejection of commodity culture as decadence found its ultimate expression in a profitable and monopolized commodity produced only at Bayreuth, so his rejection of oppressive politics found its expression in a politics that openly advocated oppression.

CHAPTER 5

Ethics and Finitude in the Late Feuerbach

Feuerbach's *Essence of Christianity* made the apparently simple gesture of reducing God to man, of transforming religion into psychology and anthropology. His followers—Hess, Dittmar, Wagner, and others—struggled to work out the implications of that gesture for politics. They searched for an authentic, purely human mode of politics, in opposition to inauthentic official and religious culture. During the mid-1840s, when Hess was closest to Feuerbach, his concept of revolution involved the critique of false idols, from God to state to money. In later years, he sought to find proof in the very order of the universe that humanity had a higher goal, combining the rediscovered infinite potential of humanity with an almost new-age cosmology. Dittmar's revolution involved a non-Christian Weltanschauung of conflict, struggle, and redemption. The pagan Germanic world she sought to recreate contrasted sharply with the provincial and patriarchal Darmstadt she inhabited. Wagner's search for new meaning in the rebirth of the authentic human raised questions about the ultimate meaning of the world and of humanity, once one gave up the objective existence of a personal God. Either the fallen modern world would end in fire, to be replaced by a new, human world, or it would just end, and the human would experience a kind of redemption in being released from evil into nothingness—a kind of nihilistic Christian perspective.

Hess, Dittmar, and Wagner sought to find the meaning of religion, its "hieroglyphics," in Dittmar's term, in myth. This was the approach pioneered by Feuerbach, Strauss, and other German researchers in the mid-nineteenth century.[1] Hess, Dittmar, and Wagner each made use of Feuerbach's ideas differently, and each no doubt would have troubled Feuerbach in some way. But they all responded to a gap between theory and practice in his thinking. That gap originated in his articulation of the presence of the finite and the infinite in the human. On the one hand, Feuerbach demanded that individual humans understand themselves within the limited, finite bounds of their own nature, and that references to superhuman, transcendental concepts be dropped. On the other hand, he insisted that the critique of the superhuman would reveal the infinite potential that lay within humanity itself. Language expressed the contradiction: while Peter may have been able to eat the food in front of him today, his ability "to eat" was grammatically infinite, not limited to the quality or quantity that he confronts. Language thus went beyond actuality. The connection between the limited Peter in practice and the unlimited Peter in theory opened up the question of what, then, should be done with this knowledge, a question whose difficulty was indicated in Feuerbach's own ambivalent revolutionary practice in 1848. Feuerbach expected, on the one hand, something dramatic and truly revolutionary in 1848, a practice that would involve blood, death, and rebirth in a new world; on the other hand, he showed a resigned, disappointed side already in the first months of revolution. The actual world did not contain the potential of an infinite grammar.

The new world of human love and community did not appear. Feuerbach found himself back in Bruckberg, far from urban life and intellectual conversation, deprived of his fellow radicals, depressed about the state of Germany and Europe. He threw himself into a massive research project on myth, which he viewed as his mature statement, with definitive evidence from religious and mythical texts, to support his theory of religion.[2] The work reached the public in 1857: *Theogony, According to the Sources of Classical, Hebrew, and Christian Antiquity.*[3] As the title indicated, he explored the origins of the gods, not as the theologians represented them, but as Homer and as the prophetic texts of the Old and New Testaments did: as individual stories about human actions and desires. In myth, Feuerbach found a truth of human finitude, expressed in hunger, thirst, love, and death, and a truth of human essence as a being that, though rooted in matter, was capable of thinking beyond the existing order of things in its dreams and wishes.[4] The material human being's essence was contradictory. Such a being might fear death and long for immortality at one moment but seek an end to self at another, when the world no longer seemed "home." Feuerbach's interest turned, then, to the way that concrete circumstances that created a particular personality also determined that person's notion of infinite potential. For the late Feuerbach, religion opened up the specific cultural world that specific people lived in, rather than some transhistorical human essence.

The final works of Feuerbach reveal how complete his break was with the tradition of philosophical thinking since Descartes, and what problems he posed for the entire endeavor of thinking about the world of knowledge and morality in the future. He abandoned philosophical abstraction for concrete stories, a decision not unlike that of Richard Rorty.[5] He never returned to careful philosophical analysis, and indeed seemed ever less interested in continuity among his works. Instead of essays, he wrote aphorisms and lines of thought. Yet his later work is dissatisfying; it pulls in two different directions. On the one hand, he seemed to shift his attention ever more to the concrete individual and his or her desires, all understood fully within the sensual-material world. The result might well have been an ethics of hedonism; indeed, his stress on the drive for happiness pointed in that direction.[6] But on the other hand, he rejected egoistic individualism, though not on moral but on ontological grounds. He now conceptualized the self as finite, as "porous" in the sense of being ontologically open to the world, and as possessing a "spirit" that was part of its existence in the world. His turn against idealism thus did not amount to a naïve materialism, but rather a more complex notion of the human self. Both his account of the self and his exploration of myth and religion showed the individual in constant, inescapable interaction with the physical world and human community: the individual was always both material and social. Feuerbach's search for a new ethics and politics that was always inevitably intertwined with nature and society led him to search for an authentic way of taking into account the "Thou" who stands against and defines the "I". But his theory remained suspended between an individualistic hedonism and a communitarianism that implied limits to individual desire. It is even more confusing that his few statements on German politics implied a liberal defense of individual rights that did not fully conform to his theoretical communitarianism. In the end, Feuerbach's theory, though posing interesting questions that would be central to German discussion later in the century, provided little guidance when it came to hard questions of responsibility, both individual and political.

Feuerbach and the New Materialism of the 1850s

Feuerbach had already turned to materialism, as defined against philosophical idealism in the traditions of Descartes and Hegel, before 1848. Thereafter, he participated in debates over materialism in the 1850s, which served as a kind of ersatz public discussion about radicalism in the highly censored period of reaction after the revolution. The leading materialists who participated in the debates came out of German radical traditions, and all were influenced by Feuerbach. The biologist Karl Vogt, for example, politicized in Giessen in the 1830s, came to know Bakunin, Proudhon, and

Herwegh while in Paris in 1845; he was a leading radical in the Frankfurt Parliament and had to escape Germany disguised as a woman. Vogt knew Feuerbach already before the revolution, and they corresponded on political matters thereafter. Vogt's friend Ludwig Büchner, brother of Georg Büchner (and therefore no doubt connected to the Dittmars in Darmstadt), trained in medicine and wrote the famous work *Kraft und Stoff*. This book, translated into many European languages, sought to make materialism into a new, freethinking Weltanschauung that would replace traditional religion. Büchner was likewise influenced by Feuerbach, whom he cited throughout the text.[7] Most closely connected to Feuerbach was the Dutch physiologist and German nationalist Jakob Moleschott, who attended Feuerbach's lectures in Heidelberg and became a personal friend. All three were prominent in public discussions during the first half of the 1850s through their defenses of materialism and atheism in the form of works of natural science. In a period when the forces of reaction had driven into exile or silenced so many politically radical voices, their works of natural science became a new locus for discussing radical politics.[8] At the famous 1854 meeting of the German Natural Researchers and Doctors, scientists took up again the great intellectual debate of the Vormärz over the existence of God and the soul.[9] Just as in the 1840s, questioning the existence of a personal God implied a critique of the monarchical state. But the intellectual climate of the 1850s was much different. The new debate took place without any admixture of complex notions of matter and metaphysics. Hegel was dead and forgotten.

After hearing Feuerbach's lectures in Heidelberg, Moleschott published a book in 1850 on diet and nutrition, one of the first of its kind. Titled *The Doctrine of Nourishment: For the People*, the book treated the physiology of consumption and the organization of the body, then turned to the way different foods worked their way through the body. The book was implicitly political from the start, insofar as it treated all humans equally.[10] Works for the general public on issues of diet and self-help, like works of popular religiosity, are not without their democratic ramifications; they open up specialized knowledge for the nonspecialist and provide some breach in the monopoly over knowledge held by priest, doctor, or scientist. Indeed, *Hours of Devotion* by the Swiss liberal novelist Heinrich Zschokke, a work of popular religiosity, had influenced Feuerbach in his youth and even foreshadowed elements of his later radical turn.[11] Moleschott's ideas implied a kind of self-empowerment of the individual, beyond existing authorities or the church. His own sympathies with the German radicals of 1848 (he even hoped that his homeland of the Netherlands would become part of a German revolutionary republic) lent his book additional notoriety.[12] But most controversial was his apparently neutral, scientific assertion that without phosphorus there could be no thought.[13] By making the material world the condition of thought, he reversed the hierarchy of the ideal (the soul, God) over matter; he implied furthermore that thought was a material process, an argument that went against both Judeo-Christian religion and the entire Cartesian tradition of philosophy.

Even before the full eruption of debate over the physiology of thought, Feuerbach appeared in print with his review of the work. Feuerbach heaped scorn on the Prussian state, which disarmed citizens and silenced writers yet piously proclaimed freedom of speech for the natural scientists. Natural science, he proclaimed, was in fact a threat to a dynastic state that claimed to be Christian. Nature was indifferent to politics in the sense of a dynastic politics: "Does the flea distinguish between the blood of a prince and that of a commoner [*bürgerlichen*], does lightning distinguish between a crowned and an uncrowned head?" "Where there is nature," he continued, "there is no politics, at least in the sense of the dynasties, and where there is [high] politics, there is only monstrosity [*Unnatur*]." Natural science was "communist" in the sense that it knew nothing of the distinction between noble and common. The natural scientist was a revolutionary, like Copernicus, who not only decentered the earth but also profaned the heavens. Moleschott's work on nutrition was a similarly revolutionary text, Feuerbach observed; it resolved some central problems of philosophy as well, insofar as it proved the unity of body and soul.[14]

That unity, Feuerbach continued, was literal: nourishment connected body and soul, "being means eating; what *is*, eats, and is eaten" (*Sein heisst Essen; was ist, isst und wird gegessen*).[15] Nutrition determined what people could do and even what they could think. The potato, for example, low in protein and phosphorus, provided no power for body and brain and rendered Ireland impotent against the British, who ate roast beef, according to Moleschott.[16] "Thus the victory of the reaction in our case, too, the humiliating course and result of our so-called March Revolution; for in our case, too, the greatest part of the population consists of people who cram themselves full of only potatoes" (*Kartoffelstopfer*). Lentils or peas, by contrast, would provide protein as well as phosphorus, a diet that would lay the foundation for a new revolution. For, as Feuerbach concluded, in one of the few quotations for which he is widely known, "you are what you eat" (*Der Mensch ist, was er isst*).[17]

The review dripped with sarcasm, but it was not merely a joke. There is no indication that Feuerbach did *not* believe what he wrote; indeed, food was one of the most important topics of his late work. The review also pointed up some issues that were beginning to arise in his own philosophy after he had abandoned idealism. What, for example, was the status of thought, of culture, of language, now that humans were reduced to the material world? Was all of it little more than ideology, muddy waters to be washed out by the clear, purifying streams of scientific knowledge? Feuerbach's notion that the self was essentially "porous," open to the physical environment, seemed at some points to suggest the end of the individual soul. Instead, the individual seemed a physiological machine driven by hunger and determined by what it received from the surrounding world.[18] Soulless hedonism would seem to be the logical conclusion of this conception. Feuerbach's approach seemed to reduce humans to just another part of a material world and to render religion, which was, after all, his chief concern, merely an error to be replaced by the higher insight into the world afforded by natural scientists like Moleschott.

But Feuerbach's earlier work already contained the germ of a different answer to the question he posed. For food had been important to him already in *The Essence of Christianity*, where he searched for the real, human meaning of the sacrament in the actual significance of bread and wine for life.[19] Feuerbach's assertion that humans, like all animals, ate what was around them and were eaten in kind was now tempered by a concern for the complex role of eating in specific human communities. Instead of making overall, general judgments about the human, Feuerbach began to compile all the specific ways consumption entered into human life.[20] Meaning *per se* was at issue, and not conveyed by the means that he was using to describe physiology; if the human was a porous being open to, determined by, the community, then its drive for happiness could not be conceptualized as that of a machine-like monad.

The materialism of Moleschott, Vogt, and Büchner, in contrast to Feuerbach's own project, left culture and history behind. All three sought a general, universally valid comprehension of the world, a new Weltanschauung based on the presumed eternal truths of the mechanical laws of nature.[21] The analysis of religion that Feuerbach advocated could not rest content with such an abstract and ahistorical materialism. He was not interested in describing the physiology and mechanism of the human body from an external, objective point of view, but in understanding from within the human world how people made sense of their lives. Natural science, he argued, only provides an answer for those who are asking a question that anticipates an answer in the form of natural science.[22] A geologist could describe the physical features of a rock formation as well as its geological history, for example, but not its meaning for humans. Feuerbach rejected what he called a "transcendental materialism" that sought only to answer "directly, immediately, materially" the kinds of questions that could in fact only be brought to the light of understanding "from afar, indirectly, by the long way around" (*aus der Ferne, nur mittelbar, auf Umwegen*).[23] Questions about the human will and consciousness, he implied, were not answerable from an "objective" viewpoint, but only from the point of view of a specific human subject.[24] At issue for Feuerbach was not the externally observed motion of material bodies, but the way humans, themselves finite and essentially limited, appropriated these bodies and granted meaning to them.

Religion provided access to these subjective truths of humanity. Religion opened up the fears and desires of people seeking to comprehend their world. These included the desire to make the world itself (nature) like oneself and therefore comprehensible from within rather than a cold, external force; the desire for happiness and serenity, for having a human home; the desire to have control over the essentially uncontrollable. Religion exposed the human condition concretely. Idealist philosophy, by contrast, according to Feuerbach, concealed existential reality under a set of abstractions; it was even more untrue to the world of concrete human experience than was religion.

Theogony and the Abandonment of Developmental History

Following his review of Moleschott and affirmation of a materialist conception of the individual, Feuerbach's next great work, *Theogony*, was on religion rather than science. He turned to the subject of religion because he held that a mechanical materialism that merely described the objective conditions of experience was also untrue to human experience. The product of years of poring over the classic texts of ancient mythology, this work was, in Feuerbach's own estimation, his most important work. It continued Feuerbach's break with idealist philosophy, in particular the Hegelian and post-Hegelian notions of a developmental history. *Theogony* concentrated attention on the porous ego in a concrete situation: not as a machine, but as a willing entity struggling to find meaning.

Attacking idealism meant attacking the traditions of philosophy that Feuerbach had followed until the late 1830s. Perhaps because his own break with Hegelian idealism had come at such a high personal and professional cost, Feuerbach remained sensitive to those like Stirner who claimed that his thought still contained elements of idealism.[25] In an 1861 letter to the young philosopher Julius Duboc, Feuerbach expressed annoyance that a recent book on philosophical materialism had accused him, as well as Karl Vogt and Jakob Moleschott, of having retained a concept of the species that was ideological. Feuerbach insisted to Duboc that he had already broken with that concept after Stirner's criticism of 1842.[26] The concept of the human species did remain in his work. The notion that humans were part of a historical chain of infinite progress and perfectability disappeared. The individual human took center stage. The individual was not even a coherent unit over time in the later Feuerbach. Rather, as a human encountered various situations in life and aged, and as the very material composition of his or her body changed, so did the individual's "essence." That meant a change in a one's basic sense of what constituted one's inalienable kernel of character. One's sense of what was required to live well was likewise subject to change. Indeed, Feuerbach at times even denied that character remained the same as individual cells died and were replaced by new ones: new matter, new consciousness.[27] Feuerbach had already rejected the notion of a human soul distinct from the body, and now he seemed to reject the human soul itself. His new approach to individual humans necessitated a different approach to his philosophical and religious material.

Theogony represented this new approach. As Moses Hess noted in one of the few serious reviews of the book, Feuerbach did not explain his method. If there was an introduction, it appeared far into the work.[28] Feuerbach abandoned traditional philosophy. He did not write as a Hegelian or as a Fichtean, he wrote to the young Finnish philosopher Wilhelm Bolin, but as a "Homerian" (*Homeride*), as a follower of the great poet.[29] The book began by rereading Homer against the theologians. Theology, Feuerbach claimed, found in the statement "Thus was Zeus's will accomplished" proof that Homer made the fate of man dependent on the will of the gods. Yet, before this verse, "already in the first verses of this heroic poem, the secret of theology is dissolved into its anthropological sense." The poem opens not with Zeus's wrath but with Achilles' rage: "Homer begins with the pernicious rage of Achilles; he makes Achilles the basis of Zeus, human resentment [*Unwillen*] the basis of divine will."[30]

One can say, against Hess, that Feuerbach did indeed provide an introduction to both method and problem, expressed in poetic form. Feuerbach's method was passive, intended to let the reader discover his insight into the nature of religion through the examples presented.[31] As Feuerbach wrote in an undated aphorism, he did not ask, as Kant did, what made religion possible, but rather proceeded as a natural scientist would, to research his object on the basis of empirical evidence, through the "facts of consciousness" recorded in religious texts.[32] For what Feuerbach described was how humans developed wishes that exceeded their abilities and created gods to represent those wishes. These gods stood above humans and yet originated from them. "The original appearance of the gods," Feuerbach stated, "is the wish."[33] Myths of the origin of the universe themselves originated in human needs and desires, which were their true, empirical content. The parallel with Freud, who would also turn to the language of myth, both pagan and Hebrew, to convey his arguments about the soul, is striking.

The fact that humans had wishes that expressed themselves in the form of gods related to another, existential fact about humans: they experienced *lack*. They experienced nonbeing, nonhaving, inability, hunger. And they also desired to overcome that lack: "The wish is a slave of need, but a slave with the will to freedom, a son of poverty, but of *that* poverty that is the mother of desire, of love, not only of sexual but also of neuter love, of love of things."[34] Religion expressed the revolutionary drive of human ability (*Können*), to measure up to human wish (*Wünschen*).[35] But the fact of a revolutionary drive did not eliminate the fact of a lack: humans, Feuerbach asserted, were inevitably stuck between wishful thinking and real inability.

According to Feuerbach, this basic human predicament appeared in all major religions. Even in the abstract monotheism of the New Testament, Feuerbach found the source of God in the human wish to be completely holy, heavenly, and eternal. God and God's word preexisted the world, but, Feuerbach stated, citing Paul, "he hath chosen us in him before the foundation of the world." From the start, God had man's life and redemption in mind.[36] Feuerbach found many more examples in the Old Testament, including the story of Abraham and Isaac: just as Abraham believed that God could create a child where none was possible, so he believed that God could not demand the real sacrifice of Isaac, but would resurrect Isaac if Abraham carried out the sacrifice God commanded.[37]

Hunger, thirst, death, love of community, sexual love: these human drives propelled Feuerbach's analysis in *Theogony*—not in a logical or analytical way, but from image to image, from quotation to quotation. Feuerbach spent over five years writing the book, assembling a huge array of quotations from sacred texts. He did not intend to refute religion, but rather to find a basic truth of humanity embedded in religion: the human, reduced to matter, facing incomprehensible nature, wanting what it does not have and wanting to be or do what it cannot, makes his or her way through life via a series of wishes raised up to the divine. The drive for happiness was translated into the creation of gods who bless humanity. The drive for revenge, also a form of happiness, translated into the creation of gods who curse humanity. Everything stemmed from the self-love of man.[38] It took an atheist to comprehend the truth of religion.

Religion was about humans, but it was also about a world that was not human. The critique of religion could not resolve the condition of that alienation and open the way to a true, authentic, liberated, unalienated humanity because the forces of nature confronting humans were in fact alien. No higher resolution, no grand synthesis of history could avoid that fact.[39] Creating gods and myths anthropomorphized nature, which in turn served to make nature graspable. Yet, Feuerbach argued, the gods consisted of both human wishes embodied in a divine form and of elements not reducible to the human—and that nonreducibility made gods so terrifying. Religious texts sought to anthropomorphize forces of nature: for example, the wind was divine breath. Religious texts also sought to articulate the terror humans felt when they faced elements of nature over which they had no control, and to articulate the wished-for ability to overcome fear, in the form of a god standing above nature.[40] The God of the New Testament remained, for Feuerbach, anthropomorphic: the natural elements of earth, from grass to the sun, were the products of His human-like creative will.[41] He had already noted in *The Essence of Christianity* that the anthropomorphic notion of God put the laws of nature at the disposal of a human-like will. His later work suggested, though did not fully develop, a residual fear that the Christian God Himself was incomprehensible.[42]

Theogony did not represent a turn to political quietism in Feuerbach's thinking. He was disgusted by the passive political implications of Schopenhauer's Buddhist "nihilism" as well as his idealism, and alarmed by his popularity.[43] Feuerbach's late work, rather, suggested a politics situated in nature. He still espoused the political ideas of revolutionary republicanism: that individual people had a concrete place in the world, that they had wishes that demanded satisfaction, and that they had a sense of community deriving from the direct recognition of other subjects (the I-Thou relationship of the early 1840s). The revolutionary impulse in humans lay in the "fiery, infinite, and intractable drive for happiness," he still maintained.[44] But now Feuerbach emphasized that these drives and wishes were part of an individual human's concrete being, and so were limited. Thus Odysseus's essence lay in his drive to return home, even at the cost of death; Achilles' essence lay in his drive to die a hero rather than die an unheroic old man; the Greeks loved their fatherland.[45] The Christians (or at least their theologians) had a different, abstract notion of what it meant to be a human, one that was separate from sun, sleep, sex, nectar, and homeland.[46]

Feuerbach's late work also implied a legitimate role for religion—an important shift from his work of the early 1840s. Religion was implicated in the effort of a political community to connect what it wished for (*Wünschen*) and what it could do (*Können*). The noble striving for higher social standing, for example, was not in itself aristocratic, but implied the drive to align human values with human reality; this Feuerbach distinguished from an institutionalized aristocracy:

> The will to become an excellent person or social superior [*eine Exzellenz*] is human, good-natured, cordial, comradely [*duzbrüderlich*], popular, democratic; but the perfected Excellency [*Exzellenz*] abolishes this sincerity and community

with the common people; he wishes to know nothing more of the humble conditions of his origin, indeed he denies his origin, declares criminal the principles and strivings to which he owes his existence, his excellence. The gods do not originate for political reasons, as the old atheists mistakenly maintained, but they maintain themselves in the end only—and admittedly only temporarily—through means that directly contradict their origin and original essence, through the arts and weapons of political and spiritual despotism.[47]

The prolonged existence of the religious myth of nobility served, then, to solidify caste hierarchy. From the community arose the ideals of humanity, expressed by way of communal practices, in the form of myth. This source of meaning Feuerbach viewed in the quote above as democratic, popular—and its institutionalization in fixed forms as despotic. The will to create gods and narrate myths found its roots in human essence, but that essence was not the nature of the isolated individual monad, but rather of human community as it searched for meaning. The formation of an aristocracy fragmented the human community. And what made despotism despotic was the reification or isolation of the individual, the attempt to fix its form apart from the flux of physiological and communal change. Feuerbach's critique of despotism was a kind of existentialist, even implicitly anarchist ethics, which left to the specific community the freedom to create its own myths out of its particular confrontation with human limitation and need. "Freedom" in Feuerbach's conception was neither abstract nor absolute, but rather change embedded in nature and society.

History in the sense of flux or change was thus central to Feuerbach's later work on religion. The subject matter of his work was empirically and historically specific: how people actually conceptualized their concrete relationship to nature in the form of religion and myth. Feuerbach insisted that his research was modeled on that of the empirically based natural sciences. "Hegel," he wrote, "stands a man on his head. I stand him on his feet, which rest on geology."[48] This is an interesting statement, for on the one hand, geology is a historical science, looking at the natural development of Earth, but on the other hand it seeks universal truths about the nature of matter. Feuerbach also sought to produce both contextually specific accounts of myth and religion and a more general account of human community and religiosity. From his new perspective, all communities were, to paraphrase Ranke, equidistant from God; all were struggling with a general existential question in specific context.

By implication, an overarching, developmental account of religion, such as had played a role in *The Essence of Christianity* and characterized so much

Young Hegelian thinking, became implausible. The idea that the world, by means of human consciousness, was becoming conscious of itself, that some kind of ultimate appropriation of the object by the subject was possible, made little sense if nature was understood as alien and in fact utterly uninterested in humanity. Materialists disdained such idealistic notions of the universe. Nevertheless, many retained a grand theoretical conception of humanity's progress from the dark ages to the world of natural science and objective fact. Many materialists even considered Luther to represent the turning point of world history. Even the late Feuerbach sometimes showed this tendency: in one of his undated aphorisms, Feuerbach asserted: "The East [*Das Morgenland*] concerns itself with what preexists humans; Christianity with the afterlife; the present or future concerns itself only with the existence of man."[49] Such a statement still reflected the developmental schema of *The Essence of Christianity*. But *Theogony* showed a different approach. The progressive development of the world, however pared down and interpreted positivistically, gave way in *Theogony* to concrete analyses of individually situated people confronting their surroundings. In the final years of his life, Feuerbach became ever less interested in distinct "Christian" or "Jewish" or "pagan" traditions. He turned to the individual stories, the individual traditions came apart, and what he was left with was not Christianity or Judaism, but rather humanity in its concrete manifestations.

Feuerbach's new approach resulted in a different, more positive interpretation of the Jewish creation myth, as Francesco Tomasoni has pointed out in an important essay.[50] In *The Essence of Christianity* of 1841, Judaism's God, by creating the world ex nihilo, supposedly reflected a selfish tendency to deny the world its value. Feuerbach represented Judaism as fundamentally egoistic and arrogant, despising rather than loving the world.[51] Judaism represented here a phase in the development of humanity in which humans had left the pagan gods behind and rejected the world, only to be partially redeemed by Christianity. In that work, Feuerbach had even cited approvingly the work of Georg Friedrich Daumer, a friend of Feuerbach's father and an eccentric anti-Semite who published several works propagating the myth of Jewish human sacrifice. Feuerbach broke personally and intellectually with Daumer by 1851. In *Theogony*, Feuerbach maintained that the myth of the creation of the world contained clues about the real human logic behind it: a *human* desire or wish for creation preceded the creation of the world.[52] Within the wish for creation lay the wish for the good, for happiness: thus, the will that preceded the creation was a will for the good. The Church Fathers merely elucidated the point insofar as they connected the wish for the good with God's act. The fundamental essence (*Grundwesen*) of God was the unity of will and potential, the solution to human weakness in the face of the world. In this basic sense, the Christian and Jewish God was doing the same work as the pagan gods. The only difference, Feuerbach argued, lay in the specific notion of what should be affirmed: the Christians, for example, affirmed a being without sin and therefore perfect and without contradiction.[53]

Feuerbach's abandonment of the developmental logic of the 1840s and its attendant anti-Jewish and anti-Christian tendencies meant that he envisioned humanity as involving a plurality of forms and that he looked at the human world as individuals in a set of overlapping groups, with many different concrete wishes and self-representations. At times in *Theogony* it is even unclear whether Feuerbach believed that each religion was consistent and coherent in itself, or merely that each contained a variety of stories and themes that made sense to specific people at specific times. As Feuerbach wrote to Julius Duboc, he was interested in moral claims from the point of view of humanity, not merely from the point of view of the Old or New Testament.[54]

One implication of his turn away from developmentalism (and anti-Semitism) was that he distanced himself from the notion of radical, redemptive revolution. Feuerbach was still a revolutionary: he advocated a republic as the only dignified political system for a true humanity and he affirmed nationalism as a human alternative to the abstract state. But in the final years of Feuerbach's life redemption meant not so much humanity's coming to control the world (as it did in Hess) as it did individual humans' coming to terms with their place in a world of necessary contradiction and need. Progress came with an inbuilt pathos.

The Abandonment of the Soul: Feuerbach's Encounter with Kant

In *Theogony*, Feuerbach not only rejected Hegelian speculations about the philosophy of history, he also rejected Kant's ethical and moral theory. Feuerbach challenged Kant on two levels. First, Feuerbach rejected the abstract, rigid style of academic philosophizing in general.[55] Kant's search for the transcendental presuppositions of knowledge seemed to Feuerbach contrived and largely irrelevant. Second, he rejected the notion of a rational will separate from the material world. Kant's transcendental deduction of a rational will as the necessary precondition to moral behavior was completely alien to Feuerbach's sensualism. Practical, action-oriented judgments were for Feuerbach entirely worldly and oriented toward happiness, i.e., the empirical world. Will and the drive for happiness were identical in the religious stories *Theogony* described; his empirical data therefore suggested the real human basis of religion lay in an identification of will and happiness. Theological speculations that sought to separate the two, like Kant's stark juxtaposition between the empirical and the theoretical, represented abstractions that denied the real, sensual, human world. Feuerbach therefore objected to Kant's rejection of eudaemonism, or the notion that moral obligation was grounded in the intention to produce happiness.

By rejecting a return to Kant, Feuerbach put himself out of step with academic philosophy after 1848, which saw a rediscovery of Kant mediated by Schopenhauer. Two younger scholars close to Feuerbach, Wilhelm Bolin and Julius Duboc, were aware of these new stirrings in philosophy in the 1850s and 1860s. Both urged Feuerbach to confront this new trend, and to be explicit about how his work both dovetailed with and contradicted the early phases of neo-Kantianism. "*Theogony,*" Duboc argued, "is not what the present time needs"; instead, the time called for a new work to fight the battle against a renewed idealism in philosophy, in the spirit of Feuerbach's programmatic *Principles of the Philosophy of the Future* of 1843. Bolin suggested to Feuerbach that he write a book challenging the renewed idealism of Kuno Fischer, a former Hegelian then involved in laying the groundwork for the revival of Kant.[56]

Feuerbach did not follow up on these suggestions in print. In his correspondence, however, he laid out both his objections to Kant and his respect for the way Kant had opened up philosophy to the sensual world. Kant's work, he argued, was contradictory, on the one hand pointing toward the worst idealism of Fichte, Hegel, or Schelling, but on the other hand toward the need for sensualism and empiricism as part of knowledge.[57] Bolin agreed with Feuerbach. Bolin's own work made of Kant alternately a new Jesus who bore the cross of idealism to save us or a new Luther initiating a reformation of philosophy.[58] Whatever his sympathies with Bolin—and at times their relationship seems almost like one between father and son—Feuerbach could not return to academic philosophy, and he rejected any "regeneration of philosophy . . . that does not at the same time emanate from a regeneration of humanity, of religion, of social life."[59] The very style of neo-Kantian work left him cold.[60] Kant's abstract considerations on the conditions of knowledge were not wrong, Feuerbach wrote, just not of value, because philosophical writing without normative goals was sterile and useless. As he noted in a letter to Duboc, "I have, furthermore, the anti-scholastic and anti-pedantic caprice to represent and to express the general only *in concreto,* in the particular; the present only through the past; the philosopher not in his professorial robes but in the beggar's outfit of Odysseus or in the monk's habit of a Luther"—not because of a mere choice of style, but because of what he thought represented useful knowledge.[61]

The style of neo-Kantian philosophy suggested a separate, "higher" world of philosophical logic, which Feuerbach's critique of theology and of idealism had dismissed as absurd. The Kantian theory of knowledge looked for a priori categories like space and time that humans were forced to use as they constructed an image of the world from empirical data; for Kant, the immediate perception of the world was an impossibility, and the world's true nature was an unobservable thing-in-itself. The neo-Kantians would have considered Feuerbach's theory of knowledge crude, insofar as it simply assumed the workings of the human senses without asking about their theoretical presuppositions.[62] Feuerbach, however, denied the value of investigating the a priori categories that allowed humans to perceive, claiming instead that space and time were lived facts for beings whose selves were fully part of and open to the world.[63] The search for a priori conditions of willing or ethics in general likewise seemed irrelevant to Feuerbach. "Why? Because from the standpoint I take, that of the inseparability of the ego and alter ego, [an inseparability] that is known only through the senses, which presupposes the truth, the at least for humans absolutely essential character of sensuality and even sexuality, from this standpoint this question seemed and seems to be nonsense or even lunacy."[64] Since for Feuerbach human will existed only within time and space, any notion of a separate, free will was as senseless as believing that philosophy could precede eating.[65]

That said, the neo-Kantian articulation of the finite and limited perspective of the human, and its criticism of philosophies like that of Hegel that overreached the limits of human reason, dovetailed with Feuerbach's own philosophy of finitude. Both Kant and Feuerbach insisted on absolute limits to human knowledge that were due to the very faculties that humans used to sense the world. In a late aphorism, Feuerbach expressed admiration for Kant's skepticism, which rendered God and soul as little more than "regulative ideas" that aided the formation of perceptions and judgments "as though" (als ob) they were real beings.[66] But as he argued the transcendental assumptions necessary for theoretical or practical knowledge—the assumption, for example, of individual responsibility in Kantian ethics—always also raised the question of whether such a "regulative ideal" in fact did exist. At its most extreme, Kantian ethics, for example, might state that a human should act "as if" the human soul were eternal and invariable, immortal. As Feuerbach noted, it was easy to "leave the 'as if' out of the hypothetical [construction]; to make a real being out of this illusory being, and thus burden humanity with the hyperphysics and supernaturalism that the Kantian philosophy had disposed of!" The tendency "to make an *ideal object* into an *object per se*" imposed itself on humans with the force of necessity.[67] The "merely" hypothetical always ran the risk of being hypostatized, of being made into an object—and even into a godlike object, replicating the logic outlined in *The Essence of Christianity*. Religion, or the creation of idols, was an essential part of the human experience, and even skeptics were not immune to its logic. What Feuerbach saw as Hegel's fundamental error in dealing with Kant, the process of making the thing-in-itself into a real subject of history, seemed all too human.

In a sense, though, Feuerbach's criticism of neo-Kantianism revealed a tension in his own thinking. On the one hand, his insistence on the concrete and particular was part of an explicit polemic against abstraction. On the other hand, his very attempt to say something in general about religion, even if by way of empirical example, necessarily implied some abstraction or generality about human nature. His method led him into a dilemma: to be concrete meant to say nothing in general about humans and the world, yet to be abstract meant to risk reifying—and deifying— concepts. The tension between the concrete and the abstract helps explain Feuerbach's inability to develop a satisfying approach to politics in his last decades.

Like later liberal neo-Kantians, Feuerbach advocated the freedom of expression and other liberal freedoms. In practice, then, he advocated individual rights. But like Vormärz radicals, including Hess, Feuerbach was skeptical about making rights into a political goal in themselves, since rights did not strengthen the community but rather the individual. For Feuerbach and the radicals, traditional, liberal rights implied a political decision for a certain kind of social order based on possessive individualism. Even though calls to expand rights to new arenas and to new groups had played a role in all emancipatory movements since the French Revolution, the German radicals, especially in the Vormärz, attacked rights (even as they praised the human rights proclaimed in the French Revolution as a necessary but now past moment in political development). As Chapter 2 discussed, for Moses Hess, in his most "Feuerbachian" period, rights served to separate individuals from each other, and thereby promoted selfishness and private property.[68] Political action should aim at substance, not at abstract rights that were blind to the concrete reality of life. It should aim at happiness and harmony, not the regulation of conflict. The "rights" demanded by socialists like Hess or socialist feminists like Louise Otto were specific and collective: the right of workers to organize in associations in order to reach the full potential of natural, associated humanity, for example.[69] Rights, in other words, were merely means to a better life; they served a eudaemonistic project. The radical critique of rights mirrored Feuerbach's critique of abstraction.

The late Feuerbach, too, stressed a concrete yearning for happiness in place of the abstract yearning for formal rights. As he declared in the first lines of his posthumously published work on moral philosophy, "What lives, loves, even if only itself, its own life"; "it wants to be, and it wants a certain kind of being, a happy being."[70] Different beings had different kinds of happiness: there was a specific kind of turtle-happiness, snake-happiness, and dinosaur-happiness.[71] And there were many different kinds of human happiness. The Buddhist drive for nothingness was a drive for happiness, though a sick and perverted one, Feuerbach asserted, in a jab at Schopenhauer.[72] The most absurd instances of a perverted drive for happiness, however, were to be found in Catholicism, whose St. Aloysius Gonzaga rejected any encounter with the opposite sex, even the sight of his own mother, whose St. Aldegundis rejoiced in her breast cancer, and whose St. Xavier drank the water he used to clean lepers.[73] But even these acts against the flesh, Feuerbach argued, expressed a concrete yearning for a pure human happiness purged of all bestial admixture.[74]

To offer an adequate account of this drive for happiness, moral philosophy had to be concrete. It could not, as in Kantian thought, turn to abstractions about rights and duties that bracketed out happiness, defined as the human drive to satisfy desires in the world. Morality and ethics resided in the concrete interactions of I and Thou, not in the transcendentally deduced, ahistorical concepts of Kantian thought. Feuerbach's distance from rights-thinking was the result not only of his critique of abstraction, but also of his particular conception of the individual. Morality did not and could not emanate from an isolated individual, since such a thing did not exist, but only from the I-Thou relationship. The Thou was never abstract but always a sensual, bodily Thou who existed objectively for the I.[75] As Duboc noted in a favorable review of Feuerbach's final essay collection of 1866, the idealists seemed to forget that the human did not appear in the world as a fully grown adult. The individual, adult human, after all, was born and raised, experiencing a long childhood where the classical idealist distinction between subject and object was only gradually worked out.[76] The abstract political subject of liberal political theory was the result of a long process, personal and psychological, cultural and historical. In Feuerbach's formulation, life preceded right: "I do not live because I have a right to live, but rather because I live, I have the incontestable right to live. Right is something secondary; something precedes right that is not right, that is more than right, and is not a human statute."[77] This proposition fit with his notion of the derivation of morality from the interactions between I and Thou. He suggested, in short, a communitarian notion of "right" in which communicative interaction, life, created right rather than resulting from right.[78] The implication was that rights served to abstract from the reality of concrete-sensual life and to formalize practical, sensual, nonformal relations. Rights were in themselves an expression of alienation, to use Marx's strong formulation.[79] Feuerbach moreover objected to abstract rights because they preserved the power of the already powerful, they cemented social inequality into place. A social republic, by contrast, was supposed to overthrow the power of the few in the name of the many and to permit the full development of human potential without being limited by formal rules. While radicals like Feuerbach, Hess, and Dittmar would never go as far as Bakunin, who advocated a system of constant destruction and constant revolution, they were nonetheless all attuned to the dangers of any set political form for free self-determination.

Feuerbach offered no sustained discussion on what his communitarian notion of "rights" might mean for political theory.[80] Clearly, though, he rejected the notion of an autonomous sphere of politics or a separate will of the state. "Neither politics nor the state is a goal in itself. The state," like God, "dissolves into people, is there for the sake of people."[81] To be there "for the sake of people" meant to be a tool for carrying out tasks that derived from the direct, "natural" interactions of people conceived as concrete, differentiated individuals rather than abstract, rights-bearing citizens. "The equal, undifferentiated, sexless ego is only an idealistic chimera, an empty thought," he observed.[82] Nature itself ensured that there was not such one-sided being by producing "a drive for happiness that one cannot satisfy, whether one wants to or not, by oneself, without satisfying another individual's drive for happiness, in short, a male and female drive for happiness." This sexual difference was the basis of the family, of feelings of "togetherness, compatibility, communality, [and] limitation of the unlimited autarchy of one's own drive for happiness."[83]

Feuerbach affirmed the ability of social individuals, people in communities, to find their own ways to happiness. But how, if not on the basis of rights that abstracted from concrete situations to allow individuals to respond to specific conditions? The conflict between his critique of rights and the necessity of rights for his political worldview was nowhere more apparent than in his approach to the condition of women. On the one hand, he made sexual difference his primary example of difference among individuals. On the other, he did not intend to cement into place a subordinate place for women. Indeed, near the end of his life he declared that he was in favor of equal legal rights for women: "Although I have always held and recognized sexual difference as an essential, not only physical but also spiritual, difference, I have never inferred from that the inferiority of the female spirit. . . . In short, the emancipation of women is a matter and a question of *general* justice and equality, which humanity now strives for."[84] The first argument, for an essential difference between the sexes, might well have led him to call for qualitatively different kinds of rights for men and women. And indeed, this kind of argument would arise in the second half of the nineteenth century, not least from some leading feminists. The second argument, however, seemed to suggest that he was advocating general rights for all humans, regardless of sex, with respect to, for example, the right to vote. That was a far more radical argument, and one that many feminists themselves did not accept.[85] Feuerbach did not consider the problem of how to relate abstract rights and concrete natures, equality and difference, at the level of political thought. This tension remained an underlying problem in his work, as his discussions about ethics and politics show.

The alternative to developing an abstract notion of human nature and potential, and with it a normative theory of which kinds of communities oppress and which enable individual development, would be to affirm all political and social conditions, including despotism, as natural and immune from criticism. Feuerbach clearly did not intend this result. His arguments about the interpenetration of I and Thou did not amount to a rejection of all individualism in favor of the community. He did not reject egoism per se, but only insofar as it existed apart from community. Concrete examples rather than abstract logic served to outline his position. One did not enjoy devouring food by oneself, but in a community, Feuerbach held. By the same token, enjoying food, even gourmet food, was not in itself wrong, so long as others had the opportunity to do so as well. What was important was to eat "basic, popular, local dishes" (*allgemeinen, volkstümlichen, landessit-tlichen Speisen*) rather than an "exotic irritant" like caviar that would separate one part of the population from another.[86] The drive for happiness per se was not a sin, indeed the drive for happiness, the drive to relieve hunger, was the project that unified all of humanity.[87] Such an assertion may seem appealing, especially given its contemporary context of racist and national-istic egoism. But it remained an assertion, and it was easy for critics like Duboc to show how the desire to make another happy could nevertheless neglect the interests of yet other people. A father was not necessarily inter-ested in any person other than his child. Kant was right: concrete passions for happiness could and did conflict, humanity was divided, a possibility that Feuerbach rarely confronted.[88] The drive for happiness could not solve the problem of how to coordinate interests.

If there were any solution to the problem of how human wills might cooperate rather than compete, it had to lie in some assumed harmony of nature. "Nature" filled the gap in Feuerbach's work, just as it did in other radical work of the time. Wagner wielded nature against artifice;

Hess asserted the natural tendency of the universe toward equilibrium following general laws of gravitation; Dittmar called for the liberation of authentic humanity's nature; even Marx preserved capitalism as part of a natural history of humanity as it moved toward its eventual victory over scarcity. "Nature" filled the gap between the finitude of humans and their potential. It also failed to solve the real dilemmas that Feuerbach's theory posed.

Nature as a Solution to Problems of Ethics

For Feuerbach, morality and ethics were necessarily embedded in the concrete relations of humans with other humans and with the world. If a standard for action could not be derived either from theological commands or from Kantian, a priori abstractions, then they had somehow to derive from these concrete relations. As noted above, resorting to an individualistic hedonism was impossible, once Feuerbach conceptualized the self as porous, i.e., as constituted by its ongoing exchanges with nature and with other selves. Feuerbach's solution was to ground action on relationships in the world that were presumed to be natural and authentic. Such a yearning for simple, authentic, and direct relations with others and with the world fit with the Rousseauian tradition of republicanism. But the difficult problem remained of how to determine what was authentic and natural. Feuerbach's late philosophy could not resolve this problem, and therefore it, like his earlier work, failed to link theory and practice.

Eating and drinking are undeniably central to concrete human existence, so it was no accident that Feuerbach turned to these activities as he tried to resolve the problems posed by his theory. Here the porous self was on display. What one ate was in fact oneself: "For what I eat and what I drink is my alter ego, my other species [*Geschlecht*], of my own nature— just as I am of its own nature." And the act of eating and drinking was what made up the truth of religion: "Eating and drinking is the everyday and therefore unadmired and even disdained incarnation, nature become human."[89] This notion was implied already in *The Essence of Christianity,* where the Host had a sublime meaning because it was connected to the miracle of everyday life: in the act of communion, the human does not actually worship Christ, but rather the miraculous powers of bread and water, the power to cleanse and nourish bodies.[90] In Feuerbach's work, consumption was important as an example of the practical cognition of the world, of imputing meaning to the world, and of setting down the criteria guiding interaction with other humans and therefore one's own being.

Feuerbach joked about eating and drinking, but he also took it very seriously. To reduce a revolution's failure to potato consumption was a deliberate provocation. But a few years later, he made a similar statement about how morality could be related to diet: "In short, the will is able to do nothing without the assistance of adequate material, corporeal means, and morality can do nothing without exercise [*Gymnastik*] and dietetics. How many moral errors derive purely from errors in diet!"[91] Perhaps he sought to shock; his point was that the human was a body, and a body was created through eating. The will could not be conceptualized apart from material life. Feuerbach's entire approach precluded the notion of an absolute, ideal freedom of the will or of reason apart from the material world. If will was related to the material world, then diet and exercise would necessarily be important for human action.[92]

Yet, if the will were at all times determined, then individual actions would lose their ethical significance: they would become effects, nothing more. Duboc confronted Feuerbach with precisely this problem already in 1853: "What is freedom, then? . . . Who is ethical? Is morality [*Sittlichkeit*] then not a temporary, local, climatic concept? Am I not able to act ethically in a subjective sense when I do something that is objectively unethical?"[93] He put the problem more bluntly in a later letter: "Can one speak of good and evil at all, if there is no ethical freedom?" At stake, for Duboc, was the "illusion" that we are autonomous and free in our decisions.[94] He did not have to spell out the implications for radicals after 1848: without a notion of good and evil, without a sense of human self-determination and a normative measure for human actions, emancipation by means of revolution was an absurd goal to begin with.

Feuerbach wrote a prompt (for him) and lengthy response to Duboc in May 1853, only a month after receiving the first letter. A first draft of the response, which Feuerbach did not send, turned quickly to the matter of eating. This discussion of eating habits had formed part of the Vormärz discussion of humanity's degradation and bestiality in the capitalist world.[95] To answer Duboc's challenge, Feuerbach's first impulse was to return to the distinction between species and individual that, as he was well aware, Max Stirner had demolished. Feuerbach divided the will into two parts, a will to eat well that was relatively distinct from the immediate desire to devour, the "species" (*Gattung*) over against the specific "type" (*Art*). Quoting from his own 1846 essay on immortality, Feuerbach wrote that a wild animal eats without considering the consequences; it is thus a "slave to the drive to feed" (*Sklave der Fressbegierde*). But "he who determines the size of the present meal by imagining the future eats with freedom and reason."[96] Feuerbach's final version of his letter to Duboc abandoned this approach and took another tack.

Freedom, Feuerbach now wrote to Duboc, was the feeling of being necessarily what one was. "The real feeling of freedom is nothing but the feeling of health, of well-being, that is, of the harmony between some
determination, action, decision, or condition and my individual nature."[97]
There was a moment when the striving for change would come to a temporary halt, as a particular wish was fulfilled: "Man has not only an impulse
to progress," Feuerbach had stated in his Heidelberg lectures, "but also an
impulse to rest once he has arrived at a stage of development corresponding
to his finite nature."[98] This "feeling of freedom" was the "feeling of harmony
between human and nature, of humans with other humans, of a person
with him- or herself." The feeling of harmony was rooted in place: the
German was in harmony with the German sun, not the African, for example. "Freedom" was "the home [Heimat] of a man, or, more correctly, the
home of a man is his freedom."[99]

Within a few days, Duboc sent off a response. He was now the one to
bring up eating and drinking, after Feuerbach had decided to avoid it. The
alcoholic, Duboc noted, drank because he had to. Indeed, it was his necessity, his nature, to drink. He might well find himself to be a slave to his
passion. Similarly, Duboc noted that he himself engaged in mental activity
beyond what his own weak constitution permitted, but in accord with his
"most inward need." Such examples showed that people could have drives
that were not necessarily in harmony with their own nature: Duboc countered Feuerbach's vague naturalism with a stark contradiction that dwelled
within a single individual. Duboc also invoked Stirner (though he claimed
himself not to have read him), who had moved beyond good and evil to
praise the "courage to lie." Following Stirner, Duboc was suggesting that
ethics were always circumstantial, never absolute, and that Feuerbach's normative distinction between species and individual was untenable.[100]

The personal and subjective sense that one acted out of necessity to quell
one's hunger or thirst ran up against the challenge of "unhealthy" desires.
There seemed to be different kinds of necessary determinations, some more
authentic than others. Feuerbach responded to Duboc by seeking to distinguish between essential and inessential necessities. Nourishment was an
essential necessity; it was related to normal health. But a specific kind of
nourishment was not. When presented with a menu in a restaurant,
Feuerbach stated, he chose the food that he wanted the most. He did not
become upset if it was no longer available, but simply chose another dish.
But he who is set on only one dish, "he *is* not free," indeed he "feels himself
not to be free" when he cannot get what he wants. If a "drive to eat or to
drink" (*Fress oder Sauftrieb*) becomes an essential part of a person, then he
does not feel himself to be a slave of his passions—as long as he has food

or drink. Yet the alcoholic has in fact long since "drunk up" (*versoffen*) his reason. He is a slave who does not feel himself to be one: "The true slave does not feel himself to be a slave, either in political or in moral matters."[101] By contrast, "[h]e who feels himself to be a slave, feels unhappy, is vexed and indignant about the domination over him, seeks to shake off the oner-ous yoke and proves by this disgust, this revolutionary effort, that this or that tendency or passion is not his characteristic or essential quality, not a quality fused with him into a unity."[102] In short, the true slave does not rebel; and the rebel, no matter how enslaved, is never a slave. The alcoholic who does not rebel against the rule of alcohol has, in Feuerbach's logic, drunk away his reason, and by analogy, the slave who does not rebel against his rulers has given up something as well. Welling up underneath these examples was Feuerbach's old, revolutionary humanism. The authentic human demanded self-control within a community, and was not a slave to God, master, or alcohol.

Duboc rejected Feuerbach's distinctions. The concept of "more" or "less" essential necessities, he argued, made no sense. Once one dispensed with the category of the essential, then ethical judgment in a world devoid of the ideal became difficult or impossible. If freedom was defined on the basis of subjective feeling, and the drinker felt free when drinking, could one truly say that he was not so? "The drinker is, according to language and strictly speaking, a human only as long as he drinks."[103] Here Duboc pointed up a contradiction: Feuerbach at the same time rejected free will and yet adopted some notion of free will related to moderation and repub-licanism. Several years later, Feuerbach attempted to solve the problem by describing different, competing wills: the thirsty person wants to drink water, but the reasoning person knows that the water is poisoned.[104] Feuerbach used a down-to-earth example to try to solve a difficult philo-sophical problem, much as Luther had tried to return to folksy examples to reconnect the individual to the gospel.

But folksiness could not solve the dilemma. In order to distinguish between healthy and unhealthy desires, Feuerbach referred to some kind of higher ability to grasp the world, to consciousness. After all, as Feuerbach noted, a brain deprived of water acted differently than a healthy brain. But his distinction still implied a basic essence and a residual idealistic concep-tualization of human consciousness and human freedom, Duboc argued. In his generally positive review of Feuerbach's late work on free will and mate-rialism, Duboc questioned whether pure affect could provide the basis for moral and ethical interaction among people with different wills. Duboc questioned, in other words, the natural harmony of the universe that people like Büchner and Hess were developing to resolve Feuerbach's problem.

Feuerbach, Duboc argued, had solved the problem by referring to some idea of "conscience" that involved recognizing and internalizing the subject position of the other person. The suffering of the other person was thus felt as one's own. But, Duboc claimed, the answer was inadequate for any complex conflict of interest. Some notion of just treatment in the abstract, some notion of "right," had to exist to explain intentions beyond the immediate one of satisfying an urge.[105]

In his final letter to Duboc, which showed signs of annoyance and impatience, Feuerbach pointed out that Duboc was calling for a return to Kantianism, exactly what Feuerbach rejected on principle:

> It is precisely my characteristic point of departure the principle that morality cannot be derived from the ego alone, as Kant, Schopenhauer, etc., maintain, but only from the I and Thou, and moreover not only from the Thou that exists in thoughts, which everyone has and must have in their head since otherwise any notion of morality or duty falls away, but rather from the sensual, bodily Thou, that exists outside of my head, that confronts me personally, which precisely for that reason, if no amicable admonitions or remonstrances help, forces upon me with physical acts the recognition of his right to life, property, honor, in short his drive for happiness.[106]

For Feuerbach, the sense of right and duty emanated from concrete situations. The individual, intertwined with the community, recognized rights and duties by necessity, as a part of his or her sensual-practical life. The "hedonist" of Feuerbach's late ethics, the individual seeking happiness, was tightly woven into a community, which limited the kinds of happiness he or she could strive for. Community was internalized as part of the desire for happiness of a social individual.

What, though, would lead a person to extrapolate from the needs of personal acquaintances to others, to members of other communities or to strangers? The deduction of normative behavior from concrete, empirical circumstances could explain very little about norms in a complex society. Precisely here, some more abstract sense of right or at least of universally valid rules would seem to be necessary. As the example of women's rights mentioned above shows, when push came to shove Feuerbach did in fact evoke general, abstract rights. But his political call for rights remained in tension with his philosophical attempt to derive rights from concrete circumstances.

In an insightful passage from *The German Ideology* from 1846, Marx foresaw the limits to Feuerbach's politics. Marx noted that Feuerbach, by framing his critique of religion (and by implication ideology critique in general) as a means to return human nature to the human, was left with an ahistorical naturalism.[107] Marx was right, except that the late Feuerbach gave up the notion of a single overarching humanity after 1848. Emancipation still involved comprehending religion as the expression of human essence, but now "humanity" was divided up into its various types, depending on climate, economy, society, and so on. Just because Achilles' true nature proved to be that of the warrior did not mean that the nature of humanity in general was that of the warrior.

From one point of view, Feuerbach's new formulation meant that he had lost his radical edge: emancipation was now connected to specific, determinate contexts, and the hope of world-historical emancipation seemed lost. He was a humanist, but without a conception of a specific emancipation of humanity per se. From another point of view, however, his demand for authenticity did leave open the possibility of constant criticism of ideology and of any myth that turned against its human subjects to cement in place an aristocracy. "In nature," Feuerbach wrote, "there is only one regime, and that regime is republican"; only republicanism, rule by representatives of the people, was in conformity with the true nature of human beings.[108] A careful philosopher, Feuerbach was at best a vague republican. Like Rousseau, he aimed at articulating a self-evident, commonsensical ethics of populist radicalism, and he pitted hierarchies, laws, institutions, and the political establishment against the concrete, solidaristic relations of family and community. In one of his last letters to Bolin, Feuerbach remarked on rereading Rousseau for the first time since his youth: Rousseau spoke "from his soul," had a "sensual, material morality," and loved the simple life of the land, all qualities that Feuerbach saw in himself as well.[109]

Feuerbach's late work on ethics contains many suggestive and interesting passages. Yet it offered even less of a critical perspective on human actions than the abstract Kantianism of his father's generation. Feuerbach himself sympathized with left-liberalism and social democracy, but his nationalism and naturalistic ethics could have just as easily flowed in a different political direction, since most of his argument relied on intuition of the self-evident, sensuous truth—and that also grounded positions on the far right as well as the left. His own hatred of war, of Prussian arrogance, and of militarism was personal, not political.[110]

In 1863, Feuerbach took a stand against the new mythic politics of Ferdinand Lassalle. Lassalle, seeking to rebuild a workers' movement in Germany, sought to make use of the Prussian Constitutional Conflict to incite the workers to cooperate with the Prussian state against the constitutional liberals. One leader of the latter was Feuerbach's friend Otto Lüning. In a letter to Lassalle, Feuerbach rejected the strategy. While he was himself a democrat, Feuerbach stated, he supported the Progressive Party's insistence on the primacy of constitutional law over the state and rights. "He who is against [the Progressives]," Feuerbach declared, "campaigns for the reaction, even if against his own intent."[111] Feuerbach—like Marx in 1848—kept his eye on the old established powers as the main enemy; only when they were vanquished and constitutional controls and individual rights were established could the workers' party make headway. (Indeed, one of the last major books Feuerbach read was the first volume of Marx's *Capital*, which appeared in 1867, and which Feuerbach cited positively in his last, unfinished work on moral philosophy.[112]) Here, then, was Feuerbach's limited defense of these individual rights that the Vormärz radicals had decried as "egoism."

Feuerbach spent his last years in obscurity, and following a stroke, he was in a debilitated state after 1868. In those years, he grew close to the Free Religious pastor Karl Scholl and others in that movement. Feuerbach enrolled as a member of the new Social Democratic Workers' Party in 1870. Since he had been suffering from a series of strokes, it is hard to say how serious his political membership was. As he himself said to a friend in 1871, "I am no longer, I am dead."[113] But certainly his radical commitments lay with the Forty-Eighters like Liebknecht and Marx, who still advocated a polity based on the participation of ordinary people, a republic that guaranteed dignity to the despised, and not with those like Friedrich Kapp who had turned to Prussian militarism and national chauvinism to achieve their aims. Feuerbach died in Nuremberg on September 13, 1872. Two days after Feuerbach's death, thousands of workers from the surrounding areas, mobilized by the new party, accompanied his body to its final resting place. Karl Scholl delivered the eulogy.[114]

CONCLUSION

The Feuerbachian Moment

Ludwig Feuerbach's great moment of fame came in the 1840s, when, as Frederick Engels wrote, "we were all Feuerbachians for a moment."[1] The problem of what came after religion did not fade away as his fame did after 1848. Being a follower of Feuerbach meant profoundly different things to different people. Hess, Dittmar, and Wagner confronted the problem of what to do after Feuerbach's critique of religion in different ways. And the world after 1848 was profoundly different. In the world of Vogt and Liebig, Darwin and Moleschott, in a world of natural science and positivism, complex readings of Luther and Hegel seemed beside the point; so did the arduous process of working oneself out from under the heavy legacy of German idealism. By the end of the century, Marx and Nietzsche became the new focal points of intellectual discussion. The problems they posed look in retrospect, however, much like the ones posed by the Feuerbachians.

Feuerbach's importance lies in the way that he posed problems about human self-perception and ethics after the end of traditional religion, after the "death of God," in Nietzsche's famous phrase. The problem that he set was, essentially, how to live as a human, as a finite creature aware of its own death. The movements to reform life that sprang up at the end of the nineteenth century resonated with the ideas put forward by Feuerbach and Hess, Dittmar and Wagner, even if direct influence did not always exist, because Feuerbach and his followers at midcentury had already explored the problems that were to preoccupy society at the end of the century. Subterranean intellectual links existed between Feuerbach and the formation of a new counterculture, but the important link lies in the basic problem of how to live—and how to die—as a human in the modern world, a problem unanswered by abstract systems, theological and otherwise.

After Religion: Love, Death, and Revolution

Feuerbach reinforced the Enlightenment conception that religion was the product of humanity rather than the revealed truth of humanity's producer. Like Enlightenment thinkers, he contended that religion's content could be reduced to human needs and passions.[2] Then he raised the question of what came after religion. The "truth" of religion in the 1841 *Essence of Christianity* still lay in a higher notion of humanity: the finite and determined, essentially limited individual stood opposite the infinite and undetermined, essentially unlimited species-being. This formulation marked only a partial break with the Christian tradition. After all, in the old theological parlance, the fallen—i.e., determined—human being stood opposite the holy, undetermined potentiality of Jesus. The animal stood opposite the angel. But this position amounted to asserting a solution rather than fully confronting the problem of meaning. After all, if religion was revealed to be the work of humanity, then the meaning religion provided humans ought now to be questioned; the holy word, imagined to be objective truth, would be revealed as essentially subjective. Stirner raised this problem most explicitly, but it was implicit in Feuerbach's own thought already in 1841, as the first chapter of this book has shown.

Feuerbach's followers, in seeking to make Feuerbach's thought concrete and practical, revealed its hidden assumptions and difficulties, including the ways it replicated aspects of the Western religious tradition. Hess, Dittmar, and Wagner all took Feuerbach in very different directions. Hess sought a natural order in the universe, a coherence to the cosmos. He sought a general unity of what is and what ought to be, in line with his starting point in Spinoza; moral truth and social reality were to coincide in the new relationships formed by labor or by nations. Dittmar turned to a radically subjectivist position, arguing that human emancipation involved choosing a Weltanschauung, and choosing ideals and values to impose on oneself. Modern, emancipatory politics should involve subordination of oneself to self-imposed ideals. Wagner combined the drive for a new society based on destruction and self-creation—a revolutionary conception—with a questioning of the ideal of life itself once the foundation of life's meaning provided by religion had disappeared. All three hoped to find or create a new center, a new worldview that would carry humanity forward to a new world. All were outsiders, even eccentrics; their solutions certainly seem eccentric. But as Feuerbachians, they were closely intertwined with the radical movement in Germany before 1848. Hess was, after all, the one who brought communism to Marx and Engels, who established ties with Karl Grün and Otto Wigand, and who engaged in philosophical and political discussions with the leaders of European radicalism, including Pierre-Joseph Proudhon and Alexander Herzen. A self-proclaimed revolutionary, he moved in the revolutionary circles that included Arnold Ruge, Mathilde Franziska Anneke (a later associate of Susan B. Anthony), and Ferdinand Lassalle. When Louise Dittmar wanted to enter the world of the radicals in the mid-1840s, she contacted Hess and Grün, who published with Carl Leske (Marx's early publisher), himself close to Dittmar's family in Darmstadt. Her brother was part of the conspiracy around Georg Büchner, and she must have known both the feminist Louise Büchner and the popular scientist and promoter of a new scientific worldview Ludwig Büchner. Her circle extended to Wilhelm Schulz, whose work on economics was so important for Marx's early turn away from Proudhon, to the radical social theorist Julius Fröbel (whose Swiss publishing house produced works by Bauer, Engels, Fallersleben, Herwegh, Ruge, Strauss, and of course Feuerbach), to the advocates of German Catholicism and Free Religion in Mannheim, Karl Scholl and Gustav von Struve. Like Dittmar, Wagner published his politically radical work with Otto Wigand in Leipzig. He was connected to Bakunin in Dresden, to the radical poet Georg Herwegh in Zurich (himself a close friend of Feuerbach), to the Feuerbachian feminist Malwida von Meysenbug, and to the liberal Berthold Auerbach, whose friendship with Moses Hess disintegrated over the issue of the limits of radicalism. These figures, however odd aspects of their thought may seem, were part of a community of radicals that spanned Europe.

Hess, Dittmar, and Wagner all grasped as an existential necessity one of Feuerbach's essential endeavors: to understand humans as the source of religion, and to understand religion as a response to the conditions humans faced in a world in which they never felt fully at home. They understood Feuerbach's affirmation of a world beyond religion—but not without the essential qualities of religion. The point was to break through the alienation imposed by attempts to force religion into abstract, theological categories, to demand immediacy and authentic community in place of the mediated, institutionalized, formalized world of official religions and officious servants of the state. Love, immediate emotional contact between I and Thou, was the password for revolutionary transformation. In Hess, love took the form of a harmonious universe, which humanity would only reach under socialism. In Dittmar, love meant a break with formal institutions that guaranteed mutual alienation and patriarchal power. It replaced false marriage with truth. In Wagner, love became the driving force as well as the intended result of the revolution—though his own work asked what the revolution was about if love ended up an illusion. Love meant the coming of immediate contact within a resurrected community, the end of the world of inauthenticity. One can find hints of this demand in Marx's work, such as his reference to a "community of free individuals, carrying on their work with the means of production in common, in which the labor power of all the different individuals is consciously applied as the combined labor power of the community."[3] But they are only hints, as Marx sought to purge his work of such speculation about the future.

Hess, Dittmar, and Wagner were preoccupied with death, too—the death of the old world, which would bring about the new, the death of the mere individual, who would give way to the health of the people in Hess. In Wagner, death competed with love for ultimate meaning in the universe. All three rejected personal immortality and the deferral of a better life to some other plane of existence. In so doing, they opened up the question of what meaning inhered in life itself, and the call to revolutionize life. For Wagner, of course, the preoccupation with death slipped into a nihilistic morbidity that sought redemption in leaving life behind. Hess sought to find an answer to the question of life's meaning in the face of death in the cosmos, as did Dittmar in the ideal of a self-determining humanity. Wagner's turn to Schopenhauer and philosophical pessimism is often taken as emblematic for the decline of the radical left in Germany. But it did not take Schopenhauer for followers of Feuerbach to discover the perils of a potentially meaningless existence; Schopenhauer provided only the crypto-Christian gloss to Wagner's pessimism.

Finally, all three called for some kind of revolution. But this was not the revolution of Karl Marx and Frederick Engels, and it was most certainly not the revolution of the Second International. The revolution had to do with a complete change in culture, in perception, in worldview, in meaning. The revolution was a cultural revolution. This revolution replaced the meaning provided by official religion, which Feuerbach, as well as his Enlightened and Romantic predecessors, had dissolved. But the cultural revolution turned away from "mere" political form to matters such as eating, drinking, homeopathic medicine, alternatives to Christianity in the form of pagan myths, and so on: to that conglomeration of ideas that would today be classified as "alternative" or even "new age" culture.

Feuerbach, in his later years, also tried to come to terms with the problem of what would come after traditional religion. His late thought marked a sharp turn against the violent, even eschatological images of revolution of the 1840s. His later writings avoided the images of the world on fire that Dittmar invoked, the glorification of death in Wagner, and the grandiose schemes for ordering the universe in Hess. Feuerbach's late emphasis on the concrete and the particular seems to be a turn away from grand ideologies of political progress. But his late writings also contained problems that he was no longer able to confront, especially concerning the status of nature for social and ethical thought. Feuerbach hoped that nature would solve the basic problems of ethics and politics. But nature remained a vague concept, and opened the door for personal sentiment to become social norm. Nature itself could become mythic, beyond question; it could itself serve as a new, dogmatic code of conduct after the presumably sharp break from religion.

Indeed, nature provides a background motif for many of the ideological tendencies that culminated in the disasters of the twentieth century. Nationalism in the late nineteenth century took on the form of a naturalism in which race dovetailed with political will. Conceptions of society as a natural organism played a role in dismantling traditional ethics, and rendering individuals up to what Marx called an "abstract capitalist": "society" as a pure force of nature.[4] Feuerbach himself flirted with scientific racism as it emerged in the work of Vogt and others though there is no indication that he ever abandoned his politics of egalitarian republicanism.[5]

Finally, Feuerbach's turn to nature seemed to obviate the need for politics and for systems to resolve real contradictions. Even after 1848, then, Feuerbach's thinking continued to be marked by the nationalism, and naturalistic antipolitical socialism that had been central to the radicalism of Moses Hess, Karl Grün, and Hermann Kriege in the 1840s. In Feuerbach's angry letter of fall 1866 to Duboc, his naturalistic conception of nationalism was clear:

> The commandment to live and to die for one's fatherland is only given and maintained by those for whom the fulfillment of the commandment is not merely a product of theoretical force of reason, which can bring forth only theoretical recognition, not action, but rather a product of the love of fatherland, the product of heartfelt, sensual necessity, by force of which they had to act as they acted; it was a product of the drive for happiness, but of *that* drive for happiness that felt and recognized in the happiness of the fatherland one's own happiness, the misfortune of the fatherland one's own misfortune.[6]

On the one hand, Feuerbach made clear that not all felt this love of fatherland. Only some periods set the ethical demand of the nation above other demands.[7] On the other hand, the long sentence pointed to a weakness in the theory. People may indeed feel the love of fatherland as a "heartfelt, sensual necessity," but that is a feeling, not a fact; it is not something that is subject to critical, empirical falsification. Indeed those who raise criticisms could be considered outsiders to the "natural" sentiment. And of course there was the basic problem of what the nation actually was. Despite nationalist assertions to the contrary, the nation is not immediately present as a sensual entity; one must engage in a series of complex and improbable abstractions to assert that tens of millions of people with multiple, often contradictory interests should feel bound together. Feuerbach had as little explanation for the "natural" feeling of national unity as did Moses Hess. Feuerbach offered nothing in the way of a critical approach to nationalism, which would become one of the scourges of humanity in the next century. He was offended by his friend Friedrich Kapp's turn to National Liberalism and Bismarck, but his own thought offered no inherent counter, either to Kapp himself or to the even more extreme turn of Kapp's son Wolfgang, for whom the infamous 1920 coup attempt against Germany's first democracy is named.[8]

Feuerbach's view of society and social norms as natural phenomena posed similar problems. So long as Feuerbach assumed that nature constituted some kind of coherent order, and that morality was rooted in these natural relations, then the justification of action turned on an interpretation of nature. By describing different drives for happiness in quasi-biological terms as necessity, Feuerbach offered a disturbing view of modern ethics. Buddhism and Catholicism were for him diseases; should not diseases be cured? Feuerbach's theory offered no reasons why a polis should not take radical steps against those that damaged its health; his theory offered no ammunition against one of his admirers on the right, Mathilde Reichardt. In a remarkable work from 1856 dedicated to Moleschott, Reichardt endorsed Feuerbach's return to nature: "Man is nature. Nature he should be: pure, unfalsified, happy nature." Nature was beauty; Reichardt affirmed nature.[9] But the nature of which she spoke was brutal; in Karl Vogt's terms, "Nature is everywhere cruel," it exposed all life to struggle and possible elimination, it was "without feeling and cold." Morality played no role in it.[10] The only thing to worship was life itself, an eternal process, according to Reichardt—and an eternal struggle, an eternal striving for the highest mountain, where death itself was converted into the immortality of the grand circulatory system itself.[11] And the only morality derived from nature was survival. Neither good nor evil existed in the world; nature could demand a sacrifice just as a tree could drop a diseased leaf.[12] Reichardt envisioned a legal order based on natural necessity, which would deliver up an individual to the demands of society. She argued, for example, that the rejection of capital punishment in modern political life reflected a weakness that should be overcome rather than a mark of progress.[13] Her argument opened the way to coercive, biological approaches to social engineering.

A Social Darwinist or eugenicist conception of humans in their natural could easily lead to brutal consequences. There is nothing in Feuerbach to indicate that he would have approved of such a course. But his approach offered little to oppose it. When he fell back on "nature" to provide social norms, his writing described a world where decisions seemed obvious; humanity's "nature" seemed stable and harmonious, not at all the same as the inhuman, stark power of nature that he analyzed as the initial source of religion.[14] Feuerbach did not accept that the social world might be founded on irreconcilable interests and mutual incomprehensibility, or fundamentally different views of the relationship between nature and action, which might only be resolved procedurally, if at all. The relationship between I and Thou might have offered some way into a conception of communicative rationality—except that he tended to embed it in physiological, especially sexual, relations. His political theory compared unfavorably to the liberal tradition since Hobbes.

But criticizing political naturalism may obscure the way "nature" opened new possibilities for imagining social change at midcentury; "nature" is not merely an oppressive, conservative ideology. Affirming nature meant affirming direct human relations, love, against the artificial institutions that stood in the way of human dialogue. Affirming nature provided a way to understand death as what gave meaning to (or took meaning from) love and life. "Nature" invoked the utopian image of humans at home with themselves and others, of an immediate community rather than the rule by artificial, autonomous systems and institutions.

After Feuerbach: Marx and Nietzsche, the Godless

Both Marx and Nietzsche, the two intellectuals who best embody the critical spirit of fin de siècle German culture, followed in the wake of Feuerbach. Marx's move beyond religion, and certainly his view of Christianity as an opiate of the people, reflected the critiques of the 1840s; Nietzsche's move beyond Christianity was deeply influenced by Wagner, and his turn against Wagner amounted to a turn against what he viewed as Christian nihilism in Wagner's later work. Both, in other words, started with the death of God. But Feuerbach's grand—and not altogether successful—gesture equating God with nature failed to satisfy the critical thinkers of the fin de siècle. Neither Marx nor Nietzsche could accept the return to nature invoked by Feuerbach. For both, history in the sense of flux and change made any bedrock assumptions about human essence questionable; for both, the world in its complexity made the relationship between fact and morality, is and ought, a problem.

Marx had already begun his critique of Feuerbach's naturalism in the 1840s, in a series of prescient notes and unpublished manuscripts; his and Engels's attacks on the "true socialists" after 1846 extended this philosophical critique of Feuerbach.[15] Marx started with a critique of idealism (strongly influenced by Feuerbach), and moved to a criticism of religion and fetishistic abstractions—but with a crucial difference. Where Feuerbach turned to general ruminations on the human in the world of nature, Marx threw himself into history: a history marked by the transhistorical place of the human in productive interaction with nature, to be sure, but still a history in which production drove development.[16] There was not a set human essence. Humans changed as their way of interacting with nature did; their mode of production, their way of producing their environment, altered human nature itself. Marx did not fall into the trap of nationalism, as had Feuerbach. He also retained a complexity in his notion of society that avoided the platitudes of naturalistic reductionism (even while ethics remained a problem). And Marx did not assume a harmonious nature: history evinced not a tendency toward harmony, but rather a tendency toward conflict. Marx's brilliance allowed him to cut through the ideological constructions around him and to lay the foundation for radical thought for the next century. To do so, however, he discarded the categories that drove the revolutionaries of the 1840s. Questions of love and death were questions of passion and pathos, not of cold, analytical rigor. His project rejected "mere" utopian thought that criticized the existing social world from the perspective either of morality or of conceptual schemes for a better world. Only the real, concrete tendencies of history itself could provide the means for radical change: "It is not enough for thought to strive for realisation, reality must itself strive towards thought." It was thus imperative for the early Marx that he find an internal source of change, such as his imagined proletariat, a class completely subject to the rules of capitalism and completely free of the illusions of past ages.[17] History itself would resolve the gap between what was and what ought to be in present society. Marx was notably never able to break fully with the humanist "warm current," in Ernst Bloch's words, of the radical tradition. But the work of thinkers like Hess, Dittmar, and Wagner reveals better the radical idea of nature that was so inspiring in Feuerbach.

For Nietzsche, too, nature also provided no escape. Whatever his use of naturalistic images, including images drawn from contemporary natural science, for Nietzsche the basic problem of meaning in human life could not be derived from nature—for nature itself was historical, changing, and provided no stable foundation for value.[18] Like Marx, Nietzsche did not fall back on some transcendental notion of value to solve his problem. History constituted humans in their concrete settings; their problem lay in finding a position, in establishing a scale of values, in short, in embracing their fate instead of seeking some transcendental way out. "Whatever has *value* in the present world," he wrote, "has it not in itself, according to its nature— nature is always value-less—but has rather been given, granted value, and *we* were the givers and granters! Only we have created the world *that concerns human beings!*"[19] Meaning and value derive from humans, not from something above humans: is this not the heart of Feuerbach's notion of the religion? Nietzsche's critique of Wagner, as Chapter 4 intimated, had a Feuerbachian ring to it: Feuerbach too would also have questioned Wagner's notion of transcendence in death that assumed the possibility of a position outside of life itself, with all the residual Christian theology.[20]

Feuerbach never attained the level of historical specificity and social theory that marked Marx's work, and his philosophical ruminations never went as far into uncharted territory as did Nietzsche's. But a similar question drove all three. Once meaning was reduced to the human, once religion was conceptualized as the result of human activity in the face of natural environment, then what happened to values, to ethics, to politics, indeed to the conception of human destiny itself? All three affirmed humans as the source of values, and all three pointed toward a conception of the world essentially alien from humans. Humans themselves had to shape their own lives within a world that in turn shaped them.

Marx and Nietzsche were, of course, just two of the many thinkers seeking to formulate a response to the loss of traditional religion—though the most penetrating. Other leading thinkers of the late nineteenth century in Germany sought new meaning in the very organization of the universe, and explicitly listed Feuerbach among their predecessors. For the biologist Ernst Haeckel, the criticisms of Feuerbach and Strauss formed the obvious starting point for any new worldview that sought to comprehend the "riddle of the universe."[21] Like Hess or Moleschott or Büchner, Haeckel found a kind of aesthetic meaning in comprehending the dynamic totality of the world; one of the leading popularizers of Darwin in Germany, he called for the unity of religion and science and asserted a basic cosmic order, the presumed cyclical process of dynamic order that constituted the totality.[22] For Friedrich Jodl, closely associated with the Ethical Culture Movement and the coeditor with Wilhelm Bolin of Feuerbach's collected works, the new age faced the imperative of reformulating ethics on the basis of a philosophical materialism. For Jodl, Feuerbach's revolutionary activities were of secondary interest; "[b]efore his prophetic gaze stood the outlines of a much greater revolution, one that reached far deeper, a revolution that would realize not only the right to a drive for happiness of individual classes, but of the broadest masses of the people"; humanity would enter into a new epoch of its historical existence.[23] The broader movement for a modern ethics extended from Haeckel's monism and Jodl's materialist ethics to other reform movements of the age, such as feminism, as Tracie Matysik has shown.[24] Dittmar had, of course, been completely forgotten in Germany by the end of the century; the calls for a reform of the basic relations between men and women, a new conception of the world, and self-imposed ideals by someone like Helene Stöcker, however, reveals deep parallels with the work of Dittmar—though Nietzsche rather than Feuerbach was her inspiration.[25] Finally, the aim to renew humanity through nationalism was part of the broader movement for reform, as one can see in Theodor Herzl's rediscovery of Hess.

The problem of the role of ethics in a modern, secular age, after all, implied the problem of how to reform the human life–world itself. Feuerbach in his village, Hess in his imagined new land of Israel, Dittmar in her new world of egalitarian gender relations, Wagner in the middle of his new opera-become-life: all were preoccupied with the construction of new social forms. As the introduction noted, these four experimented with new, esoteric worldviews, homeopathic healing, and diets. Their critiques of religion and abstraction led to new, alternative conceptions of living. Already at midcentury, one can find examples of countercultural thinking.

A direct connection can be found between Feuerbach and attempts to reform the practice of life and death at the end of the century, loosely grouped under the term *Lebensreformbewegung*, in a few cases. The Free Religious movement, discussed especially in the chapter on Dittmar earlier, for example, continued to develop in the German Empire, and closely associated with it was a new cult of cremation. Though Feuerbach himself was not concerned with the issue, the movement for cremation rather than burial implied an approach to the body and its relationship to the earth clearly distinct from that of orthodox Christianity with its belief in personal resurrection.[26] Other groups, less rationalistic, developed new cults of the sun or other chosen worldviews. It is hard to imagine Feuerbach's approving of the obsession with spirituality in the *Lebensreformbewegung*. But the point is not the specific content of the movement, which was in any case so varied that general descriptions of it are almost impossible.[27] The problem that the movement faced was Feuerbach's: what to do after traditional religion had ceased to be plausible.

For at the heart of the *Lebensreformbewegung* was the problem of what shape ethics, morality, sexuality, indeed the totality of relations between I and Thou, should take in the modern world. The world that came under attack by radicals in the 1840s had been one where the state was continuing to dominate the public sphere of politics and capital was beginning to dominate economic relations. Marx's critique of economic alienation mirrored the radical critique of political alienation. By the end of the century, Max Weber had become aware of and involved in various attempts at reforming life. He expanded Marx's analysis of the alienation essential to the capitalist economy to a number of other areas: the bureaucracy, the sciences, university life. "Love," thought of as extrasystemic, immediate contact, took on an increasingly eschatological form, as a kind of escape from systems. Weber wrote about a series of self-propelling systems that would eventually compose an iron cage of rationalism around the individual. The antibureaucratic, even antiscientific and antirationalistic, tendencies of the *Lebensreformbewegung* found their philosophical expression in Weber, despite his skepticism about the movement itself.[28] Of course, his pessimism, and indeed the era's pessimism about technical progress in general, represented a different approach to the world than Feuerbach's. The point is, however, that a counterculture organized around immediacy and authenticity, dialogue and self-expression, food and home arose in opposition to what was perceived as an alienating system of abstractions. Viewed in a broader sense, this was a reaction against the replacement of human values with functional systems.

Have we moved beyond Feuerbach today? No. Indeed, in a sense his critique of abstractions that take on a life of their own, of human alienation in modern society, has become a standard part of radicalism, whether left or right. One need only think of the different antisystem rhetorics of such disparate movements as libertarianism and antiglobalization campaigns, of the pre-1989 movements against state socialism as a system and the contemporary movements against corporate control, of the anarchist radicalism of the 1970s and the militias of the 1990s. It should also not be surprising that the turn to love might be cited as a move outside the system, whether in popular or high culture (Marcuse's radicalism of feeling in the 1970s; the invocation of Paul and communities of love in contemporary fundamentalist sects). Both the antisystemic and affective reactions against systems of control play a role in religious criticism of modernity, too. The invocation of God's rule explicitly contradicts Feuerbach's critique, but implicitly, insofar as the goal is the immediate unity of a community in love, religious antisystemic movements are not so far afield; the proximity of Hess and Dittmar to Fourier with his odd religiosity or of Wagner to a worship of the divine prince shows how thin the line is between left and right, once religion is affirmed as a means of worldly self-expression. Feuerbach's affirmation of I-Thou relationships could take the form of open dialogism, but it could also take the form of closed communities of meaning. He himself developed no criteria for judging specific communities.

These are the substantial *problems* that are with us today. Feuerbach's *method*, meanwhile, has become second nature to most in the humanities and social sciences; religion is analyzed for what it reveals about humans, not for its revelations of another, higher being. We are confronted with the difficulty of balancing on the one hand an analysis that seeks to comprehend meaning, to understand human action from the perspective of individual actors, in Weber's conception, and on the other a critical approach that questions the validity of absolute claims about God and the world. After Marx, there is no way to maintain that one can stand above the society that constructs oneself; after Nietzsche, claims to grasp scientifically the immanent processes of social development or social evolution look futile. The Feuerbachian critique of abstractions and theologizing has succeeded; the practical challenge remains.

Notes

Introduction

1. Georg Herwegh, ed., *Einundzwanzig Bogen aus der Schweiz* (Zürich: Verlag des Literarischen Comptoirs, 1843).
2. See esp. John Edward Toews, *Hegelianism: The Path toward Dialectical Humanism 1805–1841* (New York: Cambridge University Press, 1980).
3. Feuerbach to Christian Kapp, Nov. 1/3, 1837, *GW* 17:303; on the importance of Strauss's book for the educated bourgeoisie, see Rüdiger Safranski, *Romantik. Eine deutsche Affäre* (Munich: Carl Hanser, 2007), 245.
4. Karl Löwith, "Ludwig Feuerbach und der Ausgang der klassischen deutschen Philosophie" (1928), in *Sämtliche Schriften*, vol. 5, *Hegel und die Aufhebung der Philosophie im 19. Jahrhundert—Max Weber* (Stuttgart: J. B.Metzler, 1988), 4.
5. *Gedanken über Tod und Unsterblichkeit*, in *GW* 1² is the standard scholarly edition. The first edition was translated by James A. Massey as *Thoughts on Death and Immortality: From the Papers of a Thinker, along with an Appendix of Theological-Satirical Epigrams* (Berkeley: University of California Press, 1980).
6. Feuerbach, *Thoughts on Death and Immortality*, 137; Toews argues that the result was a mystical pantheism only gradually abandoned, *Hegelianism*, 192–95.
7. *Das Wesen des Christentums*, *GW* 5². Unless otherwise indicated, quotations are taken from George Eliot's 1854 translation (Amherst, NY: Prometheus, 1989) cited as *EC*.
8. I.e., an undetermined will in the case of pure reason. In the realm of law, Feuerbach stressed the way moral action was conditioned or determined by external influences or causes: see Oliver Rosbach, "Strafrecht und Gesellschaft bei Anselm von Feuerbach," *Forum historiae juris*, December 1, 2000, http://www.rewi.hu-berlin.de/FHI/zitat/0012rosbach.htm (accessed on June 30, 2008).
9. From the correspondence it appears that Feuerbach was made aware of the utopian socialists through letters from Ruge and Marx in 1844 (see the letters from Ruge to Feuerbach of Feb. 4, 1844, and May 15, 1844, and from Marx of Aug. 11, 1844, as well as Feuerbach to Friedrich Kapp, Oct. 15, 1844, all in *GW* 18:320–23, 346–52, 376–79, 395–99). A letter from Hermann Kriege to Feuerbach, April 18–19, 1845, in *GW* 19:19, suggests that Feuerbach agreed with the "true socialist" critique of society but questioned whether the masses

were ready for revolution; see also Werner Schuffenhauer, *Feuerbach und der junge Marx. Zur Entstehungsgeschichte der marxistischen Weltanschauung*, 2nd ed. (Berlin: Verlag der Wissenschaften, 1972), 127–28, and Jens Grandt, *Ludwig Feuerbach und die Welt des Glaubens* (Münster: Westfälisches Dampfboot, 2006), 115–17.

10. In English, Wolfram Siemann's (1985) *The German Revolution of 1848–49*, trans. Christiane Banerji (New York: St. Martin's, 1998) provides an overview of the basic story from a social history perspective, and remains a standard account despite the wealth of new literature coming out of the 150th anniversary of the revolution; see a similar disaggregating approach to the revolution in Jonathan Sperber's excellent *Rhineland Radicals: The Democratic Movement and the Revolution of 1848–1849* (Princeton, NJ: Princeton University Press, 1991), and Dieter Dowe, et al., eds., *Europe in 1848: Revolution and Reform*, trans. David Higgens (New York: Berghahn, 2001). Overview of the voluminous German-language literature in Hans Fenske, "Ein reichgedeckter Büchertisch: Neue Literatur zur Revolution 1848/49," *Historisches Jahrbuch* 120 (2000), 331–57.

11. Karl Löwith, *From Hegel to Nietzsche: The Revolution in Nineteenth-Century Thought*, trans. David E. Green (New York: Holt, Rinehart and Winston, 1964); Georg Lukács, *The Destruction of Reason*, trans. Peter Palmer (Atlantic Highlands, NJ: Humanities Press, 1980).

12. Löwith, *From Hegel to Nietzsche*, 183; Lenin describes the management of the planned economy as "something like the mild leadership of a conductor of an orchestra" in "The Immediate Tasks of the Soviet Government" (1918), *Selected Works in Three Volumes* (Moscow: Progress, 1977), 2:611.

13. On "Baunscheidtismus," a variety of acupuncture, see Hess to Otto Ule, Summer or Fall 1863, *Briefwechsel*, 454, referring to an article submitted to Ule's journal *Der Gedanke*; on homeopathic medicine, Hess to Sophie von Hatzfeldt, Nov. 18, 1865, *Briefwechsel*, 511.

14. As he wrote in a letter to Theodor Uhlig on Oct. 22, 1850, "Look, just as we need a water-cure to heal our bodies, so we need a fire-cure in order to remedy (i.e. destroy) the cause of our illness—a cause that is all around us," in *SL*, 219.

15. Dittmar, *Zur Charakterisirung der nordischen Mythologie im Verhältniss zu andern Naturreligionen. Eine Skizze* (Darmstadt: Leske, 1848), 23.

16. Feuerbach, "Die Naturwissenschaft und die Revolution" (1850), in *GW* 10³, 367.

17. See Bakunin, *Statism and Anarchy*, trans. and ed. Marshall S. Shatz (New York: Cambridge University Press, 1990); Bakunin praises Feuerbach for having pushed the work of destroying metaphysics as far as possible within the realm of philosophy at page 131.

18. Letter to Gustav Bäuerle, May 31, 1867, in *GW* 21:302–3, cited in Manuela Köppe, "Zur Entstehung von Ludwig Feuerbachs Schift 'Über Spiritualismus und Materialismus, besonders in Beziehung auf die Willensfreiheit,'" in

Materialismus und Spiritualismus. Philosophie und Wissenschaften nach 1848, ed. Andreas Arndt and Walter Jaeschke (Hamburg: Felix Meiner, 2000), 43–44.

19. Dittmar, *Zur Charakterisirung der nordischen Mythologie,* 4.

20. "Zur Beurteilung der Schrift: Das Wesen des Christentums'" (1842), *GW* 9³:241; Toews, *Hegelianism,* 329–30.

21. Edmund Silberner, *Moses Hess: Geschichte seines Lebens* (Leiden, The Netherlands: Brill, 1966), 5.

Chapter 1

1. Josef Winiger, *Ludwig Feuerbach: Denker der Menschlichkeit* (Berlin: Aufbau, 2004), 37, 47–48. Jens Grandt, *Ludwig Feuerbach und die Welt des Glaubens* (Münster: Westfälisches Dampfboot, 2006) 12–13, makes too much of an activist of the young Feuerbach; Alfred Schmidt, in his description of an unpolitical, loner student, who is, however, radical in his thoughts, presents a more realistic description, in his introduction to Feuerbach, *Anthropologischer Materialismus. Ausgewählte Schriften* (Frankfurt: Ullstein, 1985), 12–13.

2. Ludwig Feuerbach, *Thoughts on Death and Immortality: From the Papers of a Thinker, along with an Appendix of Theological-Satirical Epigrams,* trans. James A. Massey (Berkeley: University of California Press, 1980), 179; Grandt, *Ludwig Feuerbach,* 11–12, 27–34, who describes the anger in some parts of the *Thoughts on Death and Immortality;* John Edward Toews, *Hegelianism: The Path toward Dialectical Humanism 1805–1841* (New York: Cambridge University Press, 1980), 175–99.

3. Toews, *Hegelianism;* see also David McLellan, *The Young Hegelians and Karl Marx* (London: Macmillan, 1969), for a brief overview of the history.

4. Toews, *Hegelianism,* 131–34; and Warren Breckman, "Eduard Gans and the Crisis of Hegelianism," *Journal of the History of Ideas* 62 (2001): 543–564, with further references.

5. Toews, *Hegelianism,* 230–31, 260–70; see also Marilyn Chapin Massey, *Christ Unmasked: The Meaning of the Life of Jesus in German Politics* (Chapel Hill: University of North Carolina Press, 1983).

6. Toews, *Hegelianism,* 288–336; more sympathetic to Bauer: Harold Mah, *The End of Philosophy, the Origin of "Ideology": Karl Marx and the Crisis of the Young Hegelians* (Berkeley: University of California Press, 1987), 45–86; Douglas Moggach, *The Philosophy and Politics of Bruno Bauer* (New York: Cambridge University Press, 2003).

7. *Pierre Bayle, GW* 4²; centrality of this work to Feuerbach's development noted in Marx W. Wartofsky, *Feuerbach* (New York: Cambridge University Press, 1977), 110–34, and Winiger, *Ludwig Feuerbach,* 129–42.

8. Wartofsky, *Feuerbach,* 135–95; the article in question is "Zur Kritik der Hegelschen Philosophie," *GW* 9³:16–62.

9. Wartofsky, *Feuerbach,* 173.

10. See Todd Weir, "The Fourth Confession: Atheism, Monism, and Politics in the *Freigeistig* Movement in Berlin, 1859–1924" (PhD diss., Columbia University, 2005, 31).

11. Van A. Harvey, *Feuerbach and the Interpretation of Religion* (New York: Cambridge, 1997); Karl Löwith, *From Hegel to Nietzsche: The Revolution in Nineteenth-Century Thought,* trans. David E. Green (New York: Holt, Rinehart and Winston, 1964). The tension between the skeptic and the utopian is long standing in Feuerbach scholarship, as noted in Francesco Tomasoni, "Feuerbach und die Skepsis: Zur Relativität und Absolutheit der menschlichen Werte," in *Ludwig Feuerbach (1804–1872): Identität und Pluralismus in der globalen Gesellschaft,* ed. Ursula Reitemeyer, Takayuki Shibata, and Francesco Tomasoni (Münster: Waxmann, 2006), 33–34.

12. In general on the influence of Feuerbach, S. Rawidowicz, *Ludwig Feuerbachs Philosophie: Ursprung und Schicksal* (Berlin: Reuther und Richard, 1931); on the tension between the finite and the infinite, Benjamin Wildish Canter, "Feuerbachian Imagination and the Reversal of Hegelian Ontology in *The Essence of Christianity* (1841)" (PhD diss., Memorial University of Newfoundland, 2003), 10–11, 53; and Arsenio Ginzo Fernández, "Filosofía de la finitud y utopia en L. Feuerbach" in *O homen integral: Antropologia e utopie em Ludwig Feuerbach,* ed. Adriana Veríssima Serrão (Lisbon: Centro de Filosofia de Universidade de Lisboa, 2001), 231–56.

13. On the fundamentalist, Pietist turn in state policy—against the Hegelians—see Toews, *Hegelianism,* 245–54; David A. Barclay, *Frederick William IV and the Prussian Monarchy 1840–1861* (Oxford: Clarendon, 1995); James A. Massey, "The Hegelians, the Pietists, and the Nature of Religion," *Journal of Religion* 58 (1978): 108–29.

14. Foreword to the first edition of *Das Wesen des Christentums, GW* I²: 6. Unless otherwise indicated, quotations are taken from George Eliot's 1854 translation of the second edition of 1843 (Amherst, NY: Prometheus, 1989); cited as *EC* in the text that follows.

15. On the veiled logic of the book, Wartofsky, *Feuerbach,* 202.

16. *EC,* 271.

17. Connecting this aspect of Feuerbach to Marx, Nietzsche, and Heidegger: Ginzo Fernández, "Filosofía de la finitud y utopia en L. Feuerbach," in *O homen integral,* 231–56.

18. *EC,* 5.

19. Ibid.

20. Ibid.

21. Ibid., 6.

22. Ibid., 11.

23. "Die Grundsätze der Philosophie der Zukunft," in *GW* 9³: par. 54, 335–36; Harvey, *Feuerbach,* 144, notes parallels to Marx at his most humanist; see also Werner Schuffenhauer, *Feuerbach und der junge Marx. Zur Entstehungsgeschichte der marxistischen Weltanschauung,* 2nd ed. (Berlin: Verlag der Wissenschaften, 1972), 113–15.

24. See in particular Feuerbach, *Thoughts on Death and Immortality*, esp. 107–73, and Wartofsky, *Feuerbach*, 110, 439–40n1, on the Hegelian aspects of the work.
25. *EC*, 83.
26. A point noted already by Friedrich Albert Lange, *Geschichte des Materialismus und Kritik seiner Bedeutung in der Gegenwart* (Iserlohn: Baedeker, 1873), 284–85.
27. Canter, "Feuerbachian Imagination," 91–92.
28. *EC*, 7–8.
29. Ibid., 8.
30. Ibid., 11.
31. Ibid., 7.
32. Ibid., 11–12.
33. See, for example, ibid., xiv (preface to the second edition), where Feuerbach describes his method as a simple reversal: the dream of religion is reduced to the "simple daylight of reality and necessity."
34. Ibid., 92.
35. Ibid., 170.
36. Ibid., 171.
37. Ibid., 137–39.
38. Ibid., 71–73.
39. Ibid., 62, 147–48.
40. Ibid., 70.
41. Ibid., 178.
42. Ibid., 23.
43. Ibid., 83.
44. Ibid., 153.
45. Harvey, *Feuerbach*, 49–50.
46. "The other world is . . . the fulfillment of a wish," *EC*, 178.
47. Ibid., 29–30.
48. Max Stirner, *The Ego and Its Own*, ed. David Leopold (New York: Cambridge University Press, 1995), 55.
49. Ibid., 47. Carlo Ascheri, following a similar argument, refers to the *EC*'s primary intention as "anthropo-theist" rather than "atheist": *Feuerbachs Bruch mit der Spekulation* (Frankfurt: Europäische Verlagsanstalt, 1969), 96.
50. Further references on the German Catholics see below Chapter 3, n.2. Feuerbach himself corresponded with the German Catholic preacher Friedrich Ferdinand Kampe, but in the 1840s remained aloof from the movement, which did, after all, assert the existence of a divine creator. Indeed, in a letter of March 11, 1845, to Christian Kapp, Feuerbach referred to the movement as a "monstrosity" (*Missgeburt*) (*GW* 19:13); he softened his view in a letter from March 29, though for political reasons (*GW* 19:17). Compare, however, his more moderate comments after the revolution in a letter to Kampe of June 21, 1850, reflecting both the growing secularization of the movement and Feuerbach's respect for their actions in the revolution: *GW* 19:237–38; see also editorial comments at *GW* 19:439. The criticism of Feuerbach's humanism

and appeal to the masses by Stirner and Bauer reflected their turn in the mid-1840s to a more arcane and, in my estimation, antidemocratic ideology; compare, however, Mah, *The End of Philosophy*, 82–84, and Moggach, *The Philosophy and Politics of Bruno Bauer*.

51. *EC,* 21.
52. Ibid., 151–52.
53. Ibid., 113.
54. Ibid., 114.
55. Ibid., 116.
56. Ibid., 115.
57. Marx, "On the Jewish Question," in *MECW* 3:170, 173.
58. Further explorations in Paul Lawrence Rose, *German Question/Jewish Question: Revolutionary Antisemitism from Kant to Wagner* (Princeton, NJ: Princeton University Press, 1990).
59. *EC,* 31.
60. Ibid., 32.
61. Ibid., 114.
62. Ibid., 121.
63. Warren Breckman argues that Feuerbach was probably exposed to French socialist thought already in the 1830s in *Marx, the Young Hegelians, and the Origin of Radical Social Theory: Dethroning the Self* (New York: Cambridge University Press, 1999), 196–99; if so, however, then on the level of a general feeling rather than specific understanding.
64. *EC,* 254.
65. Harvey (*Feuerbach*, 85–86) argues that Feuerbach's critique of Judaism was not directed at a "race" and was therefore not the same as anti-Semitism. He goes on to assert that Feuerbach was not making "an invidious comparison of Judaism with Christianity but, on the contrary, was making the point, quite unrepresentative of the time, that Christianity as a religion has simply radicalized and individualized the egoism already present in Judaism." In fact, Feuerbach's account is not out of the ordinary for the time. The universalism and individualism of Christianity displaces the limitations of Judaism in a number of other radical thinkers. There is little to distinguish Feuerbach in this respect from, for example, Bruno Bauer, who argued that the overcoming of Christianity meant the prior overcoming of Judaism, and that until Jews gave up their religion they could not be emancipated: "The Jewish Problem" (1843), in Lawrence S. Stepelevich, ed., *The Young Hegelians: An Anthology* (Atlantic Highlands, NJ: Humanities, 1983), 187–97. Wartofsky (*Feuerbach*, 319–21) provides a more accurate reading of these passages. By contrast, see Rose's reading of anti-Semitism at the heart of German radicalism, an argument that allows him to make Wagner little more than an acolyte of Feuerbach in racism: *Wagner: Race and Revolution* (New Haven, CT: Yale, 1992). Distinctions within anti-Semitic thinking as well as change over time drop out of Rose's analysis, and he points to a permanent racial and anti-Semitic core. While Feuerbach's anti-Semitism was evident, it was ordinary; the radical anti-Semitism

of Richard Wagner, by contrast, would call into question the humanity of the Jews. And the distinction between Bauer and Wagner on the one hand, with their concrete, prejudice-laden images of the Jew, contrasts sharply with the images used by Feuerbach. In later years, furthermore, Feuerbach would turn against this reading and develop a more sympathetic reading of ancient Judaism, with its stronger focus on nature: Francesco Tomasoni, "Heidentum und Judentum: Vom schärfsten Gegensatz zur Annäherung. Eine Entwicklungslinie vom 'Wesen des Christenthums' bis zur 'Theogonie,'" in Walter Jaeschke and Tomasoni, ed., *Ludwig Feuerbach und die Geschichte der Philosophie* (Berlin: Akademie, 1998), 148–66, and in Chapter 5 of this book.

66. *EC,* 196.
67. Ibid., 184.
68. Ibid., 271.
69. Of the many descriptions, see, especially, the succinct statement by Endre Kiss, "Ludwig Feuerbachs Eudämonismus als philosophische und universalgeschichtliche Option," in Hans-Jürg Braun, ed., *Solidarität oder Egoismus. Studien zu einer Ethik bei und nach Ludwig Feuerbach* (Berlin: Akademie, 1994), 81–89.
70. Wartofsky puts Feuerbach's discussion of the I-Thou relationship, knowledge, and that attempt to overcome idealism in the context of Feuerbach's entire intellectual trajectory: the "dialectic of consciousness" of Hegel is gradually transformed into a dialectic of sensibility (*Feuerbach*, 20). See also Harvey, *Feuerbach*, 35.
71. *EC,* 82.
72. Ibid., 83.
73. Ibid., 82.
74. Ibid., 59.
75. McLellan, *The Young Hegelians and Karl Marx*, offers a succinct and clear chronological account.
76. "Zur Beurteilung der Schrift 'Das Wesen des Christentums,'" *GW* 9^3:229–42.
77. These texts are collected in *Entwürfe zu einer neuen Philosophie*, ed. Walter Jaeschke and Werner Schuffenhauer (Hamburg: Felix Meiner, 1996), with an extensive apparatus. Three of the four works are available in English translation: *Principles of the Philosophy of the Future*, trans. Manfred Vogel and ed. Thomas E. Wartenberg (Indianapolis, IN: Hackett, 1986); "Provisional Theses for the Reformation of Philosophy," in *The Young Hegelians: An Anthology*, trans. Lawrence S. Stepelevich (Atlantic Highlands, NJ: Humanities, 1983), 156–71. Not reliable is the translation of "Die Notwendigkeit einer Veränderung" as "The Necessity of a Reform of Philosophy" in Zawar Hanfi, trans., *The Fiery Brook: Selected Writings of Ludwig Feuerbach* (Garden City, NY: Anchor, 1972), 145–52.
78. "Notwendigkeit einer Veränderung," 120.
79. Ibid., 122; "Provisional Theses," 158–59. Predictably, Feuerbach found in Judaism the leading example of such a fate, and by implication at least seemed to assert that Judaism was sterile, dead.
80. "Notwendigkeit einer Veränderung," 123–25.
81. Ibid., 126.

82. See esp. the essays on the Württemberg constitution in Hegel, *Political Writings*, trans. T. M. Knox (New York: Oxford University Press, 1998).

83. "Provisional Theses for the Reformation of Philosophy," in *The Young Hegelians: An Anthology*, 167; see also Schuffenhauer, *Feuerbach und der junge Marx*, 45–51.

84. "Provisional Theses," 157.

85. Ibid., 158.

86. Ibid., 157.

87. Ibid., 161.

88. Ibid., 168.

89. See esp. Marx's conception of the human as a "*universal* and therefore a free being" in the 1844 manuscripts, in *Early Writings, MECW* 3:275, and his distinction between the unconscious creations of nature, such as a beehive, and conscious, human construction, in *Capital: A Critique of Political Economy, MECW* 35:188. See also Schmidt, introduction to *Anthropologischer Materialismus*, 49–51, and Jaeschke and Schuffenhauer, "Einleitung," in Ludwig Feuerbach, *Entwürfe zu einer Neuen Philosophie*, xxiii–xxiv, correcting Cold War–era attempts to reduce the relationship between Marx and Feuerbach.

90. See Karl Grün's programmatic "Feuerbach und die Socialisten" (1845), in Manuela Köppe, ed., *Ausgewählte Schriften* (Berlin: Akademie, 2006), 423–43, and Moses Hess, "Über die sozialistische Bewegung in Deutschland" (1845), in *PSS*[1], 284–306, esp. 292–95. Exceptionally clear description of "true socialism" can be seen in Heinz Pepperle's introduction to Karl Friedrich Köppen, *Ausgewählte Schriften in zwei Bänden* (Berlin: 2003), 1:52–54; and also in Francesco Tomasoni, *Ludwig Feuerbach und die nicht-menschliche Natur. Das Wesen der Religion: Die Entstehungsgeschichte des Werkes, rekonstruiert auf der Grundlage unveröffentlichter Manuskripte*, trans. Alf Schneditz (Stuttgart: Frommann-Holzboog, 1990), 32–33.

91. *Principles of the Philosophy of the Future*, 10.

92. Ibid., 12–17.

93. Ibid., 39.

94. Ibid., 64–65.

95. Ibid., 40–44.

96. The image of the porous ego in "Einige Bemerkungen über den 'Anfang der Philosophie' von Dr. J. F. Reiff" (1841), in *GW* 9[3]:151; see esp. Udo Kern's "'Individuum sein heisst . . . Kommunist sein.' Zum kommunistischen Wesen des Menschen bei Ludwig Feuerbach," in *Ludwig Feuerbach (1804–1872)*, 85–103.

97. *Principles of the Philosophy of the Future*, 52–53.

98. *EC,* 91.

99. Ibid., 92.

100. Ibid., 92.

101. As noted by Karl Löwith, "Ludwig Feuerbach und der Ausgang der klassischen deutschen Philosophie," 19. The crucial Hobbesian question of why human

should be god rather than devil to fellow human raised in Hassan Givsan, "Homo homini deus est—der Wendepunkt der Weltgeschichte," in *Ludwig Feuerbach (1804–1872)*, 67–82.

102. Feuerbach to Ruge, June 1843, *GW* 18:342–43.

103. In the context of rejecting attempts to recruit him for Marx and Ruge's new journal, Feuerbach wrote that "Germany can only be cured by poison—not by fire and sword"—a rejection of open revolution, but not of violence, see Feuerbach to Ruge, June 20, 1843, *GW* 18:272.

104. On the change, see Ascheri, *Feuerbachs Bruch*, and the introduction by Jaeschke and Schuffenhauer to Feuerbach, *Entwürfe zu einer Neuen Philosophie*, xx–xxii.

105. Ludwig Feuerbach, *The Essence of Faith According to Luther*, trans. Melvin Cherno (New York: Harper and Row, 1967), 41. Convincing argument on the centrality of this book for Feuerbach's shift to sensualism in Harvey, "Feuerbach on Luther's Doctrine of Revelation: An Essay in Honor of Brian Ferrish," *Journal of Religion* 78 (1998): 317; see also Arve Brunvoll, *"Gott ist Mensch": Die Luther-Rezeption Ludwig Feuerbachs und die Entwicklung seiner Religiosität* (Frankfurt: Peter Lang, 1996).

106. Feuerbach, *Essence of Faith*, 50; the point about Luther's turning from God to man already made in the second paragraph of the *Principles of the Philosophy of the Future*. Brunvoll, *"Gott ist Mensch,"* 103–7, investigates Feuerbach's reading of Luther and his exclusion of Calvinist accounts of an unknowable, terrifying God.

107. Feuerbach, *Essence of Faith*, 91–92.

108. Ibid., 107. Feuerbach claims to cite Luther here, but I have been unable to trace the quotation.

109. Ibid., 116–17, citing Luther.

110. Marx recognized that, publishing excerpts in the Parisian journal *Vorwärts*: see *GW* 9³:xvi–xvii, and Marx to Feuerbach, Aug. 11, 1844, *MECW* 3:354–56.

111. Letter of Jan. 27, 1845, to Otto Wigand, in *GW* 19:9. Julius Duboc, who knew Feuerbach well, read Feuerbach's response as the defensive reaction of a radical surprised to be challenged from the left, in *Das Ich und die Übrigen (Für und wider M. Stirner)* (Leipzig: Wigand, 1897), 5–10.

112. "Über das 'Wesen des Christentums' in Beziehung auf Stirners 'Der Einzige und sein Eigentum'" (1845), in GW 9³:435.

113. See esp. the critique of Feuerbach's passivity in Marx and Engels's *German Ideology, MECW* 5:40–41; Alfred Schmidt, however, argues for a more complex interaction of activity and passivity in his introduction to *Anthropologischer Materialismus*, esp. 35–43, 54–57; and Schuffenhauer, *Feuerbach und der junge Marx*, 111–12, who notes Feuerbach's critique of mechanical materialism.

114. "Wesen der Religion" (1846), in *GW* 10³: par. 2, p. 4; see esp. Tomasoni's *Ludwig Feuerbach und die nicht-menschliche Natur*, esp. chap. 1, which argues for the fundamental importance of this text in Feuerbach's coming to terms with the critiques of Stirner and Rudolf Haym.

115. Letter of Feb. 7, 1845, to Otto Wigand in *GW* 19:5.

116. Letter of Feb. 25, 1845, to Otto Wigand in *GW* 19:9. Breckman, *Marx*, 218. On the relationship with the Kapp family see Hans-Martin Sass, *Ludwig Feuerbach in Selbstzeugnissen und Bilddokumenten* (Hamburg: Rohwolt, 1978), 102–6.

117. "Die Notwendigkeit einer Veränderung," 133.

118. Feuerbach to Ruge, mid-April, 1844, *GW* 18:339.

119. "Fragmente zur Charakteristik meines philosophischen curriculum vitae," *GW* 10³:270; Winiger, *Ludwig Feuerbach*, 123.

120. Letter of Mar. 3, 1848, to Otto Wigand in *GW* 19:145. For a closer account of the following, see Jens Grandt, *Ludwig Feuerbach*, 135–58; Grandt makes of Feuerbach a more determined radical than does my analysis.

121. Letter of Mar. 11, 1845, to Christian Kapp, in *GW* 19:12.

122. Letter of Mar. 3, 1848, to Otto Wigand in *GW* 19:145–6.

123. Letter of June 6, 1848 to Bertha Feuerbach in *GW* 19:157; see also Winiger, *Ludwig Feuerbach*, 258–68, and Grün, "Redaktionelle Vorbemerkungen," in *Ausgewählte Schriften*, 742–43; Grandt paints a less passive picture, in *Ludwig Feuerbach*, 135–44.

124. Ludwig Bamberger, *Erinnerungen*, ed., Paul Nathan (Berlin: Georg Reimer, 1899), 108.

125. Letter of June 30, 1848, to Bertha Feuerbach in *GW* 19:167; Sass, *Ludwig Feuerbach*, 109.

126. Letter of July 14, 1848, to Bertha Feuerbach in *GW* 19:169–71.

127. Letter of June 6, 1848, to Bertha Feuerbach in *GW* 19:167.

128. Letter of June 6, 1848, to Wilhelmine, Elise, and Leonore Feuerbach, in *GW* 19:159.

129. Sass, *Ludwig Feuerbach*, 110–11; Erich Thies, *Ludwig Feuerbach zwischen Universität und Rathaus, oder die Heidelberger Philosophen und die 48er Revolution* (Heidelberg: Verlag Brigitte Guderjahn, 1990); Ludwig Feuerbach, *Lectures on the Essence of Religion*, trans. Ralph Manheim (New York: Harper and Row, 1967). An important part of the lectures was foreshadowed by Feuerbach's 1846 essay on "The Essence of Religion" cited above, which turned from man to nature, and from the Christian God to the pagan gods.

130. Sass, *Ludwig Feuerbach*, 110.

131. Letter of Feb. 12, 1849, to Bertha Feuerbach in *GW* 19:204.

132. Letter from Keller to Wilhelm Baumgartner of Jan. 28, 1848, in *Gesammelte Briefe*, ed., Carl Helbling (Bern: Benteli, 1950), 273–75.

133. Feuerbach, *Lectures on the Essence of Religion*, 217.

134. Grandt, *Ludwig Feuerbach*, 98–99.

135. Feuerbach, *Lectures on the Essence of Religion*, 100, 113–14, 174.

136. Ibid., 311.

137. Ibid., 274.

138. Ibid., 285.

139. Ibid., 37; Luis Miguel Arroyo, "War Feuerbach ein 'Verkenner des Bösen'? Der Humanismus Feuerbachs und der Abgrund der Existenz," in *Ludwig Feuerbach (1804–1872)*, 53–65; this interpretation directed against Karl Barth's influential interpretation in "Ludwig Feuerbach" (1920), in *Theology and Church: Shorter*

Writings, 1920–1928, trans. Louise Pettibone Smith (New York: Harper and Row, 1962), 235.

140. Feuerbach, *Lectures on the Essence of Religion*, 1–2.
141. Ibid., 100–1.
142. Ibid., 137.
143. Thies, *Ludwig Feuerbach*, 72–78.
144. Grün, "Redaktionelle Vorbemerkungen," 744; Winiger, *Ludwig Feuerbach*, 286.
145. Keller, letter to Hegi of Mar. 27, 1851, in *Gesammelte Briefe*, 290; Wolfgang Deppert, "Beziehungen zwischen Philosophie und Dichtung am Beispiel von Feuerbachs Philosophie und Kellers Dichtung," in Volker Mueller, ed., *Ludwig Feuerbach: Religionskritik und Geistesfreiheit* (Neustadt am Rübensberge: Angelika Lenz Verlag, 2004), 287–325; Barth, "Ludwig Feuerbach," 218–19, 222.

Chapter 2

1. "Fragmente zur Charakteristik meines philosophischen curriculum vitae," *GW* 10³:180.
2. "Deutschland und Frankreich," in *PSS*, 176.
3. See the letter from Kriege to Feuerbach of Apr. 18/19, 1845, referring to a now lost letter from Feuerbach, in *GW* 19:19–20. The relationship between Feuerbach and Kriege is apparent mostly through several adulatory letters sent by Kriege; Feuerbach decided in early 1845 to burn most of those letters, fearing that the police would search his home after Kriege's expulsion from Leipzig and eventual emigration to the United States. See the summary in Josef Winiger, *Ludwig Feuerbach: Denker der Menschlichkeit* (Berlin: Aufbau, 2004), 234–37, and on Kriege, see Alfred Wesselmann, *Burschenschaftler, Revolutionär, Demokrat: Hermann Kriege und die Freiheitsbewegung 1840–1850* (Osnabrück: Der Andere Verlag, 2002).
4. On faith in Hess see Shulamit Volkov, "Moses Hess: Problems of Religion and Faith," *Studies in Zionism* 3 (1982): 1–15.
5. See for example the important introduction by Theodor Zlocisti to Moses Hess, *Jüdische Schriften* (Berlin: Louis Lamm, 1905), who finds at Hess's core a "Jewish racial predisposition," "innate and inherited Messianism" (xciii); Shlomo Avineri puts Hess's Judaism at the center as well, but provides a more subtle interpretation in *Moses Hess: Prophet of Communism and Zionism* (New York: New York University Press, 1985), and Shlomo Na'aman provides a detailed reading of the messianic and emancipatory elements that run throughout Hess's work, relating them to the contexts of liberalism, Jewish emancipation, and the social question: *Emanzipation und Messianismus. Leben und Werk des Moses Hess* (Frankfurt: Campus Verlag, 1982). Kenneth Koltun-Fromm's *Moses Hess and Modern Jewish Identity* (Bloomington: Indiana University Press, 2001) examines the persistent notion of a coherent narrative of "return" in works on Hess.
6. On Hess's early life, see esp. Edmund Silberner, *Moses Hess: Geschichte seines Lebens* (Leiden: Brill, 1966) and Na'aman, *Emanzipation und Messianismus*.
7. Silberner, *Moses Hess*, 2–3; and diary entry in *NQHF*, 39.

8. Hess to M. Levy, Apr. 1831, in Moses Hess, *Briefwechsel*, 47, where he refers to himself as a "truly pious Jew, but only insofar as a pious *human*." See also Horst Lademacher, introduction to Moses Hess, *Ausgewählte Schriften* (Wiesbaden: Fourier, 1981), 8–9, quoting Hess's diaries on Judaism's supersession by Christianity, and Na'aman, *Emanzipation und Messianismus*, 42–46.

9. Silberner, *Moses Hess*, 13–14.

10. "Studien zur heiligen und profanen Geschichte" (1864), in *Jüdische Schriften*, 56.

11. Silberner, *Moses Hess*, 31–32, citing diary entries in which Hess compares himself with John the Apostle.

12. Marx and Engels, *The German Ideology*, in *MECW* 5:27.

13. Volkov, "Moses Hess," 5. Warren Breckman notes the importance of immanence to Hess, but underplays the important distinctions between Hess as a follower of Spinoza, and those in the Hegelian tradition: *Marx, the Young Hegelians, and the Origin of Radical Social Theory: Dethroning the Self* (New York: Cambridge University Press, 1999), 192–95. See also John Edward Toews, *Hegelianism: The Path toward Dialectical Humanism 1805–1841* (New York: Cambridge University Press, 1980), 238–42, on Hess's "sacred history;" he likewise places Hess too firmly in the Hegelian tradition.

14. Moses Hess, *The Holy History of Mankind and Other Writings*, ed. Shlomo Avineri (New York: Cambridge, 2004), 54–55.

15. Ibid., 19–21.

16. Ibid., 22–23.

17. Ibid., 27–32.

18. Ibid., 38. See also Breckman, *Marx*, 181–82.

19. Hess, *Holy History of Mankind*, 48–51.

20. Ibid., 44–45.

21. Ibid., 56.

22. The difference between Hess and Fourier at this point was still significant, however, as Hess still sought to find redemptive truth from within the Bible and sacred history, while Fourier derived his prophecy of the new world from a peculiar reading of the everyday world around him, which he thought betrayed the intentions of the benevolent deity. On the connection between socialist and religious utopian communities, see Michael Graetz, "Humanismus, Sozialismus und Zionismus," in Myriam Yardeni, ed., *Les juifs dans l'histoire de France* (Leiden, The Netherlands: Brill, 1980), 161–64; Carl J. Guarneri, "Reconstructing the Antebellum Communitarian Movement: Oneida and Fourierism," *Journal of the Early Republic* 16 (1996): 463–88, as well as his now-classic work *The Utopian Alternative: Fourierism in Nineteenth Century America* (Ithaca, NY: Cornell University Press, 1991), and Donald E. Pitzer, ed., *America's Communal Utopians* (Charlotte: University of North Carolina Press, 1997).

23. Hess, *Holy History of Mankind*, 72–74.

24. Ibid., 80.

25. Ibid., 80–82; later elaborated in "Socialism and Communism," in *Holy History of Mankind*, 107. Avineri notes how close this language is to Marx's famous

description of the reduction of humans to animalistic functions in his 1844 manuscripts, *Moses Hess*, 38.
26. See esp. Avineri, *Moses Hess,* 35–38.
27. Hess, *Holy History of Mankind,* 86–88.
28. Ibid., 90.
29. Ibid., 94.
30. Ibid., 89.
31. Breckman notes that Hess, along with Eduard Gans and August von Cieskowski, "linked social solidarity to millenarian expectations of a new age of humanity"; neither of the latter, however, used Old Testament rhetoric to do so: "Eduard Gans and the Crisis of Hegelianism," *Journal of the History of Ideas* 62 (2001): 543–64.
32. Hess, *Holy History of Mankind,* 74. Compare the different reading of the *Holy History* in Kultun-Fromm, *Moses Hess,* 21–26, which focuses on individual identity, alienation, and the return to Adam: stressing identity takes away from Hess's radical, transformative side.
33. Hess, *Die europäische Triarchie,* in *PSS,* 86–87.
34. Avineri, *Moses Hess,* 61, asserts that Hess drew his model of the human as species-being directly from Feuerbach in *Die europäische Triarchie,* but I have found no evidence of that borrowing.
35. Hess, *Die europäische Triarchie,* 112.
36. Ibid., 113. Breckman puts Hess into a broader context of critics of Christianity as alienation in *Marx,* 181.
37. The crisis in Cologne became a cause célèbre in the late 1830s, especially after the Young Hegelians were blamed for undermining religion and morality. See Gisela Mettele, *Bürgertum in Köln 1775–1870. Gemeinsinn und freie Assoziation* (Munich: Oldenbourg, 1998), 238–44; Thomas Nipperdey, *Deutsche Geschichte 1800–1866. Bürgerwelt und starker Staat* (Munich: C. H. Beck, 1983), 418–20; Winiger, *Ludwig Feuerbach,* 147–50; Breckman, *Marx,* 140–41; Harold Mah, *The End of Philosophy, the Origin of "Ideology": Karl Marx and the Crisis of the Young Hegelians* (Berkeley: University of California Press, 1987), 107–10.
38. Hess, *Die europäische Triarchie,* 126–27.
39. Ibid., 139–40.
40. Ibid., 141–42.
41. Ibid., 128, 142–43.
42. Ibid., 127.
43. Ibid., 143–44; Silberner, *Moses Hess,* 81; Silberner also notes how distanced Hess felt from Judaism in the early 1840s (ibid., 111).
44. Silberner, *Moses Hess,* 82, argues that *The European Triarchy* expressed Hess's increasingly radical views on private property in subdued fashion to avoid the censors.
45. Hess, *Die europäische Triarchie,* 124–26.
46. Of the many accounts of Hess's encounter with Feuerbach, see esp. Silberner, *Moses Hess,* 113, 128, 190–91, 196–97, 199–200; Georg Lukács's dogmatic critique of 1926, "Moses Hess and the Problems of Idealist Dialectics," in

Political Writings 1919–1929, trans. Rodney Livingstone (London: New Left Books, 1972), 181–223; Emil Hammacher, "Zur Würdigung des 'wahren' Sozialismus," *Archiv für die Geschichte des Sozialismus und der Arbeiterbewegung* 1 (1911): 41–100; and more recently the remarks of Hou Cai, "Moses Hess und Ludwig Feuerbach," and Junji Kanda, "Moses Hess und der gescheiterte Weg von Hegel zu Feuerbach," both in Hans-Jürg Braun, et al., eds., *Ludwig Feuerbach und die Philosophie der Zukunft* (Berlin: Akademie, 1990), 593–642.

47. "Deutschland und Frankreich in Bezug auf die Centralisationsfrage," in *PSS*, 176.

48. Silberner, *Moses Hess*, 91–104.

49. Silberner and Na'aman give the best summaries of Hess's activities.

50. "Philosophie der Tat," in *PSS*, 210.

51. Ibid., 210–211.

52. "Über die sozialistische Bewegung in Deutschland," in *PSS*, 287; "Die letzten Philosophen," in *PSS*, 384. In a sense, this criticism was misplaced, as Grandt has argued in a different context, since it had as much to do with temperament as with ideas: *Ludwig Feuerbach*, 73–105, esp. 77–78.

53. "Philosophie der That," in *PSS*, 213.

54. Feuerbach, "Provisional Theses for the Reformation of Philosophy," in Lawrence S. Stepelevich, ed., *The Young Hegelians: An Anthology* (Atlantic Highlands, NJ: Humanities, 1983), 156–58.

55. "Über die sozialistische Bewegung in Deutschland," in *PSS*, 285.

56. "Über das Geldwesen," in *PSS*, 337–38.

57. "Die Eine und ganze Freiheit!," in *PSS*, 227.

58. Ibid., 228.

59. Ibid., 228–29.

60. "Briefe aus Paris," in *PSS*, 270.

61. Ibid., 268–69; "Über die sozialistische Bewegung in Deutschland," in *PSS*, 288.

62. Ibid., 293; Andreas Arndt, "'Neue Unmittelbarkeit': Zur Aktualisierung eines Konzepts in der Philosophie der Vormärz," in Walter Jaeschke, ed., *Philosophie und Literatur im Vormärz: Der Streit um die Romantik (1820–1854)* (Hamburg: Felix Meiner, 1998), 220–21.

63. "Über die Noth in unserer Gesellschaft und deren Abhülfe," in *PSS*, 318.

64. "Fortschritt und Entwicklung," in *PSS*, 284.

65. "Über die Noth . . . ," in *PSS*, 313.

66. "Über das Geldwesen," in *PSS*, 334.

67. Ibid., 324, 337.

68. Ibid., 342.

69. "Briefe aus Paris," in *PSS*, 266.

70. "Philosophie der That," in *PSS*, 218.

71. "Über das Geldwesen," in *PSS*, 339.

72. "Die letzten Philosophen," in *PSS*, 388.

73. "Qu'est ce que la Proprieté? Par P. J. Proudhon," in *PSS*, 258.

74. "Was wir wollen," in *PSS*, 235.

75. Ibid., 235. See also Hammacher, "Zur Würdigung des 'wahren' Sozialismus," 70–72, 77, on the end of politics in "true socialism."
76. "Was wir wollen," in *PSS*, 235: "Jede neue Schöpfung ist ein Sprung, geht aus dem Nichts, der Negation der alten Zustände hervor." See also "Philosophie der That," in *PSS*, 216.
77. "Die letzten Philosophen," in *PSS*, 389. Hess included Feuerbach in this critique from 1845, the same time when Hess was cooperating with Marx and Engels to develop the arguments of *The German Ideology*. But his criticism of Feuerbach remained ad hominem: that Feuerbach remained an individual thinker and did not himself take action (ibid., 384). This was a qualitatively different kind of criticism than the ones leveled against Bauer and Stirner, whose very theories were aimed against those calling for social change.
78. "Philosophie der That," in *PSS*, 225.
79. Hess, "Socialism and Communism," in *Holy History of Mankind*, 107.
80. Ibid., 110–11.
81. "Über das Geldwesen," in *PSS*, 330.
82. "Über die sozialistische Bewegung in Deutschland," in *PSS*, 289.
83. See esp. Dieter Dowe, *Aktion und Organisation. Arbeiterbewegung, sozialistische und kommunistische Bewegung in der preussischen Rheinprovinz 1820–1852* (Hanover: Verlag für Literatur und Zeitgeschehen, 1970); see esp. Engels's language in "Progress of Social Reform on the Continent," in *MECW* 3:392–408.
84. See esp. "Bestimmung des Menschen," in *PSS*, 275–77, for an argument by Hess on these lines.
85. *The German Ideology*, in *MECW* 5:23, against the Young Hegelians, and the long-winded attack on the "true socialists" in ibid., 453–539, esp. 466–67.
86. "Über das Geldwesen," in *PSS*, 331.
87. Ibid., 345.
88. Paul Lawrence Rose, *German Question/Jewish Question: Revolutionary Antisemitism from Kant to Wagner* (Princeton, NJ: Princeton University Press, 1990), 313–17.
89. "Über das Geldwesen," in *PSS*, 333.
90. [Zwei Reden über Kommunismus], in *PSS*, 352.
91. "Über die Noth . . . ," in *PSS*, 320.
92. "Über das Geldwesen," in *PSS*, 334.
93. "Qu'est ce que la Proprieté? Par P.J. Proudhon," in *PSS*, 258.
94. "Über die Noth," in *PSS*, 314–15.
95. "Bestimmung der Menschen," in *PSS*, 277.
96. "Fortschritt und Entwicklung," in *PSS*, 284.
97. [Zwei Reden über Kommunismus], in *PSS*, 349–50.
98. Charles Fourier, *The Theory of the Four Movements*, ed. Gareth Stedman Jones and Ian Patterson (New York: Cambridge University Press, 1996), 50.
99. Ernst Bloch's attempt to address the problem of entelechy in the context of a crude, power-oriented state socialism in the German Democratic Republic is relevant here. Few socialists have understood as well as Bloch the intellectual contexts and problems of German socialism at its origin. See Peter C. Caldwell,

Dictatorship, State Planning, and Social Theory in the German Democratic Republic (New York: Cambridge University Press, 2003), 97–140.

100. "Rother Kathechismus für das deutsche Volk," in *PSS*, 448.

101. "Wesen der Religion," in *GW* 10³:52.

102. In this sense, Hess never made the complete break with Hegelian historicism that Feuerbach did, who emphasized the gap between the immediate individual and the species: Kanda, "Moses Hess," 622–23, 641–42.

103. See esp. "Die letzten Philosophen," in *PSS*, 384, 393; Marx, "Theses on Feuerbach," Thesis 5, in *MECW* 5:7; Marx, "Circular against Kriege," in *MECW* 6:35–51.

104. Hess, "Philosophie der That," in *PSS*, 213; Marx's critique of Proudhon from the *Economic and Philosophical Manuscripts*, in *MECW* III: 280: "Society is then conceived as an abstract capitalist." Hess, "Über die Noth . . . ," in *PSS*, 325, writes of a new "oriental despotism" of the French socialists. On the context of these discussions, see Na'aman, *Moses Hess*, 194–95.

105. Hess, "Entwurf" of 1844, in *NQHF*, 45; Marx, "Economic and Philosophic Manuscripts," 357, on the self-mediated birth of mankind.

106. Hess, "Entwurf" of 1844, in *NQHF*, 54; "Über die Noth in unserer Gesellschaft," in *PSS*, 322, and esp. "Über das Geldsystem," in *PSS*, 339ff.

107. "Qu'est ce que la Proprieté," in *PSS*, 260–61.

108. "Über die Noth in unserer Gesellschaft," in *PSS*, 314–15.

109. Hess, "Entwurf" of 1844, in *NQHF*, 46; see also "Über die Noth in unserer Gesellschaft," in *PSS*, 315.

110. "Über die Noth in unserer Gesellschaft," in *PSS*, 320; see also Hess, "A Communist Credo," in *Holy History of Mankind*, 125, on a revolutionary "religion of love and humanity."

111. Hess to Marx, July 28, 1846, in *Briefwechsel*, 165.

112. Marx, "Critique of Hegel's Philosophy of Right. Introduction" (1843), in *MECW* 3:186; "Economic and Philosophic Manuscripts," in *MECW* 3:280.

113. Marx and Engels, "Manifesto of the Communist Party," in *MECW* 6:494; opposite argument in Lukács, "Moses Hess"—who, however, is completely on target in his complaints about Hess's turn to "all kinds of wildly mythological, cosmic or racial theories" to support his moralizing call for harmony (222).

114. On the Weitling affair and Hess's reaction, see Na'aman, *Moses Hess*, 199–201.

115. On the authorship of different parts of *The German Ideology*, and on Hess's connection with Marx, proximity to Marx in Brussels, and eventual break with him, see Silberner, *Moses Hess*, 249; Na'aman, *Moses Hess*, 180–81, notes that Engels subverted Hess's contribution, providing a different title that implied that Hess was the main object of attack rather than the author of the attack. "Die letzten Philosophen" translated as "The Recent Philosophers" in *The Young Hegelians*, 359–75.

116. "Folgen einer Revolution des Proletariats," in *PSS*, 427–44; the second article, which contains the parallels with Marx (noted by Avineri), is translated in *Holy History of Mankind*, 128–35.

117. See Silberner, *Moses Hess,* 273–82, and Na'aman, *Moses Hess,* 204–8; Mönke provides context from a position sympathetic to Marx and Engels, in "Einleitung," *PSS,* xcvi–xcvii.
118. "Rother Katechismus für das deutsche Volk," in *PSS,* 448. As late as 1847, Engels was still using the form of a catechism to present the position of the Communists: Herwig Förder and Martin Hundt, "Zur Vorgeschichte des Kommunistischen Manifests: Der Entwurf des 'Kommunistischen Glaubensbekenntnis' vom Juni 1847," *Die bürgerlich-demokratische Revolution von 1848/49 in Deutschland* (Dadiz: Topos, 1978), 243–75.
119. Ibid., 456.
120. Cited from an unpublished manuscript from Feb. 1848 in Silberner, *Moses Hess,* 283.
121. Jürgen Herres, *1848/49: Revolution in Köln* (Cologne: Janus, 1998), 15–20.
122. Herres, *1848/49,* 48–53, Jonathan Sperber, *Rhineland Radicals: The Democratic Movement and the Revolution of 1848–1849* (Princeton, NJ: Princeton University Press, 1991), 211–13, and 224–30, which provides an excellent and unflattering portrait of Gottschalk.
123. Full account in Silberner, *Moses Hess,* 283–301.
124. Silberner, *Moses Hess,* 290–91, quoting a journalistic report by Hess from June 28, 1848.
125. Hess, "A Communist Credo," 126.
126. "Bestimmung des Menschen" (1844), in *PSS,* 276.
127. Silberner, *Moses Hess,* 167–69, finds no evidence to back up the claim that Sybille Pesch was a prostitute; Hess's family and the police, however, believed this to be the case, probably because of her social background.
128. Hess to Moleschott, Dec. 18, 1853, in *Briefwechsel,* 290: on his aim to ground the history of humanity in the natural sciences. See also Lademacher, "Einleitung," 36.
129. Silberner, *Moses Hess,* 338–39; see also the statement to this effect in Hess's important article series "Naturwissenschaften und Gesellschaftslehre," *Das Jahrhundert* 1 (1856): 258.
130. Hess, "Genesis des kosmischen, organischen und sozialen Lebens. Ein Versuch, Natur und Geschichte in ihrer Einheit darzustellen" (1855), in *NQHF,* 60.
131. "Naturwissenschaften und Gesellschaftslehre," *Das Jahrhundert* I (1856), 245; Hess, "Genesis des kosmischen . . . ," in *NQHF,* 64
132. Hess, "Genesis des kosmischen . . . ," in *NQHF,* 64. The reference to the law of gravity as a basis for harmony throughout the universe is in Fourier as well: *The Theory of the Four Movements,* 16.
133. "Entstehungs- und Entwicklungsgeschichte," *Das Jahrhundert* 2 (1857), 864.
134. Hess, "Genesis des kosmischen . . . ," in *NQHF,* 67.
135. Ibid., 58–59.
136. "Entstehungs- und Entwicklungsgeschichte," *Das Jahrhundert,* 866.
137. Andreas W. Daum, *Wissenschaftspopularisierung im 19. Jahrhundert. Bürgerliche Kultur, naturwissenschaftliche Bildung und die deutsche Öffentlichkeit 1848–1914* (Munich: Oldenbourg, 1998), esp. 193–235.

138. See the letter from Martin May to Hess, Oct. 12, 1856, in *Briefwechsel*, 316, inviting Hess to contribute to *Das Jahrhundert*; and from Friedrich August Reckahn to Hess, Jan. 10, 1857, on Hess's project of combining social and natural sciences, in *Briefwechsel*, 320–21.

139. Mathilde Reichardt, *Wissenschaft und Sittenlehre. Briefe an Jakob Moleschott* (Gotha: Hugo Schenke, 1856).

140. Hess, "Naturwissenschaften und Gesellschaftslehre," *Das Jahrhundert* II (1857), 287. See also Hess's great admiration for Marx—combined with criticism of his authoritarian character—in Hess's letter to Herzen from the beginning of Apr. 1859, *Briefwechsel*, 256. This respect for Marx remained until the end of Hess's life—but also a growing criticism of Marx's tendency to work with abstract categories like "wage labor" rather than to confront practical methods of implementing collective production such as worker cooperatives: see Hess's letter to Johann Philipp Becker of Aug. 10, 1869, in *Briefwechsel*, 584–86.

141. The critique of philosophical and financial speculation appears often; see for example "Populäre naturwissenschaftliche Schriftsteller," *Das Jahrhundert* 2 (1857), 1120, 1133–34.

142. *Grundrisse*, in *MECW* 18:159.

143. Marx, *Capital*, in *MECW* 35:8, 10.

144. "Physische Beschaffenheit und Geschichte der Weltkörper," *Das Jahrhundert* 2 (1857), 703, 410.

145. Hess, "Der deutsche Humanismus," *Das Jahrhundert* 2 (1857), 1051.

146. Ibid., 1055–56.

147. Note also Hess's rejection of Schopenhauer, whose work he correctly saw as an abstract Christian rejection of the world: *The Revival of Israel: Rome and Jerusalem, the Last Nationalist Question*, trans. Meyer Waxman (Lincoln: University of Nebraska Press, 1995), 238–40, cited hereafter as *Rome and Jerusalem*. Hess likewise left unanswered Schopenhauer's challenge to the assumption that there was any meaning in the universe.

148. "Briefe über Israels Mission," *Jüdische Schriften*, 41–42. See also Hess's letter to Leopold Löw from the first half of 1862, in which he criticizes radical (i.e., liberal) Judaism for not being "radical" enough, for retaining abstract concepts of theology rather than turning to the "natural makeup" (*Naturanlage*) of the Jewish race (*Volk*), in *Briefwechsel*, 384–85.

149. On the context of his turn, Rose, *German Question/Jewish Question*, 318–19.

150. Hess, "A Communist Credo," 124, 125.

151. Hess, *Rome and Jerusalem*, 87.

152. Ibid., 45.

153. Ibid., 47–48, 64–65.

154. Ibid., 100–1.

155. Indeed, in a letter of Jan. 2, 1836, to Wolfgang Menzel, Hess states that "I know little more about my mother than that I bitterly cried upon her death," *Briefwechsel*, 50. For a general critique of these claims, see Na'aman, *Moses Hess*, 32–33.

156. Silberner, *Moses Hess*, 387, 467.
157. Hess, *Rome and Jerusalem*, 88.
158. Indispensable guide to the tradition of radical anti-Jewish thought: Rose, *German Question/Jewish Question*.
159. See the account in Silberner, *Moses Hess*, 242–45; and Na'aman, *Moses Hess*, 184–85. For more on the context, and on the unresolved question of how much Hess's critique of anti-Semitism already existed during the Damascus Affair in 1840, see Silberner, *Moses Hess*, 62–64; Jonathan Frankel, *The Damascus Affair: "Ritual Murder," Politics, and the Jews in 1840* (New York: Cambridge University Press, 1997), 323–25, and the critique by Kultun-Fromm, *Moses Hess*, 51.
160. Mikhail Bakunin, *Statism and Anarchy,* 12; and Fourier, *The Theory of the Four Movements,* 233.
161. Hess, *Briefwechsel,* 377.
162. Hess, *Rome and Jerusalem,* 58–60; and Zlocisti, "Vorwort," *Jüdische Schriften.*
163. Zlocisti, introduction to *Jüdische Schriften,* cii.
164. Hess, *Rome and Jerusalem,* 99–100.
165. Ibid., 93–95.
166. Ibid., 104–5.
167. Explicitly stated in "Mein Messiasglaube" (1862), in *Jüdische Schriften,* 6–7: "Religion, philosophy, and politics leave me cold when they do not help the situation of the working classes through institutions that put an end to all caste spirit and class rule. . . . The conservative observances of Judaism only have a significance for us Jews, namely, that of conserving our nationality for future creations."
168. Hess, *Rome and Jerusalem,* 141–43.
169. Ibid., 52. See also "Briefe über Israels Mission," 29–30 denouncing German liberal Judaism's alleged copying of Protestant rationalism, radical individualism, and the loss of any connection to the nation. There he also sees as the essence of Christianity the separation of the individual from all social bonds, be they family, fatherland, or humanity (37–38). See also "Noch ein Wort über meine Missionserfüllung" (1865), *Jüdische Schriften,* 68–69.
170. Hess, *Rome and Jerusalem,* 46–47; and "Einleitung in die 'Religiöse Revolution im XIX Jahrhundert' von François Huet" (1868), in *Jüdische Schriften,* 99: "Hier ist nicht das Individuum, sondern die Nation unsterblich."
171. Ibid., 214; and "Briefe über Israels Mission," 39–40n. against the German and French materialists, who fail to account for religion and to search for a higher intelligence in the universe. See also Berthold Auerbach's telling criticism of Hess's reliance on subjective categories to sense the next stage of world history, in his letter of Apr. 8, 1861, *Briefwechsel,* 375–76.
172. Ibid., 252; on Hess's polygenetic theory, Kultun-Fromm, *Moses Hess,* 76–77, 80–81.
173. Hess, *Rome and Jerusalem,* 68–69; Hess would become more critical a year later: "Einleitung," 104–5. Hess's secret letter to Napoleon III of March 1859,

of which only a draft exists, promised that German Rhinelanders held secret sympathies for the French; that was probably intended strategically rather than as a statement of fact. See Hess, *Briefwechsel,* 357–62, as well as Hess's letter to Friedrich Hermann Semmig of Apr. 27, 1859, in ibid., 363–67, which lays out clearly the possibility that Napoleon's actions in support of Italian unification could be due to fear, vanity, or opportunism rather than sincere belief. Whatever Napoleon's intentions, Hess argued, he was still the "executor of the estate of a deceased republic." See also "Rechte der Arbeit," a lecture that Hess held before Lassalleans in the Rhineland in 1863, where he praises Napoleon III's recognition of the rights of labor against the bourgeoisie: *Ausgewählte Schriften,* 354. Hess rejected the overtly monarchist intentions of Lassalle's followers, however: Bernhard Becker to Hess, Jan. 17, 1868, in *Briefwechsel,* 533.

174. Hess, *Rome and Jerusalem,* 148–49, 156–57, 168–69, 122–23, 159.

175. Ibid., 226; see also his criticism of racial domination, as expressed in both Panslavism and Pangermanism, in a letter to *Volksstaat* of Aug. 21, 1870, in *Briefwechsel,* 604–5.

176. "Rechte der Arbeit," reprinted in *Ausgewählte Schriften,* 346–65; Silberner, *Moses Hess,* 361–67; and Na'aman, *Moses Hess,* 276–98 provide contextual readings of Hess's "red Bonapartism." See also Hess's diary entry from 1852, in which he already sees an opening for dictatorship once the proletariat has proven unable to take power, cited in Lademacher, "Einleitung," 33.

177. Letter to the *Social-Demokrat,* Jan. 20, 1867, in *Briefwechsel,* 535; and letter to Johann Philipp Becker of Oct. 12, 1868, in *Briefwechsel,* 563–64.

178. Hess to Lassalle, Dec. 9, 1863, in *Briefwechsel,* 458–60.

179. On race and society, see "Briefe über Israels Mission," 19–20, and his posthumous work, *Dynamische Stofflehre. I. Kosmischer Theil. Allgemeine Bewegungserscheinungen und ewiger Kreislauf des kosmischen Lebens* (Paris: Verlag von Mme. Syb. M. Hess Wittwe, 1877), 38–39, 44–45.

180. Hess, *Rome and Jerusalem,* 165.

181. Hess, *Briefwechsel,* 241.

182. Fourier, *Theory of the Four Movements,* 282–88.

183. Hess, *Briefwechsel,* 243.

184. This is the stated purpose of *Dynamische Stofflehre,* 9–10; see also ibid., 15, on the eventual overcoming of myth.

185. Silberner, *Moses Hess,* 355–57; Hess to Otto Ule, Summer or Fall 1863, in *Briefwechsel,* 454.

186. Indeed, *Dynamische Stofflehre,* chap. 1 seeks to combine all of these ideals into a coherent totality that must culminate in social democracy (esp. 46–47).

187. "Wesen der Natur," *GW* 10^3:51–52 (par. 43).

188. Ludwig Feuerbach, *The Essence of Faith According to Luther,* trans. Melvin Cherno (New York: Harper and Row, 1967), 79.

Chapter 3

1. Malwida von Meysenbug, *Memoiren einer Idealistin*, 6th ed. (Berlin: Schuster und Loeffler, 1900), 267, and the discussion of her use of Feuerbach in Ann Taylor Allen, *Feminism and Motherhood in Germany, 1800–1914* (New Brunswick, NJ: Rutgers University Press, 1991), 54–55; Gabriele Schneider, "Die Emanzipation des Individuums. Fanny Lewald und der Junghegelianismus," in Lars Lambrecht, ed., *Philosophie, Literatur und Politik vor den Revolutionen von 1848. Zur Herausbildung der demokratischen Bewegungen in Europa* (Frankfurt: Peter Lang, 1996), 525–40; in the same volume, see Irina Hundt, "Junghegelianer-Frauenbewegung. Eine Fragestellung zum Problem des Zusammenhangs," 511–24; Martin Henkel and Rolf Taubert, *"Das Weib im Conflict mit den socialen Verhältnissen": mathilde franziska anneke und die erste deutsche frauenzeitung* (Berlin: edition egalité, 1976), 15. For an overview of women feminist writers who became involved with revolutionary publishing, see Marion Freund, *"Mag der Thron in Flammen glühn!" Schriftstellerinnen und die Revolution von 1848/49* (Königstein/Taunus: Ulrike Helmer, 2004); see esp. 68–71 on Louise Aston and her connection to the Young Hegelians in Berlin.
2. On the German Catholics, see Friedrich Wilhelm Graf, *Die Politisierung des religiösen Bewusstseins. Die bürgerlichen Religionsparteien im deutschen Vormärz: Das Beispiel des Deutschkatholizismus* (Stuttgart: Frommann-Holzboog, 1978); Horst Groschopp, *Dissidenten. Freidenkerei und Kultur in Deutschland* (Berlin: Dietz, 1997), 82–91; Todd Weir, "The Fourth Confession: Atheism, Monism, and Politics in the Freigeistig Movement in Berlin, 1859–1924" (PhD diss., Columbia University, 2005); Werner Schuffenhauer, "Feuerbach und die freireligiöse Bewegung seiner Zeit," and Eckhart Pilick, "Bewusstsein des Unendlichen—Feuerbachs Religionskritik und die Freie Religion," both in *Religionskritik und Geistesfreiheit*, ed. Volker Mueller (Neustadt: Angelika Lenz Verlag, 2004), 33–42, 79–113; and the extensive work by Catherine Prelinger: "A Decade of Dissent in Germany: A Historical Study of the Society of Protestant Friends and the German-Catholic Church" (PhD diss., Yale University Press, 1954); Catherine Prelinger, "Religious Dissent, Women's Rights, and the Hamburger Hochschule für das weibliche Geschlecht in Mid-Nineteenth-Century Germany," *Church History* 45 (1976): 42–55; and Catherine Prelinger, *Charity, Challenge, and Change: Religious Dimensions of the Mid-Nineteenth-Century Women's Movement in Germany* (New York: Greenwood, 1987). On their approach to women, in addition to Prelinger, see Andrea Lotz, "'Die Erlösung des weiblichen Geschlechts. Frauen in deutsch-katholischen Gemeinden," in Carola Lipp, ed., *Schimpfende Weiber und patriotischen Jungfrauen. Frauen im Vormärz und in der Revolution 1848/49* (Moos: Elster, 1986), 232–47.
3. "Erwiderung," in *Das Wesen der Ehe von Louise Dittmar nebst einigen Aufsätzen über die soziale Reform der Frauen* (Leipzig: Wigand, 1849), 112; this book, cited hereafter as *WdE*, contains all or most of what Dittmar published in her short-lived journal *Soziale Reform*, all copies of which have now been lost.

4. For example, Dagmar Herzog in her *Intimacy and Exclusion: Religious Politics in Pre-Revolutionary Baden* (Princeton, NJ: Princeton University Press, 1996), 154–55.

5. Louise Dittmar, *Der Mensch und sein Gott in und ausser dem Christenthum* (Offenbach: André, 1846), which states on the title page that the work was written "von einem Weltlichen."

6. Georg Simmel, "Female Culture," in Guy Oakes, trans., *Georg Simmel: On Women, Sexuality, and Love* (New Haven, CT: Yale University Press, 1984), 65–101; Gabriele Käfer-Dittmar makes clear the power relation that Simmel obscures: Dittmar "usurped a purely male domain," *Louise Dittmar (1807–1884). Un-erhörte Zeitzeugnisse* (Darmstadt: Justus-von-Liebig Verlag, 1992), 22.

7. Ruth-Ellen Boettcher Joeres, *Respectability and Deviance: Nineteenth-Century German Women Writers and the Ambiguity of Representation* (Chicago: University of Chicago Press, 1998), 83–85.

8. See esp. Käfer-Dittmar's introduction to *Louise Dittmar (1807–1884);* Christine Nagel, *"In der Seele das Ringen nach Freiheit"—Louise Dittmar. Emanzipation und Sittlichkeit im Vormärz und in der Revolution 1848/49* (Königstein/Taunus: Ulrike Helmer, 2005); Christina Klausmann, "Louise Dittmar (1807–1884): Ergebnisse einer biographischen Spurensuche," and Ruth-Ellen Boettcher Joeres, "Spirit in Struggle: The Radical Vision of Louise Dittmar (1807–1884)," both in *Out of Line/Ausgefallen: The Paradox of Marginality in the Writings of Nineteenth-Century German Women,* ed. Joeres and Marianne Burkhard, Amsterdamer Beiträge zur neueren Germanistik 28 (Amsterdam: Rodopi, 1989), 17–29, 279–301; Herzog, *Intimacy and Exclusion,* 140–66.

9. "Erwiderung," 109.

10. Nagel, *"In der Seele,"* 57.

11. Ibid., 53–55.

12. Ibid., 70.

13. Ibid., 58.

14. Ibid., 68–9; Nagel also notes that the Leske family held its own salon. It cannot be accidental that her first two works were published by the Leske Verlag. See also Carola Lipp on the opening up of public spaces for women before 1848: "Frauen und Öffentlichkeit. Möglichkeiten und Grenzen politischer Partizipation im Vormärz und in der Revolution 1848/49," in *Schimpfende Weiber,* 271–307.

15. Klausmann, "Louise Dittmar," 34.

16. On the uses of the "German Michel" during the revolutionary years, see Karl Riha, "Deutscher Michel: Zur literarischen und karikaturistischen Ausprägung einer nationalen Allegorie im neunzehnten Jahrhundert," in Jürgen Link and Wulf Wülfing, eds., *Nationale Mythen und Symbole in der zweiten Hälfte des neunzehnten Jahrhunderts* (Stuttgart: Klett-Cotta, 1991), 146–71.

17. "Erwiderung," 110.

18. See Wilhelm Schulz, *Die wahrhaftige Geschichte vom deutschen Michel und seinen Schwestern* (Zurich: Verlag des literarischen Comptoirs, 1843).

19. Walter Grab, *Ein Mann der Marx Ideen gab. Wilhelm Schulz. Weggefährte Georg Büchners. Demokrat der Paulskirche* (Dusseldorf: Droste, 1979).
20. Noted by Herzog, *Intimacy and Exclusion,* 147.
21. Louise Dittmar, *Bekannte Geheimnisse* (Darmstadt: Leske, 1845), 1–2.
22. Ibid., 3. In 1849, Dittmar continued to criticize a one-sided education oriented toward learning how to earn a living (*Brodstudium*) rather than humanity "Der Selbstzweck der Menschheit," in *WdE,* 7–8.
23. Dittmar, *Bekannte Geheimnisse,* 4.
24. Ibid., 29–32.
25. Ibid., 36; on the surprising rebellion of the apes in the fable, see Joeres, "Spirit in Struggle," 290. Translation of the fable in *The Queen's Mirror: Fairy Tales by German Women, 1780–1900,* ed. and trans. Shawn C. Jarvis and Jeannine Blackwell (Lincoln: University of Nebraska Press, 2001), 197–99.
26. Dittmar, *Bekannte Geheimnisse,* 45.
27. Louise Dittmar, *Vier Zeitfragen. Beantwortet in einer Versammlung des Mannheimer Montag–Vereins* (Offenbach: André, 1847), 23.
28. Dittmar, "Religion und Philosophie," in *Skizzen und Briefe aus der Gegenwart* (Darmstadt: Leske, 1845), 22–23.
29. On "oriental" stagnation, see ibid., 23.
30. Dittmar, "Gewinn der Uebereinstimmung," in *Skizzen und Briefe,* 22: "But now I am in accord with myself."
31. Dittmar, "Freiheit der Ueberzeugung," in *Skizzen und Briefe,* 47.
32. Ludwig Feuerbach, *The Essence of Faith According to Luther,* trans. Melvin Cherno (New York: Harper and Row, 1967), 91–94; Feuerbach, *EC,* 14.
33. Dittmar, "Notwendigkeit des Handelns," in *Skizzen und Briefe,* 27.
34. Letter from Dittmar to Moses Hess of July 21, 1845, in *NQHF,* 96–97; on Dittmar and Grün, see Manuela Köppe, introduction to Grün, *Ausgewählte Schriften,* ed. Manuela Köppe, 2 vols (Berlin: Akademie, 2006), 184–85; on Schulz, Gabriele Käfer-Dittmar, introduction to *Louise Dittmar,* 22–23, and Schulz's use of Proudhon and others in *Die Bewegung der Produktion. Eine geschichtlich-statistische Abhandlung zur Grundlegung einer neuen Wissenschaft des Staats und der Geschichte* (Zürich: Verlag des literarischen Comptoirs, 1843).
35. Dittmar, "Arbeit und Genuss," *Skizzen und Briefe,* 29; Hess, "Socialism and Communism," in *The Holy History of Mankind and Other Writings,* ed. Shlomo Avineri (New York: Cambridge University Press, 2004), 107.
36. Dittmar, "Consequenz," in *Skizzen und Briefe,* 30–31.
37. Dittmar, "Besteuerung der Armen," in *Skizzen und Briefe,* 72; the criticism of modernity as a "system of isolation" reappears in 1849, in "Die Girondisten," in *WdE,* 4.
38. Herzog, *Intimacy and Exclusion,* 145, Nagel, *"In der Seele,"* 116–18; Nagel notes Dittmar's critique of a leveling communism, on page 112 (see "Die Girondisten," 4); but this critique did not distinguish her from Grün, from Hess, even from Karl Marx, all of whom criticized the leveling tendencies of the "crude communists" of the French Revolution.

39. Dittmar, "Gewinn der Uebereinstimmung," 33–34.
40. Dittmar, "Immer bleibt für die Frau etwas Unfreiheit," in *Skizzen und Briefe,* 87–88; "Die geträumte männliche Natur," in ibid., 94–95, on the mistake of trying to determine women's nature in advance on the basis of masculine assumptions.
41. Grün, "Ueber Wahre Bildung" (1844), in *Ausgewählte Schriften,* 408. Criticisms by Marx and others have made clear how poor Grün's work on social theory was. His criticisms of contemporary sexism and anti-Semitism, however, have been ignored—also by latter-day readers of the Young Hegelians. See, for example, Grün's trenchant criticism of the prejudices and poor reasoning in Bruno Bauer's anti-Semitic work on the Jews: *Die Judenfrage: Gegen Bruno Bauer* (Darmstadt: Leske, 1844), a work that gives the lie to attempts to restore Bauer's standing as political philosopher today.
42. Dittmar, "Mehr als grosse Dichter thut uns Noth," in *Skizzen und Briefe,* 56.
43. See Karl Esselborn, *Der Deutschkatholizismus in Darmstadt* (Darmstadt: Verlag der "Litera," 1923).
44. Dittmar, "Nothwendigkeit des Handelns," in *Skizzen und Briefe,* 27.
45. Dittmar, *Der Mensch und sein Gott,* x.
46. Already implicit in ibid., 43–49.
47. Ibid., vii.
48. Dittmar, *Lessing und Feuerbach, oder Auswahl aus G.C. Lessing's theologischen Schriften nebst Originalbeiträgen und Belegstellen aus L. Feuerbach's Wesen des Christenthums* (Offenbach: André, 1847), 35–38.
49. Ibid., 42.
50. Dittmar, *Der Mensch und sein Gott,* 4.
51. Ibid., 13–14.
52. Ibid., 14
53. Ibid., 25–26.
54. Ibid., 39.
55. Ibid., 50–52; see esp. Julius Fröbel's remarks on "purified religion" in *System der socialen Politik,* 2nd ed. (Mannheim: Grohe, 1847), 1:534–36.
56. Dittmar, *Der Mensch und sein Gott,* 63–64.
57. Ibid., 65–66, 74–75.
58. Ibid., 80. Dittmar's position contradicted that of, for example, Bruno Bauer, who maintained that Jews had first to give up their Judaism and become Christian before they could be fully emancipated from religion; in another respect, however, her post-Christian universalism was to trump any remaining "particularist" or minority religion. On liberalism and Jewish difference, see Herzog, *Intimacy and Exclusion,* 53–84, 154–55.
59. Dittmar, *Der Mensch und sein Gott,* 83.
60. *Lessing und Feuerbach,* 44, 88.
61. Connection to Fröbel is stressed in Nagel *"In der Seele"* although she provides little evidence of a direct link between the two. The connection to German Catholicism is clearer, since Ronge played a very important role in Darmstadt

itself, and since the radicals Scholl and Gustav von Struve, who would invite Dittmar to give her first public lecture in Mannheim, were influenced by it. See Käfer-Dittmar, *Louise Dittmar,* 28–29.

62. Ruth-Ellen Boettcher Joeres, *Die Anfänge der deutschen Frauenbewegung. Louise Otto-Peters* (Frankfurt: Fischer, 1983), 57–59, 74–77.

63. See esp. Nagel, *"In der Seele,"* 77–79, 92–94; Kaufmann, "Louise Dittmar," 26–27.

64. Dittmar, *Vier Zeitfragen,* iii.

65. Ibid., 2–3.

66. Ibid., 4–5.

67. Ibid., 9.

68. Ibid., 9.

69. Ibid., 11. Putting individual self-assertion at the foundation of political thought was central to the work of Julius Fröbel, with whose work Dittmar was acquainted. See Nagel, *"In der Seele,"* 118–30; and Fröbel, *System der socialen Politik,* 1:57, 460–65 (in defense of egoism in the sense of individual self-fulfillment).

70. Dittmar, *Vier Zeitfragen,* 13–15.

71. Ibid., 18.

72. Ibid., 20.

73. Ibid., ii.

74. Ibid., v–vi, 22–23; Joeres, "Spirit in Struggle," 284.

75. Dittmar, *Vier Fragen,* 25–26.

76. In this sense, then, the distinction between religious reform and Dittmar's and Feuerbach's critique of religion, in Klausmann, "Louise Dittmar," 28, is not accurate; see also Jens Grandt's attempt to distinguish clearly between Feuerbach's atheism and the religiosity of the German Catholics in *Ludwig Feuerbach und die Welt des Glaubens,* 111–13.

77. Louise Otto, "Die Nibelungen als Oper," *Neue Zeitschrift für Musik* 23 (1845), 129.

78. On Hecker and the failed uprising in Baden, see esp. Veit Valentin's *Geschichte der deutschen Revolution von 1848–1849* (1931; repr., Weinheim: Beltz Quadriga, 1998), I:483–501, and Sabine Freitag, *Friedrich Hecker: Two Lives for Liberty,* trans. Steven Rowan (St. Louis: St. Louis Mercantile Library, 2006).

79. Louise Dittmar, "Germania (Deutsches Bundeslied)," in *Brutus-Michel,* 2nd ed. (Darmstadt: Leske, 1848), 17.

80. Dittmar, "Hecker," in *Brutus-Michel,* 6:

> Hinaus denn Storm, greif um dich gier'ge Flamme,
> Entfesselt sei die Kraft des wilden Leu!
> Was sie zermalmt, es sei ihr kühn geopfert,
> Der Freiheit Altar fordert Opfermuth!
> Hinaus, hinaus! schliesst nicht den Friedenstempel
> Bis unsre Feinde das Palladium fliehn.

81. Dittmar, *Vier Zeitfragen*, 25, an idea emphasized by Bonnie S. Anderson, *Joyous Greetings: The First International Women's Movement, 1830–1860* (New York: Oxford University Press, 2000), 101.

82. Klausmann, "Louise Dittmar," 28–29. The content of these lectures is not known, although Klausmann cites Kathinka Zitz-Halein, who describes Dittmar's lectures on the emancipation of women in Mainz as "teachings with which a real woman can never declare herself in agreement, which strip her of all her femininity and strive to make of her a man-woman" (*Mannweibe*). Stanley Zucker, *Kathinka Zitz-Halein and Female Civic Activism in Mid-Nineteenth-Century Germany* (Carbondale: Southern Illinois University Press, 1991), 85–88, suggests that Dittmar may have coauthored several essays on women's emancipation in the *Mainzer Zeitung* during the revolution—a plausible thesis given the content, but unfortunately unproveable.

83. Feuerbach to Wigand, Aug. 8, 1848, in *GW* 19:175; on the following, see esp. Manuela Köppe, "Louise Dittmar (1807–1884). 'Die Freiheit des Geistes,'" in *Vom Salon zur Barrikade. Frauen der Heinezeit* (Stuttgart: J. B. Metzler, 2002), 281–98.

84. Feuerbach to Wigand, Aug. 16, 1848, in *GW* 19:178.

85. "An Ludwig Feuerbach," poem in Louise Dittmar, *Wühlerische Gedichte eines Wahrhaften. Gesammelt von Louise Dittmar* (Mannheim: Bensheimer, 1848), 15–16, cited in Köppe, "Louise Dittmar," 285–86; the original version of the poem, now lost, was apparently included with Dittmar's letter of Aug. 25, 1848, to Feuerbach, in *GW* 19:180–81.

> Stürzt der "Judas aller Zeiten": das "Verräther-Gold" vergeht
> Und der echte Stein der Weisen: lautrer "Menschenwerth" ersteht:
> Und die Menschheit ist erstanden, sie verlässt der "Thierheit" Spur,
> Einet sich dem 'höchsten Wesen': folgt der *Freiheit der Natur*.

86. Dittmar to Feuerbach, Aug. 25, 1848, in *GW* 19:180.

87. Feuerbach to Wigand, Oct. 7, 1848, in *GW* 19:187.

88. The history of *Die sociale Reform* in Köppe, "Louise Dittmar," 286–88.

89. Dittmar, "An Ludwig Feuerbach."

90. Louise Dittmar, *Zur Charakterisirung der nordischen Mythologie im Verhältniss zu andern Naturreligionen Eine Skizze* (Darmstadt: Leske, 1848), 19. Dittmar's work was not original; it pulled together aspects of Herder, the Brothers Grimm, and the Romantics, who had all tried to make sense of Nordic myths as national texts expressing the soul of the people. Of the many works, see esp. Wolf-Daniel Hartwich, *"Deutsche Mythologie": Die Erfindung einer nationalen Kunstreligion* (Berlin: Philo, 2000), who includes important further references.

91. Dittmar, *Zur Charakterisirung der nordischen Mythologie*, 4.

92. Ibid., 14–16.

93. Joeres, *Die Anfänge der deutschen Frauenbewegung*, 121–26, contains Otto's most important statements on the matter; see also Otto's "Die Nibelungen als Oper," *Neue Zeitschrift für Musik* 23 (1845), 49–52, 129–30, 171–72.

94. Dittmar, *Zur Charakterisirung der nordischen Mythologie,* 23.
95. Ibid., 6–7. Dittmar used the spelling employed by Friedrich Heinrich von der Hagen in his translations of the sagas; I have used the standard forms in Jesse L. Byock's translation of *The Saga of the Volsungs* (London: Penguin, 1999).
96. Dittmar, *Zur Charakterisirung der nordischen Mythologie,* 8–9.
97. Ibid., 13–14, 16–17; see Hartwich, *"Deutsche Mythologie,"* 54–56, on parallel readings of the twilight of the idols.
98. Dittmar, *Zur Charakterisirung der nordischen Mythologie,* 24.
99. Ibid., 31–32.
100. Ibid., 26–27.
101. Ibid., 40.
102. Feuerbach, *EC,* 101.
103. Dittmar, *Zur Charakterisirung der nordischen Mythologie,* 47–48. It is hard to miss the parallel in Ernst Bloch's famous formulation of socialism as a search for a *Heimat* in the world: Ernst Bloch, *Das Prinzip Hoffnung* (Frankfurt: Suhrkamp, 1959), 1628. Indeed, at times Bloch's classic formulations seem closer to the Feuerbachian radicals of the Vormärz than to the Marxism-Leninism he confronted.
104. Dittmar, *Zur Charakterisirung der nordischen Mythologie,* 49–50.
105. "Die Kunst in der Kirche," in *WdE,* 9–12.
106. "Wesen der Ehe," in *WdE,* 73.
107. Marx and Engels, "Circular Against Kriege," in *MECW* 6:35–51.
108. "Wesen der Ehe," in *WdE,* 47; "Die monarchische Weltanschauung," in *WdE,* 3, refers to a "system of attraction" (i.e., gravity) in the universe that provides for a natural order—against the capricious centrality of the sun/monarch.
109. "Wesen der Ehe," in *WdE,* 48.
110. On this section in context, see esp. Herzog, *Intimacy and Exclusion,* 12, 36–37, 158–60; Thomas Nipperdey, *Deutsche Geschichte 1800–1866. Bürgerwelt und starker Staat* (Munich: C. H. Beck, 1983), 298–300.
111. "Wesen der Ehe," in *WdE,* 48–49.
112. Ibid., 52–53.
113. Ibid., 53, 57. The distinction between marriage based on love and a marriage of convenience was also central to the German Catholics and other radicals discussing social reform at the time. See Lotz, "'Die Erlösung des weiblichen Geschlechts,'" 237; Carola Lipp, "Liebe, Krieg und Revolution. Geschlechtsbeziehung und Nationalismus," in *Schimpfende Weiber,* 356–57.
114. "Wesen der Ehe," in *WdE,* 58, 66–70.
115. Ibid., 67.
116. Ibid., 54, 61.
117. Ibid., 61–62, 65.
118. Ibid., 59.
119. Ibid., 60.
120. Ibid., 70.
121. Ibid., 55.
122. Ibid., 49, 56.

123. Ibid., 49.
124. Ibid., 56.
125. Ibid., 51.
126. Ibid., 52.
127. In this connection, Dittmar explicitly criticized Fourier's defense of "free love" ("Wesen der Ehe," in *WdE*, 51; see Charles Fourier, *The Theory of the Four Movements*, ed. Gareth Stedman-Jones and Ian Patterson [New York: Cambridge University Press, 1996], 139). Herzog provides an interesting and careful reading of these passages in *Intimacy and Exclusion*, 163–65. Herzog underplays the extent to which Dittmar also argues for the development of mind or spirit, which will organize the body; the aim was not sexual liberation, but human liberation; not to "take women's sexual and emotional perspectives seriously on their own terms" (*Intimacy and Exclusion*, 165), but to transform these perspectives, to raise women above the "raw" senses, and to affirm a freely willed monogamy.
128. Lipp, "Liebe, Krieg und Revolution," 359–63.
129. "Wesen der Ehe," in *WdE*, 71.
130. Ibid., 71.
131. Ibid., 72.
132. "Charlotte Corday," in *WdE*, 26.
133. Thomas Carlyle, *The French Revolution* (New York: Modern Library, n.d.), 609. For the description of Dittmar's place in the tradition of describing Corday, see Nagel, *"In der Seele,"* 27–42; and esp. Mechthilde Vahsen, "'Vorwärts! Die Geschichte beweist es./Freiheit sei das edelste Loos,'" in Norbert Otto Eke and Renate Werner, ed., *Vormärz-Nachmärz. Bruch oder Kontinuität?* (Bielefeld: Aisthesis, 2000), 125–38.
134. "Charlotte Corday," in *WdE*, 32.
135. Ibid., 31. Her project of portraying Corday as a woman driven by an ideal rather than by personal interest or love had already appeared in *Skizzen und Briefe*, 84.
136. "Das Ideal und die Wirklichkeit," in *WdE*, 23.
137. "Charlotte Corday," in *WdE*, 33.
138. Ibid., 40.
139. Ibid., 27, 30.
140. Ibid., 45; the critique of Corday and by implication Dittmar as a fanatic in the work of Luise Büchner is cited in Vahsen, "'Vorwärts!'" 136–7.
141. Otto, "Louise Dittmar's 'Soziale Reform,'" in *Die Frauen-Zeitung*, Sept. 15, 1849, repr. in *"Dem Reich der Freiheit werb' ich Bürgerinnen." Die Frauen-Zeitung von Louise Otto*, ed. Ute Gerhard, Elisabeth Hannover-Drück, Romina Schmitter (Frankfurt: Syndikat, 1980), 148; Vahsen is, I think, closer to the mark in seeing Dittmar's essay as an attempt to find a republican heroine free from the normal gender roles of the day, "'Vorwärts!'" 137.
142. Mathilde Kriege to Emma Herwegh, July 10, 1848, in Heinrich Schlüter and Alfred Wesselmann, ed., *Hermann Kriege. Dokumentation einer Wandlung vom Burschenschaftler und Revolutionär zum Demokraten (1840–1850)* (Bielefeld: Der Andere Verlag, 2002), I:385.

143. Zitz cited in Käfer-Dittmar, *Louise Dittmar,* 34; Fröbel cited in Klausmann, "Louise Dittmar," 37. See also Zucker, *Kathinka Zitz-Halein,* 85.

144. "Der Selbstzweck der Menschheit," in *WdE,* 8.

145. "Das Ideal und die Wirklichkeit," in *WdE,* 25.

146. The notion of a human individual's *Selbstzweck* occurs throughout her works. See esp. Dittmar, *Zur Charakterisirung der nordischen Mythologie,* 20, 47; Ibid., *Vier Zeitfragen,* 6–12 on the idea of the *Selbstgefühl;* and the excerpt from Fröbel's *Soziale Politik* on women's need for economic independence reprinted in *WdE,* 17–18.

147. Letter to Lorenz Diefenbach, Dec. 1852, cited in Klausmann, "Louise Dittmar," 32.

148. Absent in: Susanne Schötz, "Von 1848 nach 1865? Bausteine zur Kollektivbiographie der Gründerinnen und Gründer der deutschen Frauenbewegung," in Helmut Bleiber and Walter Schmidt, eds., *Revolution und Reform im 19. und 20. Jahrhundert* (Berlin: Trafo, 2005), 151–64.

149. Dittmar, *Zur Charakterisirung der nordischen Mythologie,* 19.

Chapter 4

1. Providing a general context: Karin Jeschke and Gunda Ulbricht, eds., *Dresden, Mai 1849. Tagungsband* (Dresden: ddp goldenbogen, 2000); focusing on the uprising as part of the campaign for the new constitution is Martina Schattkowsky, ed., *Dresdner Maiaufstand und Reichsverfassung 1849: Revolutionäres Nachbeben oder demokratische politische Kultur?* (Leipzig: Leipziger Universitätsverlag, 2000).

2. Of the many sources, see esp. Rüdiger Krohn, "The Revolution of 1848–49," in *Wagner Handbook,* ed. Ulrich Müller and Peter Wapnewski (Cambridge: Harvard University Press, 1992), 156–65; Joachim Köhler, *Richard Wagner: The Last of the Titans,* trans. Steward Spencer (New Haven, CT: Yale University Press, 2004), chap. 3; Ernest Newman, *The Life of Richard Wagner* (New York: Alfred A. Knopf, 1933–1946), 2:54–103.

3. For example, "A Communication to My Friends," is cited from the William Ashton Ellis, trans., *Richard Wagner's Prose Works* (London: Routledge and Kegan Paul, 1895–1899), 1:355–56. I have at times altered Ellis's idiosyncratic translations for the sake of clarity.

4. See Richard Wagner, *My Life* (New York: Dodd, Mead, and Co., 1911), 1:439–543.

5. See esp. Wagner's 1872 introduction to his 1849 "Art and Revolution," in *PW* 1:23–29; on Feuerbach and Wagner more generally, see Mark Berry, *Treacherous Bonds and Laughing Fire: Politics and Religion in Wagner's Ring* (Aldershot, UK: Ashgate, 2006).

6. *Opera and Drama,* in *PW* 2:153–54.

7. Stressing the continued place of radicalism in Wagner, see esp. Paul Lawrence Rose, *Wagner: Race and Revolution* (New Haven, CT: Yale University Press, 1992); Köhler, *Richard Wagner.*

8. Marx, *Capital,* in *MECW* 35:387–89.
9. Marx, *Grundrisse,* in *MECW* 27:47. Not all of Marx's images fit into his emancipatory project, however. His use of the image of the Cyclops, for example, suggests a kind of domination, rooted in big technology that was not so easily subordinate to mastery. Myth might remain embedded in the forces of production—which themselves determined relations of production.
10. Feuerbach to his mother, Oct. 22, 1820, in *GW* 17:8–9.
11. Köhler, *Richard Wagner,* 11, 23–26, esp. 24; Wagner, "German Art and German Policy," in *PW* 4:92–93, where Wagner goes on to condemn the "clever Jew" Börne for making light of Sand's deed.
12. Alwin H. Sörgel, *A Sojourn in Texas, 1846–47. Alwin H. Sörgel's Texas Writings,* trans. and ed. W. M. Von–Maszewski (San Marcos, TX: German-Texas Heritage Society, 1992), 59, 239–40.
13. Louise Dittmar, *Zur Charakterisirung der nordischen Mythologie im Verhältniss zu andern Naturreligionen Eine Skizze* (Darmstadt: Leske, 1848), 49–50.
14. Cited in Karl Grün, "Ludwig Feuerbachs Philosophische Charakterentwicklung," *Ausgewählte Schriften,* ed. Manuela Köppe, 2 vols. (Berlin: Akademie, 2006), 689.
15. Ludwig Feuerbach, "Luther as Arbiter," in Karl Marx, *Writings of the Young Marx on Philosophy and Society,* trans. and ed. Loyd D. Easton and Kurt H. Guddat (Indianapolis, IN: Hackett, 1997), 95; the text was originally attributed to Marx.
16. Feuerbach to Karl Ritter, Nov. 19, 1849, in *SL,* 180–81.
17. Discussion on the relationship between the two is briefly summarized in George G. Windell, "Hegel, Feuerbach, and Wagner's *Ring,*" *Central European History* 9 (1976): 30–32; Berry, *Treacherous Bonds,* shows a far closer relationship between them on the level of images and emotions. See also Hans Mayer, *Richard Wagner: Mitwelt und Nachwelt* (Zürich: Belser, 1978), 36–37, 69, 80–81, 94–95. On *Death and Immortality,* see Wagner to Karl Ritter, Nov. 19, 1849, in *SL,* 180–81; Wagner, *My Life,* 1:520–22; and Köhler's comments in *Richard Wagner,* 260–62.
18. Wagner to Feuerbach, Dec. 3, 1851, in *GW* 19:331–32. Herwegh's close relationship to Wagner in the Zurich years recounted in Ulrich Enzensberger, *Herwegh. Ein Heldenleben* (Frankfurt: Eichborn, 1999), 265–96; on Herwegh and Feuerbach, see S. Rawidowicz, *Ludwig Feuerbachs Philosophie: Ursprung und Schicksal* (Berlin: Reuther und Richard, 1931), 368–72.
19. Köhler, *Richard Wagner,* 470.
20. Newman, *The Life of Richard Wagner,* 2:166; Hans Dünnebier, *Gottfried Keller und Ludwig Feuerbach* (Zurich: Ketner, 1913), and Rawidowicz, *Ludwig Feuerbachs Philosophie,* 372–84, treat Keller's multifaceted and ongoing reception of Feuerbach.
21. Theodor Adorno, *In Search of Wagner,* trans. Rodney Livingstone (London: New Left Books, 1981), 14.
22. "The Vaterlandsverein Speech" of June 14, 1848, in *PW* 4:136–45; see also the letter to August von Lüttichau of June 18, 1848, defending the place of the monarch, in *SL,* 140–41.

23. Gottschalk cited in Jürgen Herres, *1848/49: Revolution in Köln* (Cologne: Janus, 1998), 19; see also Feuerbach's defense of a head of state who represents all in the "Provisional Theses for the Reformation of Philosophy" (1843), 170–71. On the Kantian–Hegelian tradition of the "republican monarchy," see Matthew Levinger, "Kant and the Origins of Prussian Constitutionalism," *History of Political Thought* 19 (1998): 241–63.

24. "Man and Established Society," in *PW* 8: 227–31. See the spirited account by Köhler, *Richard Wagner*, 221–32. On Bakunin's obscure role in the revolution, see Erhard Hexelschneider, "Michail Bakunin (1814–1876). Ein russischer Revolutionär im Dresdner Maiaufstand," in Helmut Bleiber, et al., eds., *Akteure eines Umbruchs. Männer und Frauen der Revolution von 1848–49* (Berlin: Fides, 2003), 37–81.

25. "Man and Established Society," 229–30; Wagner's radical critique of liberalism paralleled that of Hess, Marx, and others, especially after the revolution as he came to attack liberals' attempt to reform the existing state instead of destroying it, and his criticism of rights as cementing into place existing political and property relations rather than permitting the expression of love and humanity, in *Opera and Drama*, 45, 202–3.

26. "The Revolution," in *PW* 8:233.

27. Ibid., 236.

28. Ibid., 238.

29. See esp. Berry, *Treacherous Bonds*.

30. Insisting on the place of the essay in the context of Wagner's theoretical work of the time: Udo Bermbach, "Das ästhetische Motiv in Wagners Antisemitismus," in *Richard Wagner und die Juden*, ed. Dieter Borchmeyer, Ami Maayani, and Susanne Vill (Stuttgart: J. B. Metzler, 2000), 55–76.

31. *"I herewith sever my links with the Revolution!"*—which he described as merely about destruction rather than construction, in *SL*, 145–46; he echoed these notions in a letter of the time to Eduard Devrient, through whom he hoped—in vain—to influence positively the Saxon court and musical administration to consider taking him back. See Newman, *Richard Wagner*, 2:106–8.

32. *Opera and Drama*, 12, and in general Part I of that work; see also Dieter Borchmeyer, *Richard Wagner: Theory and Theater*, trans. Stewart Spencer (Oxford: Clarendon, 1991), 87–91.

33. *Opera and Drama*, 85–86.

34. Ibid., 61–63.

35. "Art and Revolution," 41–42; "The Artwork of the Future," in *PW* 1:76–77.

36. Köhler, *Richard Wagner*, 126–34; Rose, *Wagner*, 40–48; Sieghart Döhring, "Die traumatische Beziehung Wagners zu Meyerbeer," in *Richard Wagner und die Juden*, 262–74.

37. *Opera and Drama*, 87–88; "Judaism in Music," in *PW* 3:84–85. This argument parallels Bruno Bauer's insofar as it rejected the authentic place of only partially assimilated Jews in the revolutionary community, and Wagner furthermore slides into a physiological definition of Jewishness that seems to bar full assimilation. See also Marc Weiner, *Richard Wagner and the Anti-Semitic*

Imagination (Lincoln: University of Nebraska Press, 1995), 66–70, connecting Wagner's statements about Jewish speech and German language with *Der Meistersinger*.

38. *Opera and Drama*, 17, 193–94: state relies on unconsciousness of humans; 195–96; "A Communication to My Friends," 354–55. See also the fragmentary "Artisthood of the Future," published posthumously, with its attack on "divine or other" myths that sought to vindicate relations of property and authority, in *PW* 8:343–44.

39. *Opera and Drama*, 166–67; image of a new political order as a set of constantly changing voluntary associations replacing the static state and its laws in "The Artwork of the Future," 203.

40. Köhler, *Richard Wagner*, 260–63.

41. Bruce Lincoln, *Theorizing Myth: Narrative, Ideology, and Scholarship* (Chicago: University of Chicago Press, 1999), 57–58.

42. "Bruchstücke eines Dramas *Achilleus*," in *Dichtungen und Schriften*, ed. Dieter Borchmeyer (Frankfurt: Insel, 1983), 2:273; see also Köhler, *Richard Wagner*, 227, connecting the drama to Wagner's experience on the barricades, and Borchmeyer, *Richard Wagner: Theory and Theater*, 303, on its connection to the *Ring*.

43. Newman, *The Life of Richard Wagner*, 2:18–24.

44. "A Communication to My Friends," 356–61; George S. Williamson, *The Longing for Myth in Germany: Religion and Aesthetic Culture from Romanticism to Nietzsche* (Chicago: University of Chicago Press, 2004), 191–92.

45. "Artisthood of the Future," 345.

46. *Opera and Drama*, 191.

47. Ibid., 69, 325–28; "Artisthood of the Future," 349.

48. *Opera and Drama*, 152–53.

49. Ibid., 96, 154–55, 211–12, 213.

50. Ibid., 156.

51. Oedipus did not revolt against human nature: ibid., 182. See also Borchmeyer, *Richard Wagner: Theory and Theater*, 291–95. Extensive investigation of the personal roots of the incest theme in Joachim Köhler, *Richard Wagner*, who reduces everything to individual issues—which cannot explain the connection to a greater public, as Wagner's poetic theory itself would suggest.

52. *Opera and Drama*, 111.

53. "Artwork of the Future," 91–92.

54. *Opera and Drama*, 315.

55. Ibid., 316.

56. "Art and Revolution," 32–35, 47–50; *Opera and Drama*, 283; "The Artwork of the Future," 135–36; on Wagner's idiosyncratic understanding of Greek culture and history, Williamson, *Longing for Myth*, 196–99, and Borchmeyer, *Richard Wagner: Theory and Theater*, 59–72, on the ideal audience and the Greeks.

57. "Art and Revolution," 37; *Opera and Drama*, 104–5.

58. *Opera and Drama*, 195, 200–202, 205; "Artisthood of the Future," 346–47; Borchmeyer, *Richard Wagner*, 59–86.

59. "Art and Revolution," 39, *Opera and Drama*, 226–30, 254–76.

60. "Art and Revolution," 58.

61. "The Artwork of the Future," 199; the formulation fits well with Feuerbach's notion of immortality through humanity, in *Thoughts on Death and Immortality*.

62. *Opera and Drama*, 337. See also Carl Dahlhaus's important remarks on the role of both text and music, rather than the primacy of text, in Wagner's development, in *Richard Wagner's Music Dramas*, trans. Mary Whittall (New York: Cambridge University Press, 1979), 4–5, 54–55.

63. *Opera and Drama*, 375–76; "Art and Revolution," 64. The continuity of Wagner's rejection of the "mercantile aspect" of art, i.e., its commodity form, is explored in Borchmeyer, *Richard Wagner*.

64. "The Artwork of the Future," 73, 196–97.

65. Ludwig Feuerbach, *Theogonie nach den Quellen des klassischen, hebräischen, und christichen Altertums*, in *GW 7³*, 192.

66. See Williamson, *The Longing for Myth in Germany*, 202.

67. List of Wagner's readings in the area in Newman, *The Life of Richard Wagner*, 2:24–26; more recent works include Elizabeth Magee, *Richard Wagner and the Nibelungs* (Oxford: Clarendon Press, 1990) and Stanley R. Hauer, "Wagner and the *Völospá*," *19th Century Music* 15 (1991): 52–63, both of which list further specialized reading, and Stefan Arvidsson, *Aryan Idols: Indo–European Mythology as Ideology and as Science*, trans. Sonia Wichmann (Chicago: University of Chicago Press, 2006), esp. 149–62.

68. Sections of Otto's libretto were first published in the *Neue Zeitschrift für Musik* 23 (1845), 175–76, 181–83; full text as *Die Nibelungen. Text zu einer grossen historischen Oper in fünf Acten* (Gera: Verlag der Hofmeister'schen Zeitungs-Expedition, 1852).

69. Ernest Newman, *The Wagner Operas* (New York: Alfred A. Knopf, 1949), 393–404; Mayer, *Richard Wagner*, 158–69, 389.

70. Neuman, *The Wagner Operas*, 404–5; letter from Wagner to Theodor Uhlig, Nov. 12, 1851, in *SL*, 234.

71. George Bernard Shaw, *The Perfect Wagnerite: A Commentary on the Nibelung's Ring* (New York: Dover, 1967); Adorno, *In Search of Wagner*.

72. Newman, *The Wagner Operas*, 411–12.

73. Strongly argued in Warren Darcy, "'The World Belongs to Alberich!' Wagner's Changing Attitudes towards the 'Ring,'" in Stewart Spencer, ed., *Wagner's Ring of the Nibelung: A Companion* (London: Thames and Hudson, 1993), 48–52.

74. On the place of Wagner in music history, see esp. the works by Dahlhaus cited above, and Dahlhaus, "Wagner's Place in the History of Music," in *Wagner Handbook*, 91–117. The references to the bourgeois family and incest, to Wagner's own life, to the modern industrial age and yearnings for a premodern subjectivity, to revolution and anti-Semitism, are brought out in their full

complexity in the brilliant reading of Michael P. Steinberg, *Listening to Reason: Culture, Subjectivity, and Nineteenth Century Music* (Chicago: University of Chicago Press, 2004), chap. 4.

75. Adorno, *In Search of Wagner*, 100.

76. "Judaism in Music," 81; see also Newman, *Life of Richard Wagner*, 2:19–21; Weiner, *Richard Wagner and the Anti-Semitic Imagination*, 51–56.

77. On the motifs, see Newman, *The Wagner Operas*, 630–31.

78. See the English translation of "Siegfried's Death" in *PW* 8:1–52; more extensive stage directions in the prose sketch are reprinted in Otto Strobel, ed., *Skizzen und Entwürfe zur Ring-Dichtung* (Munich: F. Bruckmann, 1930), here at p. 55; Newman, *Life of Richard Wagner*, 2:347, 350–51; for the schematic chart showing the stages of composing the *Götterdämmerung*, see in Warren J. Darcy, "The Metaphysics of Annihilation: Wagner, Schopenhauer, and the Ending of the *Ring*," *Music Theory Spectrum* 16 (1994): 3. See also Berry, *Treacherous Bonds*, 255–56.

79. Newman, *Richard Wagner*, 2:356–57; Borchmeyer, *Richard Wagner: Theory and Theater*, 304–5; Windel, "Hegel, Feuerbach, and Wagner's *Ring*," 35; Darchy, "Metaphysics," 4–5, 4n8; Dahlhaus, *Richard Wagner's Music Dramas*, 93, sees this version already in the works by the end of 1848.

80. Newman, *The Wagner Operas*, 632. Berry provides an ingenious reading in *Treacherous Bonds*, 250–52, by which Wotan has in fact acted to fulfill fate, thereby rendering Erda's warning objectless; here and elsewhere in Berry's reading, however, it seems to me that ambiguity and perhaps even sloppiness on Wagner's part is papered over to present a seamless argument.

81. Translated in Dahlhaus, *Richard Wagner's Music Dramas*, 137–38; it is perhaps these words to which Friedrich Nietzsche refers as "the hope for a socialist utopia" in *The Birth of Tragedy and the Case of Wagner*, trans. by Walter Kaufmann (Toronto: Random House, 1967), 164; see also Newman, *The Wagner Operas*, 633–34. These notions of love worked out in Feuerbachian terms, and with explicit reference to sexual love as love's highest form, in letter to Röckel of Jan. 25–26, 1854, in *SL*, 300–13.

82. Wagner to Röckel, Aug. 23, 1856, in *SL*, 357–58.

83. Wagner to Röckel, Jan. 25–26, 1854, in *SL*, 306–7; reading the entire work as an attempt to learn how to die, with this letter as a crucial component: Linda Hutcheon and Michael Hutcheon, "'Alles was ist, endet': Living with the Knowledge of Death in Richard Wagner's *Der Ring des Nibelungen*," *University of Toronto Quarterly* 67 (1998): 789–811. See also the similar passage about learning to die in Feuerbach, "Die Unsterblichkeitsfrage vom Standpunkt der Anthrolopologie" (1847), in *GW* 10³, 257.

84. Newman, *The Life of Richard Wagner*, 2:355.

85. Wagner to Liszt, Dec. 16, 1854, in *SL*, 323–24; Wagner to Röckel, Aug. 23, 1856, in *SL*, 357–58. See also the letter to Theodor Uhlig, written before his exposure to Schopenhauer, where Wagner reacts to seeing the ill-treatment of animals by poor Italians: "I cannot help feeling that this race of ours has no

alternative but to perish utterly," July 22, 1852, in *SL*, 264. Note that according to Schopenhauer's doctrine, however, Brünnhilde's suicide would constitute an act of will against fate.

86. But cf. Darcy, "Metaphysics," 6.

87. Newman, *The Life of Richard Wagner*, 2:358.

88. But see Darcy's complex reading of the musical movements at the end of *The Twilight of the Gods* as themselves arguing for a Schopenhauerian interpretation, in his "Metaphysics"; Ernst Bloch similarly claims to find "the paradox of a repetition [of entire motives] that opens up a new vista," in "Paradox and the Pastorale in Wagner's Music," in *Essays on the Philosophy of Music*, trans. Peter Palmer (New York: Cambridge University Press, 1985), 163. I suspect that Wagner's music mirrored his literature rather than trumping it: both evaded clarity in order to increase the sense of portent.

89. M. Owen Lee, *Athena Sings: Wagner and the Greeks* (Toronto: University of Toronto Press, 2003); Borchmeyer, *Richard Wagner*, 289–91, 297.

90. Noted in Dahlhaus, *Richard Wagner's Music Dramas*, 104, citing the letter of Dec. 1, 1858, to Mathilde Wesendonck (*SL*, 431–32), where Wagner seeks to "correct his system" by finding redemption "not through any abstract human love, but a love engendered on the basis of sexual love, i.e. the attraction between man and woman."

91. Dahlhaus, *Richard Wagner's Music Dramas*, 98; Köhler, *Richard Wagner*, 406–7; Borchmeyer, *Richard Wagner*, 303–7, develops this interpretation in detail.

92. "To make one's intentions too obvious risks impairing a proper understanding of the work in question": Wagner to Röckel, Jan. 25–26, 1854, in *SL*, 308.

93. Berry's argument that Wagner is "resolved to let the music speak for itself" (*Treacherous Bonds*, 271) is not satisfactory: the music does not speak; if anything it obscures by creating unexplained connections.

94. Newman (*Life of Richard Wagner*, 2:430–46,522–30), and Köhler, *Richard Wagner*, 408–29, provide striking portraits of Wagner at this time.

95. As Newman put it, "Schopenhauer merely reinforced his emotions and intentions with reasons and arguments," *Life of Richard Wagner*, 2:431, a reading supported by Wagner's letter to Mathilde Wesendonck of July 6, 1858, where he announces his renunciation of her in the most Tristanian terms: *SL*, 394–97.

96. Wagner to Liszt, Dec. 16, 1854, in *SL*, 323–24.

97. Alan David Aberbach, *The Ideas of Richard Wagner: An Examination and Analysis*, 2nd ed. (Lanham, MD: University Press of America, 2003), 380–81. Adorno argues that rapture and materialism combined in the unrestrained desire for violence and destruction of the "bourgeois terrorist" and "rebel" against a set of social relations that constituted him: *In Search of Wagner*, 14–15, 144–56.

98. Dahlhaus, *Richard Wagner's Music Drama*, 63–64, on the movement toward the "dissolution of tonality."

99. Adorno, *In Search of Wagner*, 142.

100. Feuerbach, "Über Spiritualismus und Materialismus, besonders in Beziehung auf die Willensfreiheit" (ca. 1858–66), in *GW* 11^3, 54–61; quote at 56–57. Similar argument in Feuerbach's final, unfinished work "Zur Moralphilosophie," ed. Werner Schuffenhauer, in Hans-Jürg Braun, ed., *Solidarität oder Egoismus: Studien zu einer Ethik bei und nach Ludwig Feuerbach* (Berlin: Akademie, 1994), 370–74. Walter Jaeschke points out how unsatisfying this formulation is from the point of view of moral philosophy, questioning in particular the use of a vague term like "nature" and the attempt to argue from the "essence" of an individual to specific actions; the result, he suggests, approaches sophistry: "Ludwig Feuerbach über Spiritualismus und Materialismus," in Andreas Arndt and Walter Jaeschke, ed., *Materialismus und Spiritualismus* (Hamburg: Felix Meiner, 2000), 28–29.

101. Feuerbach, *Theogonie nach den Quellen des klassischen, hebräischen, und christichen Altertums,* in *GW* 7^3:213–15.

102. Does looking into his eyes imply her immediate and total love, as Newman suggests, or rather pity, as Wagner himself argued? See Newman, *The Wagner Operas,* 199–200, who looks at the musical motif for clarification, and Wagner in *Opera and Drama,* 111–12, who states that woman can, in fact, only feel love, but that love is constrained by pride.

103. Thomas Mann, letter to Paul Steegemann of Aug. 18, 1920, in *Pro and Contra Wagner,* trans. Allan Blunden (London: Faber and Faber, 1985), 67; see also his "The Sorrows and Grandeur of Richard Wagner," in ibid., pp. 124–27, noting that both the Romantic stress on sexuality, love, the night, and death, and the centrality of eroticism was different from Schopenhauer (and also, one might note, from the mid-nineteenth-century radical materialist milieu).

104. Or, in the words of Adorno, "Where the drama is at its most exalted, the commodity is closest at hand," in the form, namely, of a deluded wish-fulfillment—that is already known to be no more than delusion (Adorno's later theory of the culture industry) and a concealment of actual labor: *In Search of Wagner,* 91–92.

105. See Wagner's prose sketch of the drama, where she is dead, in *Dichtungen und Schriften,* 4:103.

106. Especially clear reading in Newman, *The Wagner Operas,* 203.

107. Indeed, in Schopenhauer love was at best the greatest illusion of the world; see Hartmut Reinhardt, "Wagner and Schopenhauer," in *Wagner Handbook,* 291–92, who argues that the climax of the opera "is directed at the torment of living in the absence of true love," which reveals a basic discrepancy between Wagner and Schopenhauer.

108. See esp. Newman, *Wagner Operas,* 205–6, 208, and on his characterization of love in Wagner as "longing without satisfaction and without end," 213.

109. On the usefulness of the potions in eliminating bourgeois inhibitions against violence, see Adorno, *In Search of Wagner;* even where his crude, almost Lukacsian reduction to social class is questionable, his often sarcastic reading hits the mark. On the potion: Mann, "The Sorrows and Grandeur of Richard Wagner," 96–97; Newman makes a similar point, but in a way more charitable to Wagner: the love potion is the occasion that provides the lovers the

opportunity to express their true feelings. Newman, *Wagner Operas,* 197–98. The deeper aesthetic question is, of course, whether the love potion has a necessary place in the play. Dahlhaus makes a similar argument about the potion of forgetfulness in the *Götterdämmerung*: it serves to bring out an essential element of Siegfried, his own immediacy, his living in the present, therefore his inability to recall obligations—which existed without the potion (91; see also Steinberg, *Listening to Reason,* 155). The solution in this case, however, is even more dubious, since it implies a kind of randomness hardly noble and heroic—although that explanation may explain the need for a potion to make Siegfried remember.

Wagner's own use of opium and other drugs does not explain the role of the love potion any more than his own manic depression explains the frequency of self-willed death in his work: see Köhler, *Richard Wagner,* 303–5, on Wagner's drug habits. For an example of the psychologizing genre, see John Louis DiGaetani, *Wagner and Suicide* (Jefferson, NC: McFarland, 2003), with further references. His references to sex, drugs, and death nonetheless speak to a powerful theme of modernity: the descent into the purely material, the search for intense personal experience, and nihilism. Drugs are thereby also associated with the loss of restraint, sexual enhancement, experience, and potential suicidal tendencies.

110. See Feuerbach, "Zur Moralphilosophie," 377–83, reading both ascetic Catholicism and Schopenhauer's Buddhism as emanations of a psychological disorder.
111. Mann, "The Sorrows and Grandeur of Richard Wagner," 128.
112. Wagner, "Communication," 375.
113. Köhler, *Richard Wagner,* 591–622; Peter Wapnewski, "The Operas as Literary Works," in *Wagner Handbook,* 86–95, stressing Parsifal's "hostility to the senses and to women" (91); compare, however, Ulrike Kienzle's reading, which sees the work as an attempt to find religiosity in a post-Christian world. On Kienzle's reading, Jesus for Wagner during his strongest Feuerbachian period had encouraged "insight into the transience of the individual and the voluntary surrender of one's own life, with death overcoming egoism"; Jesus the redeemer is redeemed through a new ethic of "reconciliation of mankind and nature": "*Parsifal* and Religion: A Christian Music Drama?" in William Kinderman and Katherine R. Syer, ed., *A Companion to Wagner's Parsifal* (Rochester, NY: Camden House, 2005), 81–130.
114. Wagner to Liszt, June 7, 1855, in *SL,* 346–47.
115. Friedrich Nietzsche, *The Twilight of the Idols and the Antichrist,* trans. R. J. Hollingdale (London: Penguin, 1948), 45.
116. Wagner to Uhlig, Oct. 22, 1850, in *SL,* 219; in a letter to Liszt of Feb. 11, 1853, Wagner furthermore associates the burning of Valhalla with the burning of the Jews: "I must now set it to music for the Jews of Frankfurt and Leipzig—it is just the thing for them!" *SL,* 281.
117. See esp. the 1869 appendix to "Judaism in Music," where Wagner names the Jew as the enemy who controls the modern world of money and information, and who persecutes those who speak the truth (i.e., Wagner himself), in *PW* 3:101–22.

118. See in particular Wagner's glowing report from 1881 on Gobineau's theory of racial difference, "Hero-dom and Christendom," in *PW* 6: 275–84; and the important collection on the topic, *Richard Wagner und die Juden,* ed. Dieter Borchmeyer, Ami Maayani, and Susanne Vill (Stuttgart: J. B. Metzler, 2000).
119. Nietzsche, *The Case of Wagner,* 171; see also Steinberg, *Listening to Reason,* 142ff, on Sigmund's radical-bourgeois subjectivity.
120. "Judaism in Music," 79–80. This notion of myth was adopted by the Nazi scholars of "Aryan" culture, as noted in Stefan Andersson, *Aryan Idols,* 227–28.

Chapter 5

1. Of the many works on myth in German and European thought, see especially the following recent works with further references: George S. Williamson, *The Longing for Myth in Germany: Religion and Aesthetic Culture from Romanticism to Nietzsche* (Chicago: University of Chicago Press, 2004); Bruce Lincoln, *Theorizing Myth: Narrative, Ideology, and Scholarship* (Chicago: University of Chicago Press, 1999); Stefan Arvidsson, *Aryan Idols.*
2. Letter to Friedrich Kapp of Nov. 3, 1859, in *GW* 20:263; letter to Wilhelm Bolin, Oct. 20, 1860, in *GW* 20:292.
3. Feuerbach, *Theogonie nach den Quellen des klassischen, hebräischen, und christichen Altertums,* in *GW* 7³.
4. The pathbreaking work of Van A. Harvey remains the most important secondary source on this neglected aspect of Feuerbach: *Feuerbach and the Interpretation of Religion* (New York: Cambridge, 1997); see also Francesco Tomasoni, *Ludwig Feuerbach und die nicht-menschliche Natur. Das Wesen der Religion: Die Entstehungsgeschichte des Werkes, rekonstruiert auf der Grundlage unveröffentlicher Manuskripte,* trans. Alf Schneditz (Stuttgart: Frommann-Holzboog, 1990), which has informed much of this chapter.
5. Making the connection between Feuerbach and Rorty is esp. Judith Sieverding, *Sensibilität und Solidarität. Skizze einer dialogischen Ethik im Anschluss an Ludwig Feuerbach und Richard Rorty* (Münster: Waxmann, 2007); see also Marina Bykova, "Subjektivität und Gattung," in *Ludwig Feuerbach (1804–1872): Identität und Pluralismus in der globalen Gesellschaft,* ed. Reitemeyer, et al. (Münster: Waxmann, 2006), 127; Peter Dews, "The Historicization of Analytical Philosophy," in *The Limits of Disenchantment: Essays on Contemporary European Philosophy* (London: Verso, 1995), 67; Warren Breckman, "The Symbolic Dimension and the Politics of Left Hegelianism," in *The Left Hegelians: Politics and Philosophy in the Hegelian School,* ed. Douglas Moggach (New York: Cambridge University Press, 2006), 84. Less certain of the compatibility, given Feuerbach's continued return to epistemological certainty, is András Gedö, "Bestandsaufnahme der philosophischen Moderne. Über Feuerbachs Philosophiegeschichtsschreibung," in *Ludwig Feuerbach und die Geschichte der Philosophie,* ed. Walter Jaeschke and Francesco Tomasoni (Berlin: Akademie, 1998), 130–31.

6. Paul Bishop, "'Elementary Aesthetics', Hedonistic Ethics: The Philosophical Foundations of Feuerbach's Later Works," *History of European Ideas* 34 (2008): 298–309.

7. Frederick Gregory, *Scientific Materialism in 19th Century Germany* (Dordrecht: D. Reidel, 1977). On the life and work of the "materialist trinity" of Vogt, Büchner, and Moleschott, and their relationship to Haeckel, see esp. Christoph Kockerbeck, ed., *Carl Vogt, Jacob Moleschott, Ludwig Büchner, Ernst Haeckel: Briefwechsel* (Marburg: Basilisken-Presse, 1999), who also notes the influence of Feuerbach; Frederick Gregory, *Nature Lost? Natural Science and the German Theological Traditions of the Nineteenth Century* (Cambridge, MA: Harvard University Press, 1992), 46–47; and Alfred Kelly, *The Descent of Darwin: The Popularization of Darwinism in Germany, 1860–1914* (Chapel Hill: University of North Carolina Press, 1981), 17–20. See the translation of the fifteenth edition of Büchner's *Kraft und Stoff* as *Force and Matter, or Principles of the Natural Order of the Universe, with a System of Morality Based Thereon. A Popular Exposition* (New York: Peter Eckler, 1891) with many references to Feuerbach. The parallels to the German Catholic movement, which also sought a new worldview beyond institutional religion, are noted in Andreas W. Daum, *Wissenschaftspopularisierung im 19. Jahrhundert. Bürgerliche Kultur, naturwissenschaftliche Bildung und die deutsche Öffentlichkeit 1848–1914* (Munich: Oldenbourg, 1998), 195–211.

8. See Dieter Wittich, "Einleitung," *Schriften zum kleinbürgerlichen Materialismus in Deutschland,* 2 vols. (Berlin: Akademie, 1971); Andreas Daum, "Science, Politics, and Religion: Humboldtian Thinking and the Transformation of Civil Society in Germany, 1830–1870," *Osiris* 17 (2002): 107–40.

9. Wittich, "Einleitung," xliii–xliv; Gregory, *Scientific Materialism,* 35–39.

10. Jakob Moleschott, *Lehre der Nahrungsmittel. Für das Volk,* 2nd ed. (Enke: Erlangen, 1853); on Moleschott's role in the study of nutrition, see Jane O'Hara-May, "Measuring Man's Needs," *Journal of the History of Biology* 4 (1971): 249–73; on his politics, see Gregory, *Scientific Materialism,* 88.

11. See Winiger, *Ludwig Feuerbach: Denker der Menschlichkeit* (Berlin: Aufbau, 2004), 54; on Zschokke, see Prelinger, "Religious Dissent, . . . Germany" 43–45.

12. Wittich, "Einleitung," xxiii.

13. Wittich documents the ongoing criticism of Moleschott, Vogt, and Büchner for reducing thought to fluids in "Einleitung," lxii.

14. Ludwig Feuerbach, "Die Naturwissenschaft und die Revolution" (1850), in *GW* 10³:347–48, 350–51.

15. Feuerbach, "Die Naturwissenschaft und die Revolution," 358.

16. Quoted in Feuerbach, "Die Naturwissenschaft und die Revolution," 366–67.

17. Feuerbach, "Die Naturwissenschaft und die Revolution," 367; Winiger argues that the essay was wholly satirical. I am not so sure. If read in conjunction with Feuerbach's considerations on the way character and matter interrelated, with the concomitant denial of the continued existence of a stable soul over time, the argument that diet may be the key to revolutionary activism or passivity seems consistent, even if not fully worked out.

18. "To be in the body means to be in the world. So many senses—so many pores, so many bare spots. The body is nothing other than the *porous self*." "Einige Bemerkungen über den 'Anfang der Philosophie' von Dr. J. F. Reiff," in *GW* 9³:151.

19. Feuerbach, *EC,* xx.

20. "Das Geheimnis des Opfers oder Der Mensch ist, was er isst" (1862), in *GW* 11³:26–52; Marx W. Wartofsky, *Feuerbach* (New York: Cambridge University Press, 1977), 415–17. On food and Feuerbach: Harald Lemke, "Feuerbachs Stammtischthese, oder vom Ursprung des Satzes: 'Der Mensch ist, was er isst,'" *Aufklärung und Kritik* 11 (2004), 117–40.

21. S. Rawidowicz, *Ludwig Feuerbachs Philosophie: Ursprung und Schicksal* (Berlin: Reuther und Richard, 1931), 148–50. Of the extensive work on "mechanical materialism," see esp. Gregory, *Scientific Materialism;* Frederick Gregory, "Scientific versus Dialectical Materialism: A Clash of Ideologies in Nineteenth-Century German Radicalism," *Isis* 68 (1977): 206–23.

22. Ludwig Feuerbach, "Nachgelassene Aphorismen," in *Sämtliche Werke,* ed. Wilhelm Bolin and Friedrich Jodl (Stuttgart: Fr. Frommanns Verlag, 1911), 10:308–9; in the introduction (x), Bolin and Jodl assert that all the aphorisms come from Feuerbach's last years in Bruckberg and Nuremberg, i.e., the last decades of his life.

23. Ibid., "Nachgelassene Aphorismen," 307.

24. Feuerbach to Gustav Bäuerle, May 31, 1867, in *GW* 20:302–3.

25. See esp. Lawrence S. Stepelevich, "Max Stirner and Ludwig Feuerbach," *Journal of the History of Ideas* 39 (1978): 451–63; Stepelevich's later work has continued to stress the importance of Stirner to Feuerbach's turn.

26. Letter to Julius Duboc of Apr. 6, 1861, in Feuerbach, in *GW* 20:39–40.

27. See his "Über Spiritualismus und Materialismus, besonders in Beziehung auf die Willensfreiheit," from around 1858 to 1866, in *GW* 20:62; "Wider den Dualismus von Leib und Seele, Fleisch und Geist" (1846), in Feuerbach, *GW* 10³:130: "with a change in my body, my self, my consciousness, also becomes something different."

28. Moses Hess, "Der deutsche Humanismus," *Das Jahrhundert* 2 (1857): 1049.

29. Letter to Wilhelm Bolin of Oct. 20, 1860, in *GW* 20:292.

30. Feuerbach, *Theogonie,* 3.

31. Karl Grün, "Ludwig Feuerbachs philosophische Charakterentwicklung," in *Ausgewählte Schriften in zwei Bänden,* ed. Manuela Köppe (Berlin: Akademie, 2005), 1:710; Arve Brunvoll, *"Gott ist Mensch": Die Luther-Rezeption Ludwig Feuerbachs und die Entwicklung seiner Religiosität* (Frankfurt: Peter Lang, 1996), 17–19, remarks on the development of the new style starting in 1844, with *The Essence of Faith According to Luther.*

32. Feuerbach, "Nachgelassene Aphorismen," 344–45.

33. Ibid., *Theogonie,* 33; Harvey, "Feuerbach on Luther's Doctrine of Revelation: An Essay in Honor of Brian Ferrish," *Journal of Religion* 78 (1998):5.

34. Feuerbach, *Theogonie,* 47–48.

35. Ibid., 48–49.
36. Ibid., 252; Paul, Eph. 1: 4.
37. Feuerbach, *Theogonie*, 44–45. Despite the differences between the philosopher of crisis and the psychologist of religion, Kierkegaard, perhaps the other most important person to confront the crisis of faith and idealism at midcentury, also argued for a simple faith that God would provide in the face of apparent proof to the contrary: Abraham believed that "God would give him a new Isaac, could return to life the one sacrificed," *Fear and Trembling/Repetition,* ed. and trans. Howard V. Hong and Edna H. Hong (Princeton, NJ: Princeton University Press, 1983), 36.
38. Feuerbach, *Theogonie,* 82–83.
39. This point already in "Das Wesen der Religion" (1846), par. 1–2, which describes "nature" not as a coherent, unified essence but in terms of its distinction from the "human": in *GW* 10³:3–4; Wartofsky, *Feuerbach,* 390–91. In his review of *Theogonie,* Arnold Ruge, by contrast, presents an image of Feuerbach still in accord with his earlier work; Feuerbach's retention of the wish as an essential aspect of humans, for example, signified his rejection of materialism as represented by Moleschott and others: "Briefe über Ludwig Feuerbach und seine Theogonie," *Deutsches Museum* 8, no. 2 (1858): 136–38, 249–51. Ruge was correct if materialism referred to a mechanical materialism, in which living beings were complex machines; Ruge ignored approaches to materialism that sought aspects of dynamism inherent in matter itself.
40. Feuerbach, *Theogonie,* 48–49; see also Ludwig Feuerbach, *Lectures on the Essence of Religion,* trans. Ralph Manheim (New York: Harper and Row, 1967), 33–34, on death and dependence.
41. Ibid., *Theogonie,* 259–65.
42. See Ibid., 291–92, where Feuerbach suggests that an incomprehensible God could not be loved, but would instead be hated; what he misses in this account of "mere" theological discussion of God's incomprehensibility is that God would in any case stand in an affective relationship to humans, whether loved or hated, trusted or feared. The suggestion that the creator of the world was evil does, of course, haunt Christianity, most important in the so-called Gnostic traditions. And the incomprehensibility of God was central to the Calvinist tradition, and helps explain the sources of Karl Barth's criticism of Feuerbach's humanism, insofar as it could not grasp evil and death: "Ludwig Feuerbach," in *Theology and Church: Shorter Writings, 1920–1928,* trans. Louise Pettibone Smith (New York: Harper and Row, 1962), 235–37; Brunvoll, *"Gott und Mensch,"* 103–7.
43. Feuerbach's critique of Buddhism paralleled his critique of Catholicism: see "Zur Moralphilosophie" (1868), ed. Werner Schuffenhauer, in *Solidarität oder Egoismus: Studien zu einer Ethik bei und nach Ludwig Feuerbach,* ed. Hans-Jürg Braun (Berlin: Akademie, 1994), 377–83; and letters to Wilhelm Bolin, June 13, 1859 and July 16, 1861, and letter to Otto Lüning of Nov. 28, 1860, in *GW* 20:243–44, 314, 371–72.
44. Feuerbach, *Theogonie,* 85.

45. Ibid., 170–74.
46. Ibid., 302–6.
47. Ibid., 65–66.
48. Ibid., "Nachgelassene Aphorismen," 318.
49. Ibid., 339.
50. Francesco Tomasoni, "Heidentum und Judentum: Vom schärfsten Gegensatz zur Annäherung. Eine Entwicklungslinie vom 'Wesen des Christentums' bis zur 'Theogonie,'" in *Ludwig Feuerbach und die Geschichte der Philosophie,* ed. Walter Jaeschke and Tomasoni (Berlin: Akademie, 1998); see also *Modernity and the Final Aim of History: The Debate over Judaism from Kant to the Young Hegelians* (Dordrecht: Klower, 2003), 186–97.
51. Feuerbach, *EC,* 112–19. This passage has been used to show Feuerbach's anti-Semitism by a number of authors, including Paul Lawrence Rose (*German Question/Jewish Question: Revolutionary Antisemitism from Kant to Weber* [Princeton: Princeton University Press, 1990], 253–55) and Lincoln (*Theorizing Myth,* 57–58).
52. Feuerbach, *Theogonie,* in *GW* 7³:246–50: "God only becomes the Creator insofar as He becomes human, but He only becomes human so that the human will be blessed," Feuerbach concludes based on a reconstruction of Thomas of Aquinas and others.
53. Ibid., 49–56.
54. Feuerbach to Duboc, end of Oct./beginning of Nov. 1866, in *GW* 21:271.
55. Feuerbach underlined this point in letters to Bolin, May 19, 1863, in *GW* 21:73–75, and to Duboc in a pointed and angry letter from fall 1866, in *GW* 21:269. On Kant and the late Feuerbach, see esp. Rawidowicz, *Ludwig Feuerbachs Philosophie,* 246–57; Howard Williams, "Ludwig Feuerbach's Critique of Religion and the End of Moral Philosophy," in *The New Hegelians: Politics and Philosophy in the Hegelian School,* ed. Douglas Moggach (New York: Cambridge University Press, 2006), 50–66; Ferruccio Andolfi, "Feuerbach und die kantische Ethik," in *Ludwig Feuerbach und die Philosophie der Zukunft,* ed. Hans-Jürg Braun, et al. (Berlin: Akademie, 1990), 381–410; Ferruccio Andolfi, "Autonomie und Heteronomie bei Feuerbach," in Braun, ed., *Solidarität oder Egoismus,* 31–44.
56. Julius Duboc to Feuerbach, Nov. 7, 1860, in *GW* 20:302; Bolin to Feuerbach, Nov. 10, 1860, in *GW* 20:305; Gregory, *Scientific Materialism,* 29–31; Klaus Christian Köhnke, *Entstehung und Aufstieg des Neukantianismus: Die deutsche Universitätsphilosophie zwischen Idealismus und Positivismus* (Frankfurt: Suhrkamp, 1986), 195–211; Thomas E. Willey, *Back to Kant: The Revival of Kantianism in German Social and Historical Thought, 1860–1914* (Detroit: Wayne State University Press, 1978), 59–68.
57. Feuerbach to Bolin, March 26, 1858, in *GW* 20:179; Feuerbach, "Nachgelassene Aphorismen," 317.
58. Bolin to Feuerbach, Oct. 4, 1860, in *GW* 20:285; see also Hans-Christoph Rauh, "Wilhelm Bolins philosophischer Briefwechsel mit Ludwig Feuerbach (1857–1871)," http://www.ludwig–feuerbach.de/Rauh_Bolin.pdf (accessed August 2007).

59. Feuerbach to Bolin, July 3, 1865, in *GW* 21:177.
60. Feuerbach to Bolin, Mar. 4, 1866, in *GW* 21:237, 239; Feuerbach to Bolin, Apr. 30, 1866, in *GW* 21:249.
61. Feuerbach to Duboc, Nov. 27, 1860, in *GW* 20:309–10.
62. See esp. Friedrich Albert Lange, *Geschichte des Materialismus und Kritik seiner Bedeutung in der Gegenwart* (Iserlohn: Baedeker, 1873), 290–91.
63. Feuerbach, "Zur Moralphilosophie," 389–92.
64. Feuerbach to Bolin, Feb. 4, 1864, in *GW* 21:104–5; Andolfi, "Feuerbach und die kantische Ethik," 395–96.
65. Feuerbach, "Über Spiritualismus und Materialismus, besonders in Beziehung auf die Willensfreiheit" (1866), in *GW* 11:64–66.
66. Feuerbach, "Nachgelassene Aphorismen," 321–22.
67. Ibid., 321–22.
68. Hess, "Über das Geldwesen," in *PSS,* 339, and in general Warren Breckman, *Marx, the Young Hegelians, and the Origin of Radical Social Theory: Dethroning the Self* (New York: Cambridge University Press, 1999).
69. See, for example, Louise Otto, "Assoziation für Alle!" in *Frauen-Zeitung,* repr. in *"Dem Reich der Freiheit,"* 59–61.
70. Feuerbach, "Zur Moralphilosophie," 365; Williams, "Ludwig Feuerbach's Critique," 59; Andolfi, "Autonomie und Heteronomie," on a new ethics combining self and other.
71. Feuerbach, "Zur Moralphilosophie," 388.
72. Ibid., 379–80. In his letters, Feuerbach made clear that Schopenhauer was a chief target of his work on moral philosophy. As did Nietzsche in later years, Feuerbach viewed Schopenhauer's attempt to transcend the world through nothingness as incoherent, since humans were simply in the world—and also as a frank ignorance of the combination of joy and suffering that comprised all essential parts of human life, including sexuality and raising children (see ibid., 385, on children, and on the combination of satisfaction and burden in sexuality, "Nachgelassene Aphorismen," 335). Schopenhauer's thoughts on sympathy, however, made sense to Feuerbach, and corresponded to his argument that sympathy was a necessary element in a porous self essentially open to the world (praising Schopenhauer's notion of sympathy, "Zur Moralphilosophie," 416–17). Schopenhauer's attempt to raise sympathy up to a metaphysical principle did not make sense, since it contradicted what Feuerbach saw as the sensual and immediate drive for happiness, and represented nothing more than a "flight into the realm of metaphysical dreams": Feuerbach to Bolin, July 16, 1861, in *GW* 20:371–72.
73. Feuerbach, "Zur Moralphilosophie," 380–82.
74. Ibid., 383.
75. Feuerbach to Duboc, end of Oct./beginning of Nov. 1866, in *GW* 21:269; Andolfi, "Autonomie und Heteronomie," 39; Wolfgang Lefèvre, "Feuerbach und die Grenzen der Ethik," in Braun, ed., *Solidarität oder Egoismus,* 132–34.
76. "Anthropologische Aphorismen," *Deutsches Museum* (1866): 340–46.
77. Feuerbach, "Nachgelassene Aphorismen," 311.

78. The communicative, of course, implied a system of symbols not immediately reducible to sensuality. In this sense, Feuerbach's own ideas of the relationship between I and Thou pointed toward a broader notion of interaction, which he himself was unable to articulate without a theory of language. See Walter Jaeschke, "Humanität zwischen Spiritualismus und Materialismus," in Adriàno Veríssimo Serrão, ed., *O Homen Integral: Antropologia e Utopia em Ludwig Feuerbach* (Lisbon: Centro de Filosofia da Universidade de Lisboa, 2001), 62–63.

79. Marx, "On the Jewish Question," in *MECW* 3:160–63.

80. See Karol Bal, "Das andere Du? Der Gewissensbegriff in der Feuerbachischen Spätethik," in Braun, ed., *Solidarität oder Egosimus,* 154–66.

81. Feuerbach, "Nachgelassene Aphorismen," 312.

82. Ibid., "Zur Moralphilosophie," 408.

83. Ibid., 409–11. See also Ibid.,"Über Spiritualismus und Materialismus," 74–81.

84. Feuerbach to Bolin, early June, 1870, in Bolin, ed., *Ausgewählte Briefe*, II: 362–63.

85. Of the many books on the topic, see esp. Ann Taylor Allen's *Feminism and Motherhood in Germany, 1800–1914* (New Brunswick, NJ: Rutgers University Press, 1991).

86. Feuerbach, "Zur Moralphilosophie," 413.

87. Ibid., "Über Spiritualismus und Materialismus," 80–81.

88. Julius Duboc, "Zur philosophischen Literatur," *Allgemeine Augsburger Zeitung,* Beilage, Oct. 19–22, 1866, 4831. See the important critique of Feuerbach's optimism and his refusal to engage with Hobbes in Hassan Givsan, "Homo homini deus est—der Wendepunkt der Weltgeschichte," in *Ludwig Feuerbach (1804–1872): Identität und Pluralismus in der globalen Gesellschaft,* ed. Ursula Reitemeyer, Takayuki Shibata, and Francesco Tomasoni (Münster: Waxmann, 2006), 67–82.

89. Feuerbach, "Über Spiritualismus und Materialismus," 179.

90. Ibid., *EC,* 236–46.

91. Ibid., "Über Spiritualismus und Materialismus," 113.

92. Florentine Fritzen outlines a history of consumption, movements for life reform, and politics in Germany, in *Gesünder leben. Die Lebensreformbewegung im 20. Jahrhundert* (Wiesbaden: Franz Steiner, 2006). One cannot miss the implicit reference to the German nationalist tradition of gymnastics, of developing a strong body to encase a strong, republican will.

93. Duboc to Feuerbach, April 29, 1853, in *GW* 20:28.

94. Duboc to Feuerbach, before May 18, 1853, in *GW* 20:31; Duboc was under the impression that his first letter had been misaddressed and never arrived.

95. See the critique of bestial eating habits in Marx, *MECW* 3:274–75, and in Hess, "A Communist Credo," 117–18.

96. Feuerbach to Duboc, May 20, 1853, in *GW* 20:33, citing "Über mein 'Gedanken über Tod und Unsterblichkeit,'" in *GW* 10^3:292. The argument paralleled his attempt in the same period to distinguish between imaginary

and real wishes based on experience. See also Feuerbach's, *Lectures on the Essence of Religion,* 277–78; Andolfi, "Feuerbach und die kantische Ethik," 386.

97. Feuerbach to Duboc, May 20, 1853, in *GW* 20:35–36.

98. Feuerbach, *Lectures on the Essence of Religion,* 278.

99. Feuerbach to Duboc, May 20, 1853, in *GW* 20:36.

100. Duboc to Feuerbach, May 25, 1853, in *GW* 20:38. That Duboc in fact fully comprehended Stirner's critique is clear from a work from many decades later: *Das Ich und die Uebrigen (Für und Wider M. Stirner)* (Leipzig: Wigand, 1897).

101. Feuerbach to Duboc, June 23/July 5, 1853, in *GW* 20:46–47.

102. Ibid., 47.

103. Duboc to Feuerbach, July 12, 1853, in *GW* 20:50–51.

104. Feuerbach, "Über Spiritualismus und Materialismus," 83–84.

105. See the review by Duboc, "Zur philosophischen Literatur," 4832, referring to need for "*Rechstbewusstseyn.*"

106. Feuerbach to Duboc, End Oct./beg. Nov., *GW* 21:269; see Rawidowicz, *Ludwig Feuerbachs Philosophie,* 250–51.

107. Marx and Engels, *The German Ideology,* in *MECW* 5:41, 57–58.

108. Feuerbach, *Lectures on the Essence of Religion,* 139.

109. Feuerbach to Bolin, March 5, 1867, in *GW* 21:289–90.

110. A more positive assessment of Feuerbach's notion of ethics, pointing out the way it shows the limits to all systems of ethics, in Hans-Martin Sass, "The 'Transition' from Feuerbach to Marx: A Re-Interpretation," *Studies in Soviet Thought* 26 (1983): 123–42.

111. Feuerbach to Lassalle, Oct. 28/Dec. 3, 1863, in *GW* 21:92. Lassalle had written to Feuerbach on Oct. 21, 1863, on the advice of Emma Herwegh, seeking approval of his theoretical and political work: *GW* 21:86–89; more context in ibid., xi. See also Feuerbach's letter of March 10, 1863, to Jakob von Khanikoff, on how socialism becomes despotic and fanatical if it denies the right to individuality, in *GW* 21:63. Duboc described conversations with Feuerbach in 1864 that revealed Feuerbach's proximity to the democrats of southern Germany, in "Aus Ludwig Feuerbachs Nachlass" (1875), repr. in Duboc, *Gegen den Strom: Gesammelte Aufsätze,* 2nd ed. (Hamburg: Hermann Grüning, 1883), 179.

112. Feuerbach to Friedrich Kapp, April 11, 1868, in *GW* 21:347; references to *Capital* in "Zur Moralphilosophie," 376–77.

113. Quoted in Winiger, *Ludwig Feuerbach,* 322.

114. As described in Georg Gärtner, *Die Nürnberger Arbeiterbewegung 1868–1908* (Berlin: Dietz Nachf, 1977), 43–44; Karl Grün reproduces Karl Scholl's speech at the grave in *Ludwig Feuerbach in seinem Briefwechsel und Nachlass, sowie in seiner philosophischen Charakterentwicklung* (Leipzig: Winter, 1874) 2:113–15; Rawidowicz notes the divergent appropriations of Feuerbach's legacies by Marxist social democracy and radical liberalism, a more accurate view of the legacy, in *Ludwig Feuerbach,* 316–17.

Conclusion

1. Engels, "Ludwig Feuerbach and the End of Classical German Philosophy," in *MECW* 26:364; on Engels's break with Feuerbach, see esp. Francesco Tomasoni, *Ludwig Feuerbach und die nicht-menschliche Natur. Das Wesen der Religion: Die Entstehungsgeschichte des Werkes, rekonstruiert auf der Grundlage unveröffentlicher Manuskripte,* trans. Alf Schneditz (Stuttgart: Frommann-Holzboog, 1990), 31–37, 53–54, and Jens Grandt, *Ludwig Feuerbach und die Welt des Glaubens* (Münster: Westfälisches Dampfboot, 2006), 86–104.

2. See esp. Karl Löwith, *From Hegel to Nietzsche: The Revolution in Nineteenth-Century Thought,* trans. David E. Green (New York: Holt, Rinehart and Winston, 1964), 76, 82.

3. Marx, *Capital,* in *MECW* 25:89.

4. Marx, *Economic and Philosophic Manuscripts,* in MECW 3:280; the context for Marx was somewhat different, insofar as he was criticizing Proudhon's call for equal wages within a market economy deprived of capitalists; the criticism in the end, though, applied as well to Feuerbach, who also sought a natural, "republican" social order without hierarchy, without asking about the coercive role that society itself could play.

5. See Tomasoni's account of Feuerbach's notes on ethnography and evolution in *Ludwig Feuerbach und die nicht-menschliche Natur,* 127–76, esp. 150–63 on colonialism and racism.

6. Feuerbach to Duboc, end of Oct./start of Nov. 1866, in *GW* 21:270.

7. See Feuerbach, "Über Spiritualismus und Materialismus, besonders in Beziehung auf die Willensfreiheit" (1866), in *GW* 11:55–57.

8. Feuerbach to Friedrich Kapp, Dec. 2, 1866, in *GW* 21:275, and Feb. 15, 1867, in *GW* 21:287–89; Kapp's letters to Feuerbach of Aug. 10, 1866, Dec. 29, 1866, and Jan. 4, 1868 (in ibid., 21:258, 281–82, 337–39) show the sharp turn toward Prussia, military power, and the yearning for Germany to become a world power on the part of the incipient National Liberal; see also his proud reference to his son Wolfgang, who has begun to come to blows with his school friends in New York who did not support Lincoln (Kapp to Feuerbach, Dec. 10, 1864, in ibid., 142). See also Hans-Ulrich Wehler's introduction to Friedrich Kapp, *Vom radikalen Frühsozialisten des Vormärz zum liberalen Parteipolitiker des Bismarckreichs. Briefe 1843–1884* (Frankfurt: Insel, 1969), 24–30.

9. Mathilde Reichardt, *Wissenschaft und Sittenlehre. Briefe an Jakob Moleschott* (Gotha: Hugo Schenke, 1856), 85; see also 10–11, 30, praising Feuerbach's theory of religion.

10. Ibid., 111, quoting Vogt.

11. Ibid., 24–26, 30–31.

12. Ibid., 110–20, 122.

13. Ibid., 123–25; at 133–34, she demands sacrifice of criminals, implying clearly capital punishment, that would nonetheless affirm their dignity as products of nature.

14. "Wesen der Natur," in *GW* 10³:2.

15. Most important, of course, was *The German Ideology,* in *MECW* 5.

16. Marx, *Capital,* in *MECW* 35:53: useful labor is an "eternal, nature-imposed necessity."

17. See esp. "Contribution to the Critique of Hegel's Philosophy of Law," in *MECW* 3:183.

18. See, for example, his scathing remarks about Rousseau's concept of nature and natural equality—which could as easily be applied to Feuerbach—in *Twilight of the Idols and the Anti-Christ* trans. R. J. Hollingdale (London: Penguin, 1948), 101: nature not as something to which one returns, but something "high, free, even frightful."

19. Bernard Williams, ed., *The Gay Science,* trans. Josefine Nauckhoff (Cambridge: Cambridge University Press, 2001), 171; see also the comments by Stefan Arvidsson, "Aryan Mythology as Science and Ideology," *Journal of the American Academy of Religion* 67 (1999): 340.

20. Nietzsche, *Twilight of the Idols,* 30; see also Nietzsche's brief remark on Wagner's fall away from Feuerbach's notion of a "healthy sensuality" to "conversion, denial, Christianity, medievalism" in *Parsifal,* in *On the Genealogy of Morals,* trans. Walter Kaufmann, *Basic Writings of Nietzsche* (New York: Modern Library 1968), 536, as well as a more sustained discussion of Nietzsche, Feuerbach, and sensuality in Paul Bishop, "Nietzsche's 'New' Morality: Gay Science, Materialist Ethics," *History of European Ideas* 32 (2006): 223–36, with further references in n7.

21. Ernst Haeckel, *The Riddle of the Universe at the Close of the Nineteenth Century,* trans. Joseph McCabe (New York: Harper, 1900), 194, 295, 309, 313; Wolfgang R. Krabbe, "Biologismus und Lebensreform," in *Die Lebensreform. Entwürfe zur Neugestaltung von Leben und Kunst um 1900,* ed. Kai Buchholz, et al. (Darmstadt: Häusser, 2001), 1:179–81, who notes the paradox—which was common for the *Lebensreformbewegung*—in the attempt to make use of a rationalist materialist to promote a worldview that was expressly idealist and mystical; as the discussion in this book has suggested, such a paradox was never far from Feuerbachianism already in the 1840s.

22. Of the many sources, see esp. Hans Schwarz, "Darwinism between Kant and Haeckel," *Journal of the American Academy of Religion* 48 (1980): 581–602.

23. Friedrich Jodl, *Ludwig Feuerbach* (Stuttgart: Frommann, 1904), 115.

24. Tracie Matysik, *Reforming the Moral Subject: Ethics and Sexuality in Central Europe, 1890–1930* (Ithaca, NY: Cornell University Press, 2008).

25. In addition to Matysik's work, with further references, see Annegret Stopczyk, "Helene Stöcker. Philosophin der 'Neuen Ethik,'" in *Die Lebensreform,* 1:157–59.

26. Jochen-Christoph Kaiser, "Freireligiöse und Feuerbestatter," in *Handbuch der deutschen Reformbewegungen 1880–1933,* ed. Diethart Kerbs and Jürgen Reulecke (Wuppertal: Peter Hammer, 1998), 537–49, with further references.

27. See esp. the huge variety of positions and people presented in the two volumes of *Die Lebensreform,* ed. Kai Buchholz, et al., 2 vols.

28. See esp. his comments on the rationalization of sexuality in "Religious Rejections of the World and Their Directions," in *From Max Weber: Essays on Sociology,* ed. H. H. Gerth and C. Wright Mills (New York: Oxford University Press, 1946), 323–59, esp. 344–46.

Bibliography

Aberbach, Alan David. *The Ideas of Richard Wagner: An Examination and Analysis.* 2nd ed. Lanham, MD: University Press of America, 2003.

Adorno, Theodor. *In Search of Wagner.* Translated by Rodney Livingstone. London: New Left Books, 1981.

Allen, Ann Taylor. *Feminism and Motherhood in Germany, 1800–1914.* New Brunswick, NJ: Rutgers University Press, 1991.

Anderson, Bonnie S. *Joyous Greetings: The First International Women's Movement, 1830–1860.* New York: Oxford University Press, 2000.

Andolfi, Ferruccio. "Autonomie und Heteronomie bei Feuerbach." In *Solidarität oder Egoismus. Studien zu einer Ethik bei und nach Ludwig Feuerbach,* edited by Hans-Jürg Braun, 31–44. Berlin: Akademie, 1994.

———. "Feuerbach und die kantische Ethik." In *Ludwig Feuerbach und die Philosophie der Zukunft,* edited by Hans-Jürg Braun, Hans-Martin Sass, Werner Schuffenhauer, and Francesco Tomasoni, 381–410. Berlin: Akademie, 1990.

Arndt, Andreas. "'Neue Unmittelbarkeit': Zur Aktualisierung eines Konzepts in der Philosophie der Vormärz." In *Philosophie und Literatur in der Vormärz: Der Streit um die Romantik (1820–1854),* edited by Walter Jaeschke, 207–33. Hamburg: Felix Meiner, 1995.

Arvidsson, Stefan. *Aryan Idols: Indo-European Mythology as Ideology and as Science.* Translated by Sonia Wichmann. Chicago: University of Chicago Press, 2006.

Ascheri, Carlo. *Feuerbachs Bruch mit der Spekulation.* Frankfurt: Europäische Verlagsanstalt, 1969.

Avineri, Shlomo. *Moses Hess: Prophet of Communism and Zionism.* New York: New York University Press, 1985.

Bailey, Robert. "The Structure of the *Ring* and its Evolution." *19th Century Music* 1 (1977): 49–50.

Bakunin, Mikhail. *Statism and Anarchy.* Translated and edited by Marshall S. Shatz. New York: Cambridge University Press, 1990.

Bal, Karol. "Das andere Du? Der Gewissensbegriff in der Feuerbachischen Spätethik." In *Solidarität oder Egoismus. Studien zu einer Ethik bei und nach Ludwig Feuerbach,* edited by Hans-Jürg Braun, 154–66. Berlin: Akademie, 1994.

Bamberger, Ludwig. *Erinnerungen.* Edited by Paul Nathan. Berlin: Georg Reimer, 1899.

Barclay, David A. *Frederick William IV and the Prussian Monarchy 1840–1861.* Oxford: Clarendon, 1995.

Barth, Karl. *Theology and Church: Shorter Writings, 1920–1928.* Translated by Louise Pettibone Smith. New York: Harper and Row, 1962.

Bermbach, Udo. "Das ästhetische Motiv in Wagners Antisemitismus." In *Richard Wagner und die Juden,* edited by Dieter Borchmeyer, Ami Maayani, and Susanne Vill, 55–76. Stuttgart: J. B. Metzler, 2000.

Berry, Mark. *Treacherous Bonds and Laughing Fire: Politics and Religion in Wagner's Ring.* Aldershot: Ashgate, 2006.

Bishop, Paul. "'Elementary Aesthetics,' Hedonistic Ethics: The Philosophical Foundations of Feuerbach's Later Works." *History of European Ideas* 34 (2008): 298–309.

———. "Nietzsche's 'New' Morality: Gay Science, Materialist Ethics." *History of European Ideas* 32 (2006): 223–36.

Bloch, Ernst. *Das Prinzip Hoffnung.* Frankfurt: Suhrkamp, 1959.

———. *Essays on the Philosophy of Music.* Translated by Peter Palmer. New York: Cambridge University Press, 1985.

Borchmeyer, Dieter. *Richard Wagner: Theory and Theater.* Translated by Stewart Spencer. Oxford: Clarendon, 1991.

Borchmeyer, Dieter, Ami Maayani, and Susanne Vill, eds. *Richard Wagner und die Juden.* Stuttgart: J. B. Metzler, 2000.

Breckman, Warren. "Eduard Gans and the Crisis of Hegelianism." *Journal of the History of Ideas* 62 (2001): 543–564.

———. *Marx, the Young Hegelians, and the Origin of Radical Social Theory: Dethroning the Self.* New York: Cambridge University Press, 1999.

———. "The Symbolic Dimension and the Politics of Left Hegelianism." In *The Left Hegelians: Politics and Philosophy in the Hegelian School,* edited by Douglas Moggach, 67–90. New York: Cambridge University Press, 2006.

Brunvoll, Arve. *"Gott ist Mensch": Die Luther-Rezeption Ludwig Feuerbachs und die Entwicklung seiner Religiosität.* Frankfurt: Peter Lang, 1996.

Buchholz, Kai, Rita Latocha, Hilke Peckmann und Klaus Wolbert, eds. *Die Lebensreform. Entwürfe zur Neugestaltung von Leben und Kunst um 1900.* 2 vols. Darmstadt: Häusser, 2001.

Büchner, Ludwig. *Force and Matter, or Principles of the Natural Order of the Universe, with a System of Morality Based Thereon. A Popular Exposition.* 15th ed. New York: Peter Eckler, 1891.

Bykova, Marina. "Subjektivität und Gattung." In *Ludwig Feuerbach (1804–1872): Identität und Pluralismus in der globalen Gesellschaft,* edited by Ursula Reitemeyer, Takayuki Shibata, and Francesco Tomasoni, 117–28. Münster: Waxmann, 2006.

Cai, Hou. "Moses Hess und Ludwig Feuerbach." In *Ludwig Feuerbach und die Philosophie der Zukunft,* edited by Hans-Jürg Braun, Hans-Martin Sass, Werner Schuffenhauer, and Francesco Tomasoni,, 593–615. Berlin: Akademie, 1990.

Canter, Benjamin Wildish. "Feuerbachian Imagination and the Reversal of Hegelian Ontology in *The Essence of Christianity* (1841)." PhD diss., Memorial University of Newfoundland, 2003.

Carlyle, Thomas. *The French Revolution.* New York: Modern Library, n.d.

Dahlhaus, Carl. *Richard Wagner's Music Dramas.* Translated by Mary Whittall. New York: Cambridge University Press, 1979.

———. "Wagner's Place in the History of Music." In *Wagner Handbook,* edited by Ulrich Müller and Peter Wapnewski, translation edited by Peter Deathridge, 91–117. Cambridge: Harvard University Press, 1992.

Darcy, Warren. "The Metaphysics of Annihilation: Wagner, Schopenhauer, and the Ending of the *Ring.*" *Music Theory Spectrum* 16 (1994): 1–40.

———. "'The World Belongs to Alberich!' Wagner's Changing Attitudes towards the 'Ring.'" In *Wagner's Ring of the Nibelung: A Companion,* edited by Stewart Spencer, 48–52. London: Thames and Hudson, 1993.

Daum, Andreas W. "Science, Politics, and Religion: Humboldtian Thinking and the Transformation of Civil Society in Germany, 1830–1870." *Osiris* 17 (2002): 107–40.

———. *Wissenschaftspopularisierung im 19. Jahrhundert. Bürgerliche Kultur, naturwissenschaftliche Bildung und die deutsche Öffentlichkeit 1848–1914.* Munich: Oldenbourg, 1998.

Deppert, Wolfgang. "Beziehungen zwischen Philosophie und Dichtung am Beispiel von Feuerbachs Philosophie und Kellers Dichtung." In *Ludwig Feuerbach: Religionskritik und Geistesfreiheit,* edited by Volker Mueller, 287–325. Neustadt: Angelika Lenz Verlag, 2004.

Dews, Peter. *The Limits of Disenchantment: Essays on Contemporary European Philosophy.* London: Verso, 1995.

DiGaetani, John Louis. *Wagner and Suicide.* Jefferson, NC: McFarland, 2003.

Dittmar, Louise. *Bekannte Geheimnisse.* Darmstadt: Leske, 1845.

———. *Brutus-Michel.* 2nd ed. Darmstadt: Leske, 1848.

———. *Lessing und Feuerbach, oder Auswahl aus G. C. Lessing's theologischen Schriften nebst Originalbeiträgen und Belegstellen aus L. Feuerbach's Wesen des Christenthums.* Offenbach: André, 1847.

———. *Der Mensch und sein Gott in und ausser dem Christenthum.* Offenbach: André, 1846.

———. *Skizzen und Briefe aus der Gegenwart.* Darmstadt: Leske, 1845.

———. *Vier Zeitfragen. Beantwortet in einer Versammlung des Mannheimer Montag-Vereins.* Offenbach: André, 1847.

———. *Das Wesen der Ehe von Louise Dittmar nebst einigen Aufsätzen über die soziale Reform der Frauen.* Leipzig: Wigand, 1849.

———. *Wühlerische Gedichte eines Wahrhaften. Gesammelt von Louise Dittmar.* Mannheim: Bensheimer, 1848.

———. *Zur Charakterisirung der nordischen Mythologie im Verhältniss zu andern Naturreligionen Eine Skizze.* Darmstadt: Leske, 1848.

Döhring, Sieghart. "Die traumatische Beziehung Wagners zu Meyerbeer." In *Richard Wagner und die Juden,* edited by Dieter Borchmeyer, Ami Maayani, and Susanne Vill, 262–73. Stuttgart: J. B. Metzler, 2000.

Dowe, Dieter. *Aktion und Organisation. Arbeiterbewegung, sozialistische und kommunistische Bewegung in der Preussischen Rheinprovinz 1820–1852.* Hannover: Verlag für Literatur und Zeitgeschehen, 1970.

Dowe, Dieter, Dieter Langewiesche, David Higgins, and Jonathan Sperber, eds. *Europe in 1848: Revolution and Reform.* Translated by David Higgens. New York: Berghahn, 2001.

Duboc, Julius. *Gegen den Strom: Gesammelte Aufsätze,* 2nd ed. Hamburg: Hermann Grüning, 1883.

———. *Das Ich und die Übrigen (Für und wider M. Stirner).* Leipzig: Wigand, 1897.

———. "Zur philosophischen Literatur." *Beilage zur Allgemeine Augsburger Zeitung,* October 19–22, 1866: 4793–94, 4809–10, 4831–32.

Dünnebier, Hans. *Gottfried Keller und Ludwig Feuerbach.* Zurich: Ketner, 1913.

Enzensberger, Ulrich. *Herwegh. Ein Heldenleben.* Frankfurt: Eichborn, 1999.

Esselborn, Karl. *Der Deutschkatholizismus in Darmstadt.* Darmstadt: Verlag der "Litera," 1923.

Fenske, Hans. "Ein reichgedeckter Büchertisch: Neue Literatur zur Revolution 1848/49." *Historisches Jahrbuch* 120 (2000): 331–57.

Feuerbach, Ludwig. *Entwürfe zu einer neuen Philosophie.* Edited by Walter Jaeschke and Werner Schuffenhauer. Hamburg: Felix Meiner, 1996.

———. *The Essence of Christianity.* Translated by George Elliot. 1855. Reprint. New York: Prometheus, 1989.

———. *The Essence of Faith according to Luther.* Translated by Melvin Cherno. New York: Harper and Row, 1967.

———. *Gesammelte Werke.* Edited by Werner Schuffenhauer. 21 vols. Berlin: Akademie, 1969ff.

———. *Lectures on the Essence of Religion.* Translated by Ralph Manheim. New York: Harper and Row, 1967.

———. *Ludwig Feuerbach in seinem Briefwechsel und Nachlass, sowie in seiner philosophischen Charakterentwicklung.* Edited by Karl Grün. Leipzig: Winter, 1874.

———. "Nachgelassene Aphorismen." In *Schriften zur Ethik und nachgelassene Aphorismen, Sämtliche Werke,* edited by Wilhelm Bolin and Friedrich Jodl, vol. 10, 297–346. Stuttgart: Frommanns Verlag, 1911.

———. *Principles of the Philosophy of the Future.* Translated by Manfred Vogel. Edited by Thomas E. Wartenberg. Indianapolis: Hackett, 1986.

———. "Provisional Theses for the Reformation of Philosophy." In *The Young Hegelians: An Anthology,* edited by Lawrence S. Stepelevich, 156–72. Atlantic Highlands, NJ: Humanities Press, 1983.

———. *Thoughts on Death and Immortality: From the Papers of a Thinker, along with an Appendix of Theological-Satirical Epigrams.* Translated by James A. Massey. Berkeley: University of California Press, 1980.

———. "Zur Moralphilosophie." Edited by Werner Schuffenhauer. In *Solidarität oder Egoismus: Studien zu einer Ethik bei und nach Ludwig Feuerbach,* edited by Hans-Jürg Braun, 353–429. Berlin: Akademie, 1994.

Förder, Herwig, and Martin Hundt. "Zur Vorgeschichte des Kommunistischen Manifests: Der Entwurf des 'Kommunistischen Glaubensbekenntnis' vom Juni 1847." In *Die bürgerlich-demokratische Revolution von 1848/49 in Deutschland,* 243–75. Dadiz: Topos, 1978.

Fourier, Charles. *The Theory of the Four Movements*. Edited by Gareth Stedman-Jones and Ian Patterson. New York: Cambridge University Press, 1996.

Frankel, Jonathan. *The Damascus Affair: "Ritual Murder," Politics, and the Jews in 1840*. New York: Cambridge University Press, 1997.

Freitag, Sabine. *Friedrich Hecker: Two Lives for Liberty*. Translated by Steven Rowan. St. Louis: St. Louis Mercantile Library, 2006.

Freund, Marion. *"Mag der Thron in Flammen glühn!" Schriftstellerinnen und die Revoluton von 1848/49*. Königstein/Taunus: Ulrike Helmer, 2004.

Fritzen, Florentine. *Gesünder leben. Die Lebensreformbewegung im 20. Jahrhundert*. Wiesbaden: Franz Steiner, 2006.

Fröbel, Julius. *System der socialen Politik*. 2nd ed. Mannheim: Grohe, 1847.

Gedö, András. "Bestandsaufnahme der philosophischen Moderne. Über Feuerbachs Philosophiegeschichtsschreibung." In *Ludwig Feuerbach und die Geschichte der Philosophie*, edited by Walter Jaeschke and Francesco Tomasoni, 97–133. Berlin: Akademie, 1998.

Geis, Lothar, ed. *Freireligiöses Quellenbuch Band I: 1844–1926*. Mainz: Freireligiöse Gemeinde Mainz, 2007.

Ginzo Fernández, Arsenio. "Filosofía de la finitud y utopia en L. Feuerbach." In *O homen integral: Antropologia e utopie em Ludwig Feuerbach*, edited by Adriana Veríssima Serrão, 231–56. Lisbon: Centro de Filosofia de Universidade de Lisboa, 2001.

Givsan, Hassan. "Homo homini deus est—der Wendepunkt der Weltgeschichte." In *Ludwig Feuerbach (1804–1872): Identität und Pluralismus in der globalen Gesellschaft*, edited by Ursula Reitemeyer, Takayuki Shibata, and Francesco Tomasoni, 67–82. Münster: Waxmann, 2006.

Grab, Walter. *Ein Mann der Marx Ideen gab. Wilhelm Schulz. Weggefährte Georg Büchners. Demokrat der Paulskirche*. Dusseldorf: Droste, 1979.

Graetz, Michael. "Humanismus, Sozialismus und Zionismus." In *Les juifs dans l'histoire de France*, edited by Myriam Yardeni, 146–64. Leiden, The Netherlands: Brill, 1980.

Graf, Friedrich Wilhelm. *Die Politisierung des religiösen Bewusstseins. Die bürgerlichen Religionsparteien im deutschen Vormärz: Das Beispiel des Deutschkatholizismus*. Stuttgart: Frommann-Holzboog, 1978.

Grandt, Jens. *Ludwig Feuerbach und die Welt des Glaubens*. Münster: Westfälisches Dampfboot, 2006.

Gregory, Frederick. *Nature Lost? Natural Science and the German Theological Traditions of the Nineteenth Century*. Cambridge, MA: Harvard University Press, 1992.

———. *Scientific Materialism in 19th Century Germany*. Dordrecht: D. Reidel, 1977.

———. "Scientific versus Dialectical Materialism: A Clash of Ideologies in Nineteenth-Century German Radicalism." *Isis* 68 (1977): 206–23.

Groschopp, Horst. *Dissidenten. Freidenkerei und Kultur in Deutschland*. Berlin: Dietz, 1997.

Grün, Karl. *Ausgewählte Schriften in zwei Bänden*. Edited by Manuela Köppe. 2 vols. Berlin: Akademie, 2006.

Guarneri, Carl J. "Reconstructing the Antebellum Communitarian Movement: Oneida and Fourierism." *Journal of the Early Republic* 16 (1996): 463–88.

———. *The Utopian Alternative: Fourierism in Nineteenth Century America.* Ithaca, NY: Cornell University Press, 1991.

Haeckel, Ernst. *The Riddle of the Universe at the Close of the Nineteenth Century.* Translated by Joseph McCabe. New York: Harper, 1900.

Hammacher, Emil. "Zur Würdigung des 'wahren' Sozialismus." *Archiv für die Geschichte des Sozialismus und der Arbeiterbewegung* 1 (1911): 41–100.

Hartwich, Wolf-Daniel. *"Deutsche Mythologie": Die Erfindung einer nationalen Kunstreligion.* Berlin: Philo, 2000.

Harvey, Van A. *Feuerbach and the Interpretation of Religion.* New York: Cambridge, 1997.

———. "Feuerbach on Luther's Doctrine of Revelation: An Essay in Honor of Brian Ferrish." *Journal of Religion* 78 (1998): 3–17.

Hauer, Stanley R. "Wagner and the *Völospá.*" *19th Century Music* 15 (1991): 52–63.

Hegel, Georg Wilhelm Friedrich. *Political Writings.* Translated by T. M. Knox. New York: Oxford University Press, 1998.

Henkel, Martin, and Rolf Taubert. *"Das Weib im Conflict mit den socialen Verhältnissen": mathilde franziska anneke und die erste deutsche frauenzeitung.* Berlin: edition egalité, 1976.

Herres, Jürgen. *1848/49: Revolution in Köln.* Cologne: Janus, 1998.

Herwegh, Georg, ed. *Einundzwanzig Bogen aus der Schweiz.* Zürich: Verlag des Literarischen Comptoirs, 1843.

Herzog, Dagmar. *Intimacy and Exclusion: Religious Politics in Pre-Revolutionary Baden.* Princeton, NJ: Princeton University Press, 1996.

Hess, Moses. *Ausgewählte Schriften.* Edited by Horst Lademacher. Wiesbaden: Fourier, 1981.

———. *Briefwechsel.* Edited by Edmund Silberner. The Hague: Mouton, 1959.

———. "Der deutsche Humanismus." *Das Jahrhundert* 2 (1857): 1033–40, 1049–55.

———. *Dynamische Stofflehre. I. Kosmischer Theil. Allgemeine Bewegungserscheinungen und ewiger Kreislauf des kosmischen Lebens.* Paris: Verlag von Mme. Syb. M. Hess Wittwe, 1877.

———. *The Holy History of Mankind and Other Writings.* Edited by Shlomo Avineri. New York: Cambridge University Press, 2004.

———. *Jüdische Schriften.* Edited by Theodor Zlocisti. Berlin: Louis Lamm, 1905.

———. "Naturwissenschaften und Gesellschaftslehre." *Das Jahrhundert* 1 (1856): 168–72, 221–24, 240–42, 258–60; 2 (1857): 19–20, 43–45, 115–17, 132–40, 169–76, 242–47, 285–91, 357–63.

———. *Neue Quellen zur Hess-Forschung.* Edited by Wolfgang Mönke. Berlin: Akademie, 1964.

———. *Philosophische und sozialistische Schriften 1837–1850. Eine Auswahl.* 2nd ed. Edited by Wolfgang Mönke. Berlin: Akademie, 1981.

————. "Physische Beschaffenheit und Geschichte der Weltkörper." *Das Jahrhundert* 2 (1857): 407–10, 432–37, 581–83, 628–32, 700–704, 726–28, 748–52, 773–76, 795–800.

————. "Populäre naturwissenschaftliche Schriftsteller." *Das Jahrhundert* 2 (1857): 889–91, 911–17, 933–40, 959–64, 1115–20, 1133–36, 1164–68, 1182–84; 3 (1858): 12–16.

————. *The Revival of Israel: Rome and Jerusalem, the Last Nationalist Question.* Translated by Meyer Waxman. Lincoln, NE: University of Nebraska Press, 1995.

Hexelschneider, Erhard. "Michail Bakunin (1814–1876). Ein russischer Revolutionär im Dresdner Maiaufstand." In *Akteure eines Umbruchs. Männer und Frauen der Revolution von 1848–49,* edited by Helmut Bleiber, Walter Schmidt, and Susanne Schötz, 37–81. Berlin: Fides, 2003.

Hundt, Irina. "Junghegelianer-Frauenbewegung. Eine Fragestellung zum Problem des Zusammenhangs." In *Philosophie, Literatur und Politik vor den Revolutionen von 1848. Zur Herausbildung der demokratischen Bewegungen in Europa,* edited by Lars Lambrecht, 511–24. Frankfurt: Peter Lang, 1996.

Hutcheon, Linda, and Michael Hutcheon. "'Alles was ist, endet': Living with the Knowledge of Death in Richard Wagner's *Der Ring des Nibelungen.*" *University of Toronto Quarterly* 67 (1998): 789–811.

Jaeschke, Walter. "Humanität zwischen Spiritualismus und Materialismus." In *O Homen Intregral: Antropologia e Utopia em Ludwig Feuerbach,* edited by Adriàno Veríssimo Serrão, 51–63. Lisbon: Centro de Filosofia da Universidade de Lisboa, 2001.

————. "Ludwig Feuerbach über Spiritualismus und Materialismus." In *Materialismus und Spiritualismus,* edited by Andreas Arndt and Walter Jaeschke, 23–34. Hamburg: Felix Meiner, 2000.

Jaeschke, Walter, and Werner Schuffenhauer. "Einleitung der Herausgeber." In Ludwig Feuerbach, *Entwürfe zu einer neuen Philosophie,* edited by Walter Jaeschke and Werner Schuffenhauer, ix–lxi. Hamburg: Felix Meiner, 1996.

Jeschke, Karin, and Gunda Ulbricht, eds. *Dresden, Mai 1849. Tagungsband.* Dresden: ddp goldenbogen, 2000.

Jodl, Friedrich. *Ludwig Feuerbach.* Stuttgart: Frommann, 1904.

Joeres, Ruth-Ellen Boettcher. *Die Anfänge der deutschen Frauenbewegung. Louise Otto-Peters.* Frankfurt: Fischer, 1983.

————. *Respectability and Deviance: Nineteenth-Century German Women Writers and the Ambiguity of Representation.* Chicago: University of Chicago Press, 1998.

————. "Spirit in Struggle: The Radical Vision of Louise Dittmar (1807–1884)." In *Out of Line/Ausgefallen: The Paradox of Marginality in the Writings of Nineteenth-Century German Women,* edited by Joeres and Marianne Burkhard., Amsterdamer Beiträge zur neueren Germanistik, vol. 28, 279–310. Amsterdam: Rodopi, 1989.

Käfer-Dittmar, Gabriele. *Louise Dittmar (1807–1884). Un-erhörte Zeitzeugnisse.* Darmstadt: Justus-von-Liebig Verlag, 1992.

Kaiser, Jochen-Christoph. "Freireligiöse und Feuerbestatter." In *Handbuch der deutschen Reformbewegungen 1880–1933,* edited by Diethart Kerbs and Jürgen Reulecke, 537–49. Wuppertal: Peter Hammer, 1998.

Kanda, Junji. "Moses Hess und der gescheiterte Weg von Hegel zu Feuerbach." In *Ludwig Feuerbach und die Philosophie der Zukunft*, edited by Hans-Jürg Braun, Hans-Martin Sass, Werner Schuffenhauer, and Francesco Tomasoni, 617–42. Berlin: Akademie, 1990.

Kapp, Friedrich. *Vom radikalen Frühsozialisten des Vormärz zum liberalen Parteipolitiker des Bismarckreichs. Briefe 1843–1884.* Edited by Hans-Ulrich Wehler. Frankfurt: Insel, 1969.

Keller, Gottfried. *Gesammelte Briefe.* Edited by Carl Helbling. Bern: Benteli, 1950.

Kelly, Alfred. *The Descent of Darwin: The Popularization of Darwinism in Germany, 1860–1914.* Chapel Hill: University of North Carolina Press, 1981.

Kern, Udo. "'Individuum sein heisst . . . Kommunist sein.' Zum kommunistischen Wesen des Menschen bei Ludwig Feuerbach." In *Ludwig Feuerbach (1804– 1872): Identität und Pluralismus in der globalen Gesellschaft*, edited by Ursula Reitemeyer, Takayuki Shibata, and Francesco Tomasoni, 85–103. Münster: Waxmann, 2006.

Kierkegaard, Soren. *Fear and Trembling/Repetition.* Edited and translated by Howard V. Hong and Edna H. Hong. Princeton, NJ: Princeton University Press, 1983.

Kiss, Endre. "Ludwig Feuerbachs Eudämonismus als philosophische und universal- geschichtliche Option." In *Solidarität oder Egoismus. Studien zu einer Ethik bei und nach Ludwig Feuerbach*, edited by Hans-Jürg Braun, 81–89. Berlin: Akademie, 1994.

Klausmann, Christina. "Louise Dittmar (1807–1884): Ergebnisse einer biographi- schen Spurensuche." In *Out of Line/Ausgefallen: The Paradox of Marginality in the Writings of Nineteenth-Century German Women*, edited by Ruth-Ellen Boettcher Joeres and Marianne Burkhard, Amsterdamer Beiträge zur neueren Germanistik, vol. 28, 17–29. Amsterdam: Rodopi, 1989.

Kockerbeck, Christoph, ed. *Carl Vogt, Jacob Moleschott, Ludwig Büchner, Ernst Haeckel: Briefwechsel.* Marburg: Basilisken-Presse, 1999.

Köhler, Joachim. *Richard Wagner: The Last of the Titans.* Translated by Steward Spencer. New Haven, CT: Yale University Press, 2004.

Köhnke, Klaus Christian. *Entstehung und Aufstieg des Neukantianismus: Die deutsche Universitätsphilosophie zwischen Idealismus und Positivismus.* Frankfurt: Suhrkamp, 1986.

Koltun-Fromm, Kenneth. *Moses Hess and Modern Jewish Identity.* Bloomington: Indiana University Press, 2001.

Köppe, Manuela. "Louise Dittmar (1807–1884). 'Die Freiheit des Geistes.'" In *Vom Salon zur Barrikade. Frauen der Heinezeit*, edited by Irina Hundt and Joseph A. Kruse, 281–98. Stuttgart: J. B. Metzler, 2002.

———. "Zur Entstehung von Ludwig Feuerbachs Schrift 'Über Spiritualismus und Materialismus, besonders in Beziehung auf die Willensfreiheit.'" In *Materialismus und Spiritualismus. Philosophie und Wissenschaften nach 1848*, edited by Andreas Arndt and Walter Jaeschke, 35–52. Hamburg: Felix Meiner, 2000.

Krabbe, Wolfgang R. "Biologismus und Lebensreform." In *Die Lebensreform. Entwürfe zur Neugestaltung von Leben und Kunst um 1900*, edited by Kai

Buchholz, Rita Latocha, Hilke Peckmann und Klaus Wolbert, vol. 1, 183–86. Darmstadt: Häusser, 2001.

Kriege, Hermann. *Hermann Kriege. Dokumentation einer Wandlung vom Burschenschaftler und Revolutionär zum Demokraten (1840–1850).* Edited by Heinrich Schlüter and Alfred Wesselmann. Bielefeld: Der Andere Verlag, 2002.

Krohn, Rüdiger. "The Revolution of 1848–49." In *Wagner Handbook,* edited by Ulrich Müller and Peter Wapnewski. 156–65. Cambridge, MA: Harvard University Press, 1992.

Lange, Friedrich Albert. *Geschichte des Materialismus und Kritik seiner Bedeutung in der Gegenwart.* Iserlohn: Baedeker, 1873.

Lee, M. Owen. *Athena Sings: Wagner and the Greeks.* Toronto: University of Toronto Press, 2003.

Lefèvre, Wolfgang. "Feuerbach und die Grenzen der Ethik." In *Solidarität oder Egoismus. Studien zu einer Ethik bei und nach Ludwig Feuerbach,* edited by Hans-Jürg Braun, 125–40. Berlin: Akademie, 1994.

Lemke, Harald. "Feuerbachs Stammtischthese, oder vom Ursprung des Satzes: 'Der Mensch ist, was er isst." *Aufklärung und Kritik* 11 (2004), 117–40.

Lenin, Vladimir Ilyich. "The Immediate Tasks of the Soviet Government." In *Selected Works in Three Volumes.* Vol. 2, 586–617. Moscow: Progress, 1977.

Levinger, Matthew. "Kant and the Origins of Prussian Constitutionalism." *History of Political Thought* 19 (1998): 241–63.

Lincoln, Bruce. *Theorizing Myth: Narrative, Ideology, and Scholarship.* Chicago: University of Chicago Press, 1999.

Lipp, Carola. "Liebe, Krieg und Revolution. Geschlechtsbeziehung und Nationalismus." In *Schimpfende Weiber und patriotischen Jungfrauen. Frauen im Vormärz und in der Revolution 1848/49,* edited by Carola Lipp, 353–84. Moos: Elster, 1986.

Lotz, Andrea. "'Die Erlösung des weiblichen Geschlechts. Frauen in deutsch-katholischen Gemeinden." In *Schimpfende Weiber und patriotischen Jungfrauen. Frauen im Vormärz und in der Revolution 1848/49,* edited by Carola Lipp, 232–47. Moos: Elster, 1986.

Löwith, Karl. *From Hegel to Nietzsche: The Revolution in Nineteenth-Century Thought.* Translated by David E. Green. New York: Holt, Rinehart and Winston, 1964.

———. "Ludwig Feuerbach und der Ausgang der klassischen deutschen Philosophie." In *Hegel und die Aufhebung der Philosophie im 19. Jahrhundert—Max Weber.* Vol. 5 of *Sämtliche Schriften,* 1–26. Stuttgart: J. B. Metzler, 1988.

Lukács, Georg. *The Destruction of Reason.* Translated by Peter Palmer. Atlantic Highlands, NJ: Humanities Press, 1980.

———. "Moses Hess and the Problems of Idealist Dialectics." In *Political Writings 1919–1929,* translated by Rodney Livingstone, 181–223. London: New Left Books, 1972.

Magee, Elizabeth. *Richard Wagner and the Nibelungs.* Oxford: Clarendon Press, 1990.

Mah, Harold. *The End of Philosophy, the Origin of "Ideology": Karl Marx and the Crisis of the Young Hegelians.* Berkeley: University of California Press, 1987.

Mann, Thomas. *Pro and Contra Wagner.* Translated by Allan Blunden. London: Faber and Faber, 1985.

Marx, Karl, and Friedrich Engels. *Collected Works.* 50 vols. New York: International Publishers, 1975–2004.

Massey, James A. "The Hegelians, the Pietists, and the Nature of Religion." *Journal of Religion* 58 (1978): 108–29.

Massey, Marilyn Chapin. *Christ Unmasked: The Meaning of the Life of Jesus in German Politics.* Chapel Hill: University of North Carolina Press, 1983.

Matysik, Tracie. *Reforming the Moral Subject: Ethics and Sexuality in Central Europe, 1890–1930.* Ithaca, NY: Cornell University Press, 2008.

Mayer, Hans. *Richard Wagner: Mitwelt und Nachwelt.* Zürich: Belser, 1978.

McClellan, David. *The Young Hegelians and Karl Marx.* London: Macmillan, 1969.

Mettele, Gisela. *Bürgertum in Köln 1775–1870. Gemeinsinn und freie Assoziation.* Munich: Oldenbourg, 1998.

Meysenbug, Malwida von. *Memoiren einer Idealistin.* 6th ed. Berlin: Schuster und Loeffler, 1900.

Miguel Arroyo, Luis. "War Feuerbach ein 'Verkenner des Bösen'? Der Humanismus Feuerbachs und der Abgrung der Existenz." In *Ludwig Feuerbach (1804–1872): Identität und Pluralismus in der globalen Gesellschaft,* edited by Ursula Reitemeyer, Takayuki Shibata, and Francesco Tomasoni, 53–65. Münster: Waxmann, 2006.

Moggach, Douglas, ed. *The Left Hegelians: Politics and Philosophy in the Hegelian School.* New York: Cambridge University Press, 2006.

———. *The Philosophy and Politics of Bruno Bauer.* New York: Cambridge University Press, 2003.

Moleschott, Jakob. *Lehre der Nahrungsmittel. Für das Volk.* 2nd ed. Enke: Erlangen, 1853.

Mueller, Volker, ed. *Religionskritik und Geistesfreiheit.* Neustadt: Angelika Lenz Verlag, 2004.

Müller, Ulrich, and Peter Wapnewski, eds. *Wagner Handbook.* Cambridge: Harvard University Press, 1992.

Na'aman, Shlomo. *Emanzipation und Messianismus. Leben und Werk des Moses Hess.* Frankfurt: Campus Verlag, 1982.

Nagel, Christine. *"In der Seele das Ringen nach Freiheit"—Louise Dittmar. Emanzipation und Sittlichkeit im Vormärz und in der Revolution 1848/49.* Königstein/Taunus: Ulrike Helmer, 2005.

Newman, Ernest. *The Life of Richard Wagner.* 4 vols. New York: Alfred A. Knopf, 1933–46.

———. *The Wagner Operas.* New York: Alfred A. Knopf, 1949.

Nietzsche, Friedrich. *The Birth of Tragedy and the Case of Wagner.* Translated by Walter Kaufmann. Toronto: Random House, 1967.

———. *The Twilight of the Idols and the Antichrist.* Translated by R. J. Hollingdale. London: Penguin, 1948.

Nipperdey, Thomas. *Deutsche Geschichte 1800–1866. Bürgerwelt und starker Staat.* Munich: C. H. Beck, 1983.

O'Hara-May, Jane. "Measuring Man's Needs." *Journal of the History of Biology* 4 (1971): 249–73.

Otto, Louise. "Die Nibelungen als Oper." *Neue Zeitschrift für Musik* 23 (1845): 49–52, 129–30, 171–72.

———. *Die Nibelungen. Text zu einer grossen historischen Oper in fünf Acten.* Gera: Verlag der Hofmeister'schen Zeitungs-Expedition, 1852.

———. *"Dem Reich der Freiheit werb' ich Bürgerinnen." Die Frauen-Zeitung von Louise Otto.* Edited by Ute Gerhard, Elisabeth Hannover-Drück, and Romina Schmitter. Frankfurt: Syndikat, 1980.

Pepperle, Heinz. "Einleitung." In *Ausgewählte Schriften in zwei Bänden,* by Karl Friedrich Köppen, 11–125. Berlin: Akademie Verlag, 2003.

Pilick, Eckhart. "Bewusstsein des Unendlichen—Feuerbachs Religionskritik und die Freie Religion." In *Religionskritik und Geistesfreiheit,* edited by Volker Mueller, 79–113. Neustadt: Angelika Lenz Verlag, 2004.

Pitzer, Donald E., ed. *America's Communal Utopians.* Charlotte: University of North Carolina Press, 1997.

Prelinger, Catherine. *Charity, Challenge, and Change: Religious Dimensions of the Mid-Nineteenth-Century Women's Movement in Germany.* New York: Greenwood, 1987.

———. "A Decade of Dissent in Germany: A Historical Study of the Society of Protestant Friends and the German-Catholic Church." PhD diss., Yale University Press, 1954.

———. "Religious Dissent, Women's Rights, and the Hamburger Hochschule für das weibliche Geschlecht in Mid-Nineteenth-Century Germany." *Church History* 45 (1976): 42–55.

Rawidowicz, S. *Ludwig Feuerbachs Philosophie: Ursprung und Schicksal.* Berlin: Reuther und Richard, 1931.

Reichardt, Mathilde. *Wissenschaft und Sittenlehre. Briefe an Jakob Moleschott.* Gotha: Hugo Schenke, 1856.

Reinhardt, Hartmut. "Wagner and Schopenhauer." In *Wagner Handbook,* edited by Ulrich Müller and Peter Wapnewski, translation edited by John Deathridge, 287–96. Cambridge, MA: Harvard University Press, 1992.

Riha, Karl. "Deutscher Michel: Zur literarischen und karikaturistischen Ausprägung einer nationalen Allegorie im neunzehnten Jahrhundert." In *Nationale Mythen und Symbole in der zweiten Hälfte des neunzehnten Jahrhunderts,* edited by Jürgen Link and Wulf Wülfing, 146–71. Stuttgart: Klett-Cotta, 1991.

Rosbach, Oliver. "Strafrecht und Gesellschaft bei Anselm von Feuerbach." *Forum historiae juris.* December 1, 2000, at http://www.rewi.hu-berlin.de/FHI/zitat/0012rosbach.htm (accessed June 30, 2008).

Rose, Paul Lawrence. *German Question/Jewish Question: Revolutionary Antisemitism from Kant to Wagner.* Princeton, NJ: Princeton University Press, 1990.

———. *Wagner: Race and Revolution.* New Haven, CT: Yale University Press, 1992.

Ruge, Arnold. "Anthropologische Aphorismen." *Deutsches Museum* 16 (1866): 340–46.

———. "Briefe über Ludwig Feuerbach und seine Theogonie." *Deutsches Museum* 8 (1858): 136–38, 249–51.

Safranski, Rüdiger. *Romantik. Eine deutsche Affäre.* Munich: Carl Hanser, 2007.

Sass, Hans-Martin. *Ludwig Feuerbach in Selbstzeugnissen und Bilddokumenten.* Hamburg: Rohwolt, 1978.

———. "The 'Transition' from Feuerbach to Marx: A Re-Interpretation." *Studies in Soviet Thought* 26 (1983): 123–42.

Schattkowsky, Martina, ed. *Dresdner Maiaufstand und Reichsverfassung 1849: Revolutionäres Nachbeben oder demokratische politische Kultur.* Leipzig: Leipziger Universitätsverlag, 2000.

Schmidt, Alfred. "Einleitung: Für eine neue Lektüre Feuerbachs." In *Anthropologischer Materialismus. Ausgewählte Schriften,* by Ludwig Feuerbach, 5–64. Frankfurt: Ullstein, 1985.

Schneider, Gabriele. "Die Emanzipation des Individuums. Fanny Lewald und der Junghegelianismus." In *Philosophie, Literatur und Politik vor den Revolutionen von 1848. Zur Herausbildung der demokratischen Bewegungen in Europa,* edited by Lars Lambrecht, 525–40. Frankfurt: Peter Lang, 1996.

Schötz, Susanne. "Von 1848 nach 1865? Bausteine zur Kollektivbiographie der Gründerinnen und Gründer der deutschen Frauenbewegung." In *Revolution und Reform im 19. und 20. Jahrhundert,* edited by Helmut Bleiber and Walter Schmidt, 151–64. Berlin: Trafo, 2005.

Schuffenhauer, Werner. *Feuerbach und der junge Marx. Zur Entstehungsgeschichte der marxistischen Weltanschauung.* 2nd ed. Berlin: Verlag der Wissenschaften, 1972.

———. "Feuerbach und die freireligiöse Bewegung seiner Zeit." In *Religionskritik und Geistesfreiheit,* edited by Volker Mueller, 33–42. Neustadt: Angelika Lenz Verlag, 2004.

Schulz, Wilhelm. *Die Bewegung der Produktion. Eine geschichtlich-statistische Abhandlung zur Grundlegung einer neuen Wissenschaft des Staats und der Geschichte.* Zurich: Verlag des literarischen Comptoirs, 1843.

———. *Die wahrhaftige Geschichte vom deutschen Michel und seinen Schwestern.* Zurich: Verlag des literarischen Comptoirs, 1843.

Shaw, George Bernard. *The Perfect Wagnerite: A Commentary on the Nibelung's Ring.* New York: Dover, 1967.

Siemann, Wolfram. *The German Revolution of 1848–49.* Translated by Christiane Banerji. New York: St. Martin's, 1998.

Sieverding, Judith. *Sensibilität und Solidarität. Skizze einer dialogischen Ethik im Anschluss an Ludwig Feuerbach und Richard Rorty.* Münster: Waxmann, 2007.

Silberner, Edmund. *Moses Hess: Geschichte seines Lebens.* Leiden, The Netherlands: Brill, 1966.

Simmel, Georg. "Female Culture." In *Georg Simmel: On Women, Sexuality, and Love,* edited and translated by Guy Oakes, 65–101. New Haven, CT: Yale University Press, 1984.

Sörgel, Alwin H. *A Sojourn in Texas, 1846–47. Alwin H, Sörgel's Texas Writings.* Translated and edited by W. M. Von-Maszewski. San Marcos, TX: German-Texas Heritage Society, 1992.

Sperber, Jonathan. *Rhineland Radicals: The Democratic Movement and the Revolution of 1848–1849.* Princeton, NJ: Princeton University Press, 1991.

Steinberg, Michael P. *Listening to Reason: Culture, Subjectivity, and Nineteenth Century Music.* Chicago: University of Chicago Press, 2004.

Stepelevich, Lawrence S. "Max Stirner and Ludwig Feuerbach." *Journal of the History of Ideas* 39 (1978): 451–63.

———, ed. *The Young Hegelians: An Anthology.* Atlantic Highlands, NJ: Humanities Press, 1983.

Stirner, Max. *The Ego and Its Own.* Translated by David Leopold. New York: Cambridge University Press, 1995.

Stopczyk, Annegret. "Helene Stöcker. Philosophin der 'Neuen Ethik.'" In *Die Lebensreform. Entwürfe zur Neugestaltung von Leben und Kunst um 1900,* edited by Kai Buchholz, Rita Latocha, Hilke Peckmann und Klaus Wolbert, vol. 1, 157–59. Darmstadt: Häusser, 2001.

Strobel, Otto, ed. *Skizzen und Entwürfe zur Ring-Dichtung.* Munich: F. Bruckmann, 1930.

Thies, Erich. *Ludwig Feuerbach zwischen Universität und Rathaus, oder die Heidelberger Philosophen und the 48er Revolution.* Heidelberg: Verlag Brigitte Guderjahn, 1990.

Toews, John Edward. *Hegelianism: The Path toward Dialectical Humanism 1805–1841.* New York: Cambridge University Press, 1980.

Tomasoni, Francesco. "Ethnologische Vorurteile und Ansätze zu einer Überwindung derselben im Fall der Hebräer." In *Solidarität oder Egoismus. Studien zu einer Ethik bei und nach Ludwig Feuerbach,* edited by Hans-Jürg Braun, 254–63. Berlin: Akademie, 1994.

———. "Feuerbach und die Skepsis: Zur Relativität und Absolutheit der mensch-lichen Werte." In *Ludwig Feuerbach (1804–1872): Identität und Pluralismus in der globalen Gesellschaft,* edited by Ursula Reitemeyer, Takayuki Shibata, and Francesco Tomasoni, 21–38. Münster: Waxmann, 2006.

———. "Heidentum und Judentum: Vom schärfsten Gegensatz zur Annäherung. Eine Entwicklungslinie vom 'Wesen des Christenthums' bis zur 'Theogonie.'" In *Ludwig Feuerbach und die Geschichte der Philosophie,* edited by Walter Jaeschke and Francesco Tomasoni, 148–66. Berlin: Akademie, 1998.

———. *Ludwig Feuerbach und die nicht-menschliche Natur. Das Wesen der Religion: Die Entstehungsgeschichte des Werkes, rekonstruiert auf der Grundlage unveröffent-licher Manuskripte.* Translated by Alf Schneditz. Stuttgart: Frommann-Holzboog, 1990.

———. *Modernity and the Final Aim of History: The Debate over Judaism from Kant to the Young Hegelians.* Dordrecht: Klower, 2003.

Vahsen, Mechthilde. "'Vorwärts! Die Geschichte beweist es./Freiheit sei das edelste Loos.'" In *Vormärz-Nachmärz. Bruch oder Kontinuität?,* edited by Norbert Otto Eke and Renate Werner, 125–38. Bielefeld: Aisthesis, 2000.

Valentin, Veit. *Geschichte der deutschen Revolution von 1848–1849.* 2 vols. Weinheim: Beltz Quadriga, 1998.

Volkov, Shulamith. "Moses Hess: Problems of Religion and Faith." *Studies in Zionism* 3 (1982): 1–15.

Wagner, Richard. *Dichtungen und Schriften. Jubiläumsausgabe in zehn Bände.* Edited by Dieter Borchmeyer. 10 vols. Frankfurt: Insel, 1983.

———. *My Life.* 2 vols. New York: Dodd, Mead, 1911.

———. *Richard Wagner's Prose Works.* Translated by William Ashton Ellis. 8 vols. London: Routledge and Kegan Paul, 1895–1899.

———. *Selected Letters of Richard Wagner.* Translated and edited by Stewart Spencer and Barry Millington. New York: W. W. Norton, 1987.

Wapnewski, Peter. "The Operas as Literary Works." In *Wagner Handbook,* edited by Ulrich Müller and Peter Wapnewski, translation edited by John Deathridge, 3–95. Cambridge, MA: Harvard University Press, 1992.

Wartofsky, Marx W. *Feuerbach.* New York: Cambridge University Press, 1977.

Weber, Max. "Religious Rejections of the World and Their Directions." In *From Max Weber: Essays on Sociology,* edited by H. H. Gerth and C. Wright Mills, 323–59. New York: Oxford University Press, 1946.

Weiner, Marc. *Richard Wagner and the Anti-Semitic Imagination.* Lincoln: University of Nebraska Press, 1995.

Weir, Todd. "The Fourth Confession: Atheism, Monism, and Politics in the Freigeistig Movement in Berlin, 1859–1924." PhD diss., Columbia University, 2005.

Willey, Thomas E. *Back to Kant: The Revival of Kantianism in German Social and Historical Thought, 1860–1914.* Detroit: Wayne State University Press, 1978.

Williams, Howard. "Ludwig Feuerbach's Critique of Religion and the End of Moral Philosophy." In *The New Hegelians: Politics and Philosophy in the Hegelian School,* edited by Douglas Moggach, 50–66. New York: Cambridge University Press, 2006.

Williamson, George S. *The Longing for Myth in Germany: Religion and Aesthetic Culture from Romanticism to Nietzsche.* Chicago: University of Chicago Press, 2004.

Windell, George G. "Hegel, Feuerbach, and Wagner's *Ring.*" *Central European History* 9 (1976): 37–57.

Winiger, Josef. *Ludwig Feuerbach: Denker der Menschlichkeit.* Berlin: Aufbau, 2004.

Wittich, Dieter. "Einleitung." In *Schriften zum kleinbürgerlichen Materialismus in Deutschland,* 2 vols., vol. 1, v–lxxxi. Berlin: Akademie, 1971.

Zucker, Stanley. *Kathinka Zitz-Halein and Female Civic Activism in Mid-Nineteenth-Century Germany.* Carbondale: Southern Illinois University Press, 1991.

Index